IN THE SIXTIES

—

D0532341

ALSO BY RAY CONNOLLY

Novels
A Girl Who Came To Stay
Trick Or Treat?
Newsdeath
A Sunday Kind Of Woman
The Sun Place
Sunday Morning
Shadows On A Wall

Biography
John Lennon, 1940-1980

Anthology of journalism
Stardust Memories

Screenplays for the cinema
That'll Be The Day
Stardust

Films and series for television
James Dean: The First American Teenager [documentary]
Honky Tonk Heroes
Lytton's Diary
Forever Young
Defrosting The Fridge
Perfect Scoundrels

Plays for radio
An Easy Game To Play
Lost Fortnight

IN THE SIXTIES

—

Edited by Ray Connolly

Assistant editor: Dominic Connolly

PAVILION

First published in Great Britain in 1995 by
Pavilion Books Limited
26 Upper Ground
London SE1 9PD

Text copyright © see p. 226

The moral right of the author has been asserted.

Text designed by AB3

Jacket designed by Nigel Partridge

Front jacket photographs: Muhammad Ali; FBI agent leaps onto moving car, Kennedy's assassination, Dallas, Texas; The Beatles (**all AP**); US helicopters in Vietnam (**Popperfoto**).

All rights reserved. No part of this publication may be reproduced, stored in a retrieval system, or transmitted in any form or by any means, electronic, mechanical, photocopying, recording, or otherwise, without the prior permission of the copyright owner.

A CIP catalogue record for this book is available from the British Library.

ISBN 1-85793-985-9

Typeset by Litho Link Ltd, Welshpool, Powys, Wales
Printed and bound in Great Britain
by Cox and Wyman

2 4 6 8 10 9 7 5 3 1

This book may be ordered by post direct from the publisher. Please contact the Marketing Department. But try your bookshop first.

For Dominic

All the editor's royalties from sales of this book
will be donated to the English Centre of International P.E.N., the
world association of writers.

CONTENTS

INTRODUCTION

—

When Harold Macmillan spoke in Cape Town on 5 February 1960 of the 'wind of change' he was, of course, talking about the continent of Africa where the growth of national consciousness was then sweeping away the vestiges of the European empires. But had he been speaking more generally about the decade which was just beginning, he could hardly have chosen a more apposite expression. Because by the beginning of the 1960s a wind of change was blowing everywhere, not just in Africa but across Europe and North America and even eventually into the Soviet empire. Indeed the era of the Sixties was about nothing so much as change; not change from the outside or by conquest, but change from within.

And there was more than that. As well as change, the Sixties' ethos was also about optimism, the belief that things could, should and would be changed for the better, because that was the right thing to do. There was, in short, a new idealism about, conceived in a time of shared privation and now funded by a sustained period of peace and greater prosperity than the world had ever known. After a great depression, six years of world war, and fifteen more of austerity a new generation was coming of age to live the dreams of their parents.

So far as Britain is concerned it has always seemed to me that the attitudes which shaped the Sixties were largely forged during the Second World War, with the Beveridge Report of 1942 and the 1944 Education Act as midwife and wet-nurse. The changes sought there represented idealism of the highest order. In health and education there was for the first time a national plan to nurture what the Liberal Democrats would today call the nation's greatest natural asset. The plan worked. By 1960 a generation of achievers, bred on notions of fairness and opportunity, was able to take advantage of the unlimited possibilities which were suddenly becoming available. This was something new.

Looking back it now almost seems as though everything happened at once. While the abolition of national service in 1960 was, in effect, adding two extra years to the young life of every boy (thus releasing all kinds of energies), Britain's loss of Empire meant that a whole class of educated young Britons was being forced to look closer to home for careers. Everywhere the barriers of class and social conformity were being examined and, in the need to fill jobs with qualified personnel, pushed aside. The contagion of a fairer society was spreading quickly, promptly demonstrated when Princess Margaret married a commoner (who was also a *photographer*!). There were more university places chasing fewer students than ever before, and *Lady Chatterley's Lover* was judged not pornographic when a jury, asked if they would wish their servants to read such a book, voted against the nation's artistic game-keepers and in favour of the individual's common sense. In 1961 the birth control pill became available on prescription for the first time, in the United States the Peace Corps, under President Kennedy, was founded and in London *Beyond The Fringe* opened, followed a few months later by the first edition of *Private Eye*. In November of that year *That Was The Week That Was* went on television, ending the BBC's traditional ban on jokes about religion, politics, royalty and sex. Then came the Beatles, and the Sixties had its troubadours.

Certainly it is the look and sounds we most readily associate with the Sixties now – the geometric Mary Quant look, the Muhammad Ali travelling circus, the pirate radio stations, Julie Christie's performance in *Darling*, Michael Caine's in *Alfie*, and Mandy Rice Davies's in the dock of the Old Bailey. But there was much else happening, a redefining of attitudes which today we take for granted. In 1965 the death penalty was abolished and the Race Relations Board set up. Two years later, in the same month that *Sergeant Pepper* was celebrating flower power, two bills, one legalizing abortion, the other homosexuality between consenting adults, were reaching the statute book. Three months earlier the nation's first Ombudsman had begun work, and breath tests had been introduced.

With almost full employment (there was great consternation when in 1966 the jobless total rose past the half million mark) it never occurred to anyone that there might not be a job waiting after education was completed. And because there were jobs there was the opportunity to fail, which is one of the best ways of learning. In l965 when BBC2 began, after a very short planning period, it almost doubled BBC Television's output overnight, and a whole generation of young producers and directors were suddenly given that opportunity. Not many failed.

There was an impudence about the time. My own generation of war babies had grown up cowed by the success of America, the country which had been so recently the friendly invader. In some respects perhaps we imagined ourselves secondhand Americans. Everything that was new and exciting seemed to happen in America first. But in the Sixties all that changed. There was a new mood in Britain reflected on a global scale by the Beatles, and winning the World Cup in 1966 didn't hurt national morale either. For a while, crazily, everything seemed possible. Little wonder that by the end of the decade a man was walking on the moon.

The juggernaut of change and endless possibility was exhilarating: the Clean Air Act of 1956 was banishing the great London smogs, a British film, *Lawrence of Arabia*, won seven Oscars, a grammar school boy in Edward Heath was voted leader of the Conservative Party for the first time, and by the end of the decade Concorde was making her maiden flight. While there was considerable disquiet at Britain's selling of arms in the Biafran War, and violence at demonstrations in Grosvenor Square against the Vietnam War, Britain was not psychologically being ripped apart by war and assassination as was America. And although 1969 saw the beginning of the troubles in Northern Ireland it was not until the Seventies that sectarian violence became an everyday occurrence.

Nor was the acceleration of change limited to Britain. In ten years the non-violent Civil Rights movement made extraordinary strides in the United States, while 1968 took students to the barricades in Paris and brought the early, (and sadly, ultimately unhappy) flowering of the Prague Spring. (The fact that it seemed possible for change to be non-violent in a totalitarian system owed much to Sixties' attitudes, even if the Czechs did eventually have to wait a further twenty-one years for democracy.)

And then there was sex . . . The pill inevitably changed everything, although not, I suspect, quite so universally quickly as legend would have us believe. For those at the heart of things, in the media, the universities, the arts, yes, attitudes somersaulted overnight. But for the average kids, for the Terrys and Julies down by the station every Friday night, these things took a little longer.

These days it is modish in some quarters to deride the very term *Sixties*, to use it pejoratively of no longer fashionable teaching techniques, of ugly, functional, urban architecture and of woolly, well-intentioned but impractical thinking. And obviously evidence can be produced to support such views. But to me that is to miss the point. For all the naïveté of the time, all the mistakes, all the youthful silliness and emphasis on style, the Sixties was an era of great idealism and startling creativity.

It was also an excellent era for written journalism, possibly the last moment in history when the word arrived before the pictures. Newspapers had remained thin long after the war, with every story pared to its absolute minimum. This produced some brilliantly concise writing but it was inevitably limiting on more complex issues. By the Sixties the papers were growing rapidly: first came the special review sections and in 1962 the first colour supplement from the *Sunday Times*. Suddenly writers and photographers were given a new freedom to report at length and they used that freedom well. A new kind of investigative journalism was being devised. Little wonder that after Margaret Laing's piece on John Bloom appeared, his Rolls Razor empire never quite looked the same.

This book, a collection of newspaper and magazine articles by over fifty writers, written during and about a fascinating time, is not intended as a history of the Sixties. It couldn't hope to be. At best it is a series of snapshots of a few of the events, people and attitudes which made up those times – from the funeral of Winston Churchill to sex, groupies and Germaine Greer, from the Eichmann trial to Muhammad Ali, the Profumo Affair and Jilly Cooper's office Christmas party. Nor is this book only about the fashionable, famous and notorious. It is also about the ordinary people who still wore ties to football matches, went to jail on a matter of principle and, like Ivy Benson's all-girls band, marched forward into the future with their attitudes shaped years in the past. Because, let's face it, the now fabled Sixties were over before many people were even aware of what was happening.

While some of the pieces reprinted here are so brilliant they would be in everyone's collections, others, like Neville Cardus's chronicle of a love story, are simply a matter of personal taste, small and personal pieces which struck a nerve and lingered in the mind. Few journalists can hope to do much more than that.

Ray Connolly
March 1995

EYE-WITNESS AT SHARPEVILLE

—

Humphrey Tyler
Observer
27 March 1960

One of the worst massacres in the history of South Africa occurred in the black township of Sharpeville in the Transvaal on this first day of civil disobedience against the pass laws. Fifty-six Africans were shot dead and 162 injured after police opened fire.

We went back into Sharpeville the back way around lunchtime last Monday, driving along behind a big grey police car and three Saracen armoured cars. As we went through the fringes of the township many people were shouting the Pan-Africanist slogan 'Iswe Lethu' (Our land). They were grinning and cheerful. Some kids waved to the policemen sitting on the Saracens and two of the policemen waved back. It was like a Sunday outing – except that Major A.T.T. Spengler, head of the Witwatersrand Security Branch, was in the front car and there were bullets in the Saracens' guns.

At the main gates of the fenced-off location, policemen were stopping all cars coming in from the outside. Spengler and the Saracens headed for the police station which is deep inside the settlement, and we followed. The policemen were by now all inside the Saracens, with the hatches battened down, looking at Sharpeville through the chinks of the armour plating. Yet the Africans did not appear to be alarmed by the cars. Some looked interested. Some just grinned.

A constable shoved the butt of his rifle against my windshield. Another pointed his rifle at my chest. Another leaned into the car, shouting, 'Have you got a permit to be in this location?' I said no, whereupon he bellowed, 'Then get out, get out, get out! Or I will arrest you on the spot. Understand?' He had a police gun in his holster and a black pistol tucked into his belt. We decided to go around the other side of the police station, where we parked in a big field.

We could see a couple of the Saracens, their tops poking starkly above the heads of the crowd, just over one hundred yards away from us. This was about seven minutes before the police opened fire. The crowd seemed to be loosely gathered around them and on the fringes people were walking in and out. The kids were playing. In all there were about 3,000 people. They seemed amiable and relaxed.

I said to Ian Berry, *Drum's* chief photographer, 'This is going to go on all day.' He replied, 'Let's hang on for a bit.' Suddenly there was a sharp report from the direction of the police station. 'That's a shot,' Berry said. There were shrill cries of *'Iswe Lethu'*

– women's voices, I thought. The cries came from the police station and I could see a small section of the crowd swirl around the Saracens. Hands went up in the Africanist salute.

Then the shooting started. We heard the chatter of a machine-gun, then another, then another. 'Here it comes,' said Berry. He leaped out of the car with two cameras and crouched in the grass, shooting pictures. The first rush was on us, then past. There were hundreds of women, some of them laughing. They must have thought the police were firing blanks. One woman was hit abut ten yards from our car. Her companion, a young man, went back when she fell. He thought she had stumbled. Then he turned her over and saw that her chest had been shot away. He looked at the blood on his hand and said, 'My God, she's gone!' Hundreds of kids were running, too. One little boy had on an old black coat, which he held up behind his head, thinking, perhaps, that it might save him from the bullets. Some of the children, hardly as tall as the grass, were leaping like rabbits. Some of them were shot, too.

Still the shooting went on. One of the policemen was standing on top of a Saracen, and it looked as though he was firing his sten gun into the crowd. He was swinging it around in a wide arc from his hip as though he were panning a movie camera. Two other police officers were on the truck with him, and it looked as if they were firing pistols. Most of the bodies were strewn in the road running through the field in which we were. One man who had been lying still dazedly got to his feet, staggered a few yards then fell in a heap. A woman sat with her head cupped in her hands.

One by one the guns stopped. Nobody was moving in our field except Berry. The rest were wounded – or dead. There was no longer a crowd and it was very quiet. Berry ran back to the car, saying, 'Let's go before they get my film.' We drove out through the main gate, looking straight ahead.

Before the shooting I heard no warning to the crowd to disperse. There was no warning volley. When the shooting started it did not stop until there was no living thing on the huge compound in front of the police station. The police have claimed they were in desperate danger because the crowd was stoning them. Yet only three policemen were reported to have been hit by stones – and more than 200 Africans were shot down. The police also have said that the crowd was armed with 'ferocious weapons' which littered the compound after they fled. I saw no weapons, although I looked carefully, and afterwards studied the photographs of the death scene. While I was there I saw only shoes, hats and a few bicycles left among the bodies.

It seems to me that tough stuff was behind the killings at Sharpeville. The crowd gave me no reason to feel scared, though I moved among them without any distinguishing mark to protect me, quite obvious with my white skin. I think the police were scared, though, and I think the crowd knew it. That final shrill cry from the women before the shooting started certainly sounded much more like a jeer than a battle-cry. And the first Africans who fled past me after the shooting started were still laughing.

This article first appeared in the South African magazine Drum *where Humphrey Tyler was a staff journalist.*

THE FRIENDLESS ONES

—

Penelope Gilliatt
Queen
April 1960

Long before the modern tabloids pack-hunted royals and soap celebrities, gossip columnists detailed the lives of lesser aristocrats and the vulgar rich. By today's standards it was all fairly tame, but when the magazine Queen *turned the tables and, with sneak photographs, put the columnists themselves under the microscope, there was outrage – leading, it is said, to sackings on some newspapers. Incidentally, although this article was printed under Penelope Gilliatt's by-line, its co-author was Jocelyn Stevens, who remained anonymous so that he might not be the target of revenge attacks from Fleet Street.*

Soon there will be no 'r' in the month, and debs will be in season again. This is not a statement guaranteed to thrill all of us; in fact, it is conceivable that it leaves much of the population cold with disinterest; but it clearly means a lot to gossip columnists. Even they cannot run for ever on Charles Clore and Suna Portman, and the yearly arrival of the debutantes with their caravan of mothers and escorts must seem heaven-sent. Soon there will be news of parties in the Zoo, and plump, excitable girls winning things at tombolas, and Lady Nostalgie de la Boue giving a dance at Hurlingham. And soon, God save us, there will be another Henrietta Tiarks.

Even without invoking value-judgements, most people would agree that the picture of life presented by gossip columns is shakily related to the observable world. Hickey-land is a limbo without worry, love or conscience. In it there is no achievement, only success; no conversation, only quotes that the most inept Victorian playwright would have hesitated to pass off as human speech; no art, merely art-personalities who are invariably presented as being bizarre, dissolute, and/or over-paid, following the ancient Philistine precept that art must be made to seem as peripheral as possible.

To be good at his job, a gossip columnist needs a number of special qualifications. First, he must be able to accept the Fleet Street mystique of 'news-getting' and of 'being a professional journalist', which will help him to surmount any sense of ordinary ethics. Then he must be able to write with unfailing brightness: a breaking marriage and a Potato Marketing Board party must be reported in exactly the same tone of voice, in short, pert sentences and with a sciolist's assurance. He must be able to interview celebrities on the telephone and tell you that they smiled, and he must get in as many bold-type names as possible, if necessary by the breathtakingly simple method of stating the people who were not present. ('Glassy-eyed debutantes searched wistfully for *James Mason*. He stars in the film. He wasn't there' – *Evening Standard*.) He must be able to collar a young man about a rumour that Princess Alexandra is coming to stay and, on being told that it's all in the air, write a headline saying, 'Princess Alexandra Engagement: Lord so-and-so says "It's all in the air".' He must have limitless effrontery, disguised by a goody-goody suggestion that he is merely upholding the public's right to know. ('Why are some people so secretive about their marriages?' said Hickey woundedly on 22 March having discovered that Dame Margot Fonteyn's husband had been married before. Why, on the contrary, should anyone have to tell Hickey?) And, above all, he must be able to write with aplomb even if he has made no attempt to find out whether his story is true. As a retired gossip writer blandly explained, 'There are some stories that checking would kill stone dead.'

A know-all manner is an essential part of the equipment. The omniscients were badly hipped by the news of Princess Margaret's engagement, but they have made up for it since. 'Now the whole world knows of the engagement of Princess Margaret and Mr Antony Armstrong-Jones,' wrote Tanfield on 29 February – with a clever implication that he had been in on the secret, but had waited politely for the Palace to have first go – 'I have news of another intriguing friendship', a hinted engagement between one of Princess Margaret's late escorts and one of Princess Margaret's ladies-in-waiting that next morning he unsheepishly admitted to be a figment of his own Royalty-fixated imagination. On 8 March Hickey said smugly, 'Margaret's engagement ring . . . FOR THE FIRST TIME I CAN REVEAL ITS FASCINATING FAMILY HISTORY', and went into a long story: 'It was given to Tony for the engagement by his mother, the Countess of Rosse. How did it reach the Countess? I will tell you . . .' Next morning it turned out to be the wrong ring. Impenetrably cocky, the writer of the column kicked off ten days later with the assertion that 'I rarely get led astray . . .'

This use of the first person is an important part of the myth. Quite illusorily, one acquires a sense that William Hickey and Paul Tanfield and John London and the rest of them are real people: bright, ungullible, relentlessly popular men who enjoy the confidence of the famous and the admiration of the most glittering (key word) hostesses in London. As the quick-witted may have suspected, this is not an accurate picture. To begin with, the columnists' names are nearly all fictional, and generally disguise a whole team of writers. There has been no real William Hickey since the original prolix gossip of the eighteenth century, who did for the Mohawks very much what his descendant has done for the Chelsea set, and who appears to have been equally remotely acquainted with the intellectual life of his day.

And in the second place, the scraps of inside information on the gossip columnists' desks have often arrived there by far from natural means. The industry at present supports in high style a whole underground movement of stringers – informers – who can apparently earn up to £30 or £40 a week by passing on pieces of news about their friends. It also provides a nice livelihood for the public relations men who specialize in 'creating' gossip-column characters. For a fee, almost anyone can be given a leg up into this distinguished category. 'Easy, if you know your way about,' I was told by a gossip writer turned PRO, with that absence of a blush which is such a striking characteristic of the gossip column world. 'Some dress manufacturer comes to you, say. You spread a report about a fantastic party he's giving, pass on a tip that he's bidding against Niarchos for a Renoir, and he's in.'

Considering the minute area of the ground covered, and the fact that plagiarism goes on freely between one paper and another as soon as the first editions are out, it is surprising that each column has developed the identity that it has. John Rolls, for instance, has a jovial and beery character; Hardcastle is an out-and-out title snob; Hickey is oddly sentimental, especially about money, and is apt to lapse now and then into an ornate set-piece about what he calls 'my world' – a smallish world chiefly inhabited by millionaires, starlets, yachts, and peers with model-girl wives. (One looks forward mildly to the day when the process is reversed for once, and a life peeress marries a male model. The Aquascutum man looks good stock.) What Hickey likes better than anything is the sight of the rich at play; to pick his way among the oily limbs on a beach in the South of France arouses him to ecstasy. This frenetic holiday-worship recurs in most gossip columns, and it is one of the many spurious aspects of the picture they present.

The ethos of Rex North's column is much more amiable and mundane than Hickey's, and the style much less paradisiacal. An inveterate back-slapper, he summons up an image of a benevolent but leery sales manager, with a tendency to produce a warm bottle of sherry from his desk after his secretary has been working late. This is not the sort of thing that you would ever catch John London doing: the *News Chronicle's* man has sober tastes. Most of his friends seem to be artists and writers, and although he makes a show of writing the kind of stories that make his colleagues guffaw, his heart is not in it. He is the only gossip columnist in London who could conceivably have found and quoted an anecdote told in the Frampton Parish Magazine. The mind boggles at the distaste he must feel in working cheek by jowl with Paul Tanfield. Generally regarded as provoking a higher weekly average of threatened libel suits than any of his fellow bloods, Mr. Tanfield projects a disagreeable character: he can stomach a more disagreeable story than anyone else in the field, and has an insatiable appetite for marriages going wrong, jobs being lost, children behaving callously to their declining parents and second-rank stars having rows with film directors. If Hickey ever wrote a book, it would be called *Success*; Tanfield's would be called *Failure*.

The methods employed by these national figures are brazen, ingenious, and practically invincible, since in any clash the ordinary citizen tends to forget that his inquisitor is not inhibited by the faintest sense of morality. Knowing that 'Yes' and 'No' are quite enough to make a long story and that 'No comment' can be given every kind of dark implication, he is inclined to yield to the reporter's common persuasion that, since something is going to appear in print anyway, it is in his own interests to answer questions. Like any blackmailed person, he often develops a curious and hopeless sense of intimacy with his tormentor, so that he is even insane enough to think that 'off-the-record' has some meaning in the mouth of a gossip-reporter. If he refuses to talk, he knows that there are plenty of back-door methods. His children will be cornered and questioned. His neighbours, or his colleagues at work, will be bribed. Friends' names will be given to lure him to the telephone or to gain an entrance for photographers. A really good newspaper-man, you see, stops at nothing: armed with a bouquet, he will even invade a hospital room barred to all visitors. Some time ago the Press was riled by Mrs. Selwyn Lloyd's wish to keep her private country address private, but they beat her: a reporter telephoned her town house pretending to be her child's godfather, told the housekeeper that he had a present that he wanted to get to the child, and, on hearing that the nurse was going down to the country the next day and would take it, waited outside the house and followed her to earth. The tenacity and fatuity of the gossip columnist on the scent of his gossip provides a new variant of Oscar Wilde's view of hunting: the unbeatable in pursuit of the unspeakably dull.

Quite apart from the inanity of the material, though, and the bullying and impertinence involved in getting it, there is a real sense in which gossip columns are socially mischievous. 'My world' is *not* a world: but it is presented as though it were, skilfully and insistently. When money is constantly represented as something glamorous in itself, for instance – when Baron Thyssen's ticker-tape machine in his drawing-room is described in emotive terms that simply do not belong to money-making – the illusion becomes pernicious. There is a point where people's natural taste for small-talk can be exploited and perverted, and a good many of our gossip columns are way over the line: their assumptions are jaundiced, materialist and smug, and the picture of the world that they project is morally as well as factually dishonest.

Penelope Gilliatt later became a well-respected film critic for the Observer *before joining the* New Yorker. *Married to playwright John Osborne for some years she also enjoyed a reputation as a novelist and wrote the film* Sunday, Bloody Sunday. *She died in 1993.*

LADY CHATTERLEY'S TRIAL

—

Kenneth Tynan
Observer
6 November 1960

To many the beginning of the sexual liberation of the Sixties can be traced directly back to the moment when an Old Bailey jury decided that D.H. Lawrence's novel Lady Chatterley's Lover *was not obscene. Within a few days Penguin Books, who had challenged the law by publishing the book, sold over 200,000 copies.*

Now that the case is over, and Lady Chatterley's adventures are speeding two-hundred-thousand-fold to every outpost of literacy in the country, it seems suddenly unthinkable that the jury could have brought in any other verdict. But it was desperately thinkable right up to three o'clock on Thursday afternoon, as anyone knows who sat through the six days of the trial, and sweated out the dragging hours of the jury's retirement; more than most people, Gerald Gardiner, counsel for the defence knew it, and looked the reverse of optimistic as he prowled up and down like a wounded lion, waiting for those twelve inscrutable citizens to come to their conclusion. How we had all stared at them, seizing on each smile, each sniffle, each sign of inattentiveness as evidence of sympathy or hostility to Lawrence's cause! The lean, middle-aged man at the right-hand end of the back row seemed prematurely grey: did this betoken sensitivity or hyper-sensitivity? And the quietly eccentric behaviour of the woman, upstage right, left many of us baffled; she was given to strange, secret smiles, and would take notes at inexplicable moments.

In front of her sat a younger woman, sedate and pretty, perhaps a teacher; some of us pictured her as the Henry Fonda character whose gentle persistence would finally win over her colleagues, as in *Twelve Angry Men*.

In all our ears there still rang the voice of Mervyn Griffith-Jones, counsel for the prosecution, high-cheek-boned and poker-backed, a veteran of Eton, Trinity Hall (Cambridge), the Coldstream Guards and many previous obscenity cases; a voice passionate only in disdain, but barbed with a rabid belief in convention and discipline; a slow, scaly voice, listening to which one almost felt that if Penguin Books were acquitted, the prostitutes would dance in the streets, as they did after Oscar Wilde's conviction.

On Lawrence as a literary artist, the voice (for so I think of Mr. Griffith-Jones, since from where I sat only his head was visible) – the voice had done some dedicated homework. 'Is that expert, artistic writing?' it would ask, having cited a passage in which a phrase was several times repeated. The mind's eye saw a man holding up one brick after another and demanding, 'Is that expert, artistic architecture?' The voice marked Lawrence as if he were an examination paper, and its interrogations had much in common with *vivas*.

It exhaled class-consciousness as effortlessly as air. Would the jury wish their servants to read Lawrence's novel? And was it natural for the lady of a great house to 'run off and copulate with his husband's game-keeper?' The voice took on a positively vengeful rasp when cross-examining people who distinguished between sex as Lawrence saw it and sex as a trivial diversion. Wasn't it true that by 'tenderness' the book actually meant tenderness towards the genital organs? (One wondered how else the voice would want them treated.) And could anyone deny that in the 'bouts' of love-making the emphasis was on the 'pleasure and satisfaction' involved? Leisurely and deadly, the voice hounded Connie Chatterley, a traitress to her class in that she not only enjoyed sex, but enjoyed it with a quasi-peasant. *A propos* of a passage in which she removed her nightdress before making love, the voice enquired why this 'striptease' was necessary; one assumed, charitably, that the question had been carelessly phrased.

Throughout the trial, one longed for a witness who might challenge Mr. Griffith-Jones in Lionel Trilling's words: 'I see no reason in Morality (or in aesthetic theory) why literature should not have as one of its intentions the arousing of thoughts of lust. It is one of the effects, perhaps one of the functions, of literature to arouse desire, and I can discover no grounds for saying that sexual pleasure should not be among the objects of desire which literature present to us, along with heroism, virtue, peace, death, food, wisdom, God, etc.'

But nobody made that answer; and we, anxious in the corridors, had all but persuaded ourselves that no jury could withstand the impact of Mr. Griffith-Jones when the verdict was returned and Lawrence exonerated.

Looking back, I think I can isolate the crucial incident, the exchange wherein the case was psychologically won. It occurred on the third morning during the testimony of Richard Hoggart, who had called Lawrence's novel 'puritanical'. Mr. Hoggart is a short, dark, young Midland teacher of immense scholarship and fierce integrity. From the witness box he uttered a word that we had formerly heard only on the lips of Mr. Griffith-Jones: he pointed out how Lawrence had striven to cleanse it from its furtive, contemptuous and expletive connotations, and to use it in the most simple, neutral way: one fucks. There was no reaction of shock anywhere in the court, so calmly was the word pronounced and so literally employed.

'Does it gain anything,' asked Mr. Gardiner, counsel for the defence, 'by being printed "f---"?' 'Yes,' said Mr. Hoggart, 'it gains a dirty suggestiveness.'

Rising in cross-examination, Mr. Griffith-Jones wanted to know what Mr. Hoggart meant by 'puritanical', receiving an answer to the effect that a puritan was a man who felt a profound sense of responsibility to his own conscience. Counsel then read out a series of excerpts from the novel. It must have been by chance that he chose the most impressive passages, the most solemnly ecstatic, the ones about 'the primeval roots of true beauty' and 'the sons of men and the daughters of women' but slowly, as he recited them, one realized that he genuinely thought them impure and revolting.

With every defiling inflection he alienated some part of his audience, seemingly unaware that what he had intended for our scorn was moving us in a way he had never foreseen; yet still he continued, bland and derisive, utterly unconscious of his increasing loneliness. Having finished, he triumphantly asked the witness whether a puritan would feel such 'reverence for a man's balls'. 'Indeed, yes,' said Mr. Hoggart, almost with compassion.

I remembered his earlier reply to the suggestion that Lady Chatterley's affair with Mellors was due solely to her husband's impotence. '*It is not,*' he said: and in those words we heard, for the first time in the trial, the stubborn, uncompromising voice of the radical English moralist.

Its volume and assurance grew as the cross-examination proceeded; and before long both jury and audience knew that the real battle had at last been joined – between all that Hoggart stood for, and all that Griffith-Jones stood for; between Lawrence's England and Sir Clifford Chatterley's England; between contact and separation; between freedom and control; between love and death.

After a career as a drama critic, mainly for the Observer, *Kenneth Tynan became a theatrical producer (Oh! Calcutta! and Soldiers) and was later literary manager at the National Theatre in London. He died in 1980.*

THE MAN IN THE GLASS CASE

—

James Morris
Guardian
12 April 1961

After being kidnapped and smuggled out of his hiding place in Argentina by Israeli agents, ex-Nazi SS officer Adolf Eichmann was put on trial in Jerusalem. Found guilty, he was later hanged for 'crimes against the Jewish people, crimes against humanity and war crimes'.

At eleven o'clock this morning, the twenty-fifth day of Nissan in the Hebrew year 5721, Adolf Eichmann, the German, appeared before a Jewish Court in Jerusalem charged with crimes against the Jewish people – and in that very sentence, I suspect, I am recording the whole significance of this tragic and symbolic hearing.

All is incidental – the controversy, the evidence, the implications, the sentence, the verdict. The point of the Eichmann trial is that it is happening at all, and that through its ritual the Jews have answered history back.

Eichmann slipped into court this morning, out of the mystery and legend of his imprisonment, almost unnoticed. Heaven knows, the courtroom was ready for him. Its parallel strips of neon lighting gave it a pale and heartless brilliance. Its great Jewish candelabra shone gilded on the wall. There sat the five Jewish lawyers of the prosecution, grave-faced, mostly youngish men, with a saturnine bearded procurator, lithe and long-limbed, elegant in his skullcap at the end of the line. There sat Dr Servatius, the German defence counsel, earnest in discussion with his young assistant.

There were the translators in their booths, and the girl secretaries at their tables, and the peak-capped policemen at the doors, and the gallimaufry of the Press seething and grumbling and scribbling and making half-embarrassed jokes in its seats. And there stood the bullet-proof glass box, like a big museum showcase – too big for a civet or a bird of paradise, too small for a skeletonic dinosaur – which was the focus and fulcrum of it all.

Nothing had been forgotten, nothing overlooked. A dozen books had been written about this moment, and a thousand newspaper articles: we only awaited the accused.

But when he came, by one of those curious half-Freudian ironies of great events, most of us were looking the other way. He slipped in silently, almost slyly, flanked by three policemen in their blue, British uniforms. No shudder ran around the courtroom for hardly anybody noticed.

'There he is,' I heard a rather self-conscious English voice somewhere behind my shoulder, rather as you sometimes hear mourners pointing out rich relatives at a funeral: and, sure enough, when I looked up at that glass receptacle, there he was.

He looked dignified enough, almost proud, in horn-rimmed glasses and a new dark suit bought for him yesterday for the occasion. He looked like a lawyer himself, perhaps, or perhaps a recently retired brigadier, or possibly a textile manufacturer of vaguely intellectual pursuits.

When I looked at him again, though, I noticed that there was to his movements a queer stiffness or jerkiness of locomotion. He hardly looked at the courtroom – he had nobody to look for – but even in his small gestures of preparation and expectancy I thought I recognized the symptoms: somewhere inside him, behind the new dark suit and the faint suggestion of defiance, Adolf Eichmann was trembling.

Like a candidate at a *viva voce* he rose to his feet, as though he were holding his stomach in, when the three Judges entered the Court: Dr Moshe Landau, Dr Benjamin Halevi, Dr Yitzhak Raveh – European Jews all three of them, and two of them from Germany itself, whence they escaped almost at the moment when the racialists came to power. They looked the very personification of justice, solemn, bare-headed and commanding.

But the proceedings opened, paradoxically, without dignity, for at this moment the myriad attending journalists found that their portable radio sets, for simultaneous translations, did not seem to work properly, and the Eichmann hearing, this moment of Jewish destiny, began to a cacophony of clicks, muffled shakings, and tapping of plastic.

'Are you Adolf Eichmann?' asked the President of the Court: and through the racket around us we heard him answer, via microphones and wires out of his glass insulation.

'Yes, sir,' he said, and the trial began.

James Morris (now Jan Morris) has published several books including Conundrum, Locations, *and* Last Letters From Hav, *which was shortlisted for the Booker Prize in 1985.*

HOME FOR CHRISTMAS

—

Marian E. Davies
Guardian
December 1961

As a popular political movement, the Committee of 100's Campaign for Nuclear Disarmament led to untypical behaviour forged by moral conviction. For the first time in a generation, normally peaceful, law-abiding, professional people were, in their passive resistance, purposely breaking the law. Marian E. Davies was one of them.

Feeling miserably ill because I am breaking the law, and hoping that I will not be sick all over the uniforms of the two smiling Bobbies who lift me from the pavement, I am gently carried into the police horsebox. 'Why can't you be a bit lighter? . . . You are not so young as some of 'em, are you? . . . Why do you do this?' Laughingly they ask me questions, politely they put me down on the floor of the horsebox next to my friend. All the way to the police station we hear cheers from our law-abiding supporters. There are twenty-one of us in the van and we all go to a police cell together, staying there long enough for the smokers to have two fags.

Then a room where the police take down our particulars: I have to guess my height; I think my eyes are brown; I have no visible scars. I am given a charge sheet which informs me that 'At 3.35 p.m. on Saturday, 9th December, 1961, you, without lawful authority or excuse, wilfully obstructed the free passage along a highway, called Princess Street, Manchester, contrary to Section 121, Highways Act, 1959.' We wait in a corridor for some considerable time. The police, by now firmly established as our friends, make sure that the women have chairs. They still fire questions at us because they are interested and impressed, glad to have first-hand knowledge of how we feel and why we act as we do. 'Many of our chaps agree with you, you know, though not when you break the law.' And in correct order we go before the magistrate; we plead guilty; a few of us make short statements; we are fined forty-two shillings.

The police cashier's office is as efficient as the most modern bank, and fines are quickly collected, though four of the twenty-one refuse to pay and are sent into the corridor again. By now the police have discovered that I have three children. They are staggered. I must pay my fine, they say. 'Lassie, change your mind, go and pay it. The magistrate will hate sending you to prison.'

And she did. She tried very hard to persuade me to change my mind. Twenty-five days in prison; she 'had no alternative but to give me the alternative'. Twenty-five days in prison, in prison until after Christmas, I should be separated from my family at this special time of the year, wouldn't I pay my fine? I could be given time in which to pay; would I sit on one side for a moment and think about it? No? Then prison it was.

Now that I was officially a prisoner I was handed over to a policewoman, who first removed my nuclear disarmament badge and the belt of my mac (did she think I would stab or hang myself? I vaguely wondered) and then took away what few personal possessions I had on me. I sat in a small cell with my three companions. I wept silently, feeling small and frightened when I thought I should be feeling big and heroic.

The Black Maria was uncomfortable; how much better they transport their horses than their prisoners! It was foggy, so the journey to the prison was cold and slow.

At the prison gates we entered a new world; our possessions were listed, a kindly officer explained some of the procedure and told me I could leave if I paid my fine. A doctor examined me. What was the blotchiness all over me? I assured her it was only nerves. Was I sure? Was I allergic to wool? Had I a rash? Then a dear nurse was more embarrassed than I was at having to ask me very intimate questions and to search my hair. I stripped and then, oh joy, I was given a hot bath and allowed to keep my own foundation garments. My prison clothing was passed to me over the unlocked bathroom door. What queer underclothes! I smiled as I wished my two teenage daughters could see them and thought wistfully of the black nylon panties I had just surrendered. But they were clean, the cardigan was cheerful, and the shoes were enormous, which was better than being too small.

Next, food and drink – but the tea was undrinkable and I didn't even sample the stodgy white bread, but this was my own fault, I was still feeling sick. More formalities, more details, maiden name, where born, husband's name, where did he live? My signature on this form and that form. And so into the prison proper.

Another official checked my particulars, assured me that I could go out whenever I agreed to pay the fine, and asked me if I would do so. Another official gave me a sheet of notepaper on which to write home, telling me that if I asked I could have another whenever I wished to write for someone to pay my fine. Would I do so?

My 'room' was cream and pink, with a green rug and a green hessian bedcover. A large mug of unsweetened, unmilked cocoa awaited me. I filled my bucket from a tap along the corridor. I was locked in with a sweet 'Good night, dear.' So this was prison. I looked round my cell – painted brick walls and iron door, tiled floor, three plain wooden chairs and two small tables, an unmade-up double bunk, 'my' single bed, buckets, bowls, chamber pots. I read, 'I love Eddie.' 'I love Bill.' 'I want my mum.' 'Dirty rotten coppers', 'I love a boy I can never have.' I had my pen and ink. Should I add a Ban the Bomb sign? But no, one doesn't write on walls, one is too well brought up. But I can write home. I wonder if my husband has been arrested, I think of my children, I weep. I pull myself together and begin my letter and find this helps; I write freely hoping it won't be censored.

So to bed, chuckling over my unglamorous nightie. But no sleep. I climb up on the top bunk and look out at Manchester. The fog has cleared a little but the air is thick and smokey. I think of my beloved hills with perhaps the moon upon them and the beautiful fresh air which comes in at my own bedroom window I weep. I pull myself together. I have got to stick this for twenty-five days.

Eventually a light goes on and I get dressed and washed and finish my letter. I sit and sit, reading the inscriptions on the wall. I reread the prison rules, but still can't understand them all. Perhaps I will be allowed a visitor. I'll read them again to find out. But I don't find out. A bell goes and I wonder what I should do. But I can't do anything; I'm locked in. I sit. Another bell goes. I hear keys being turned and people clattering down the corridor with buckets. It's like hell let loose. What a noise! My own door is unlocked. 'Good morning; you'll be allowed to empty your pail and get water as soon as the others have finished.' The others clatter back past my open door. Most of them are young girls about the same age as my elder daughter. They smile at me, such welcoming smiles. I weep. Then I collect my own water, meeting the other three Ban the Bomb prisoners (as we are obviously styled) at the tap. I go to the one and only toilet. It is filthy. It will not flush; the smell is horrible.

The four of us are taken down a separate staircase to the basement to fetch our breakfast, carrying it back up three flights of spiral stairs to our rooms. I notice for the first time that we are on the top floor. But I still can't work out the geography of the place. We are locked in our cells. The porridge was unsweetened and of the coarsest kind and had no milk on it. The bread was white and stodgy, the slice of luncheon meat highly seasoned and rather dry. I could eat nothing. The tea was lovely. I sat. I wanted to go to the toilet and didn't like to use the pot; in any case I had no toilet paper. I must ask for that. Eventually the door was unlocked, the others passed back along the corridor to empty their slops. They smiled. I felt like weeping. One whispered, 'Don't sit on the toilet, love. We aren't supposed to speak to you.' They passed back and we were allowed out to empty our slops. I asked for toilet paper and tried to use the toilet without sitting on it. It still did not flush.

We were visited by officials. Had I considered paying my fine? I could arrange to have it paid at any time. I was brought books, the classics, *Jude the Obscure*, *Mill on the Floss*, and the *Bible*. I read, but I hadn't got my reading glasses and my headache was bad but I didn't feel quite so sick. I was allowed to stand at the door of my cell and talk to my friends, a blessed time. And then we were asked if we would like a Meeting for Worship. Three of us went to a room, the door was shut and we were watched by a warder. But it was a wonderful Meeting for Worship. I thought, 'Here we sit, three Quakers all in our forties, yet the Committee of 100 is accused of being political, Communist, full of young irresponsible people.' But I soon forgot such thoughts. 'Where two or three are gathered together . . .' It was a marvellous half-hour.

And so back to our cells. I read. Then dinner-time. We went down three flights of stairs, separate from all the others, we came back, we were locked in, we ate our dinner. At least I ate a little. The soup was hot and tasty, but very solid; the main course was solid; the pudding was solid. I felt ashamed at the amount I was wasting, for it wasn't badly cooked. The governor came to see me. She was sweet. She was concerned about my family. She asked me to consider paying the fine. I wept. I lay down on my bed and thought it must be the middle of the afternoon, but then the wireless was put on in the corridor, very loud and distorted, and I recognized *Two-Way Family Favourites* which I knew ended at 1.30 p.m. How glad I was that, thanks to my three teenagers, I was up to date with all the latest pop songs.

I lay on my bed. I was visited by the Church Army Sister. She was one of the most marvellous people I have ever talked to. Of course she wanted me to pay the fine and of course I wept. We talked together for some time. And then I read (thank goodness for Thomas Hardy), though I wished I had my reading glasses. We were unlocked at last. And three of us were taken for 'exercise'. Down the three flights of stairs into a yard, walk at the same speed, in the same direction for about twenty minutes, keep to the perimeter of the oval area, mustn't cut the corners, keep going steadily round and round. But we walked together and we talked.

Back to cell, fetch water, fetch tea – solid white bread, solid bun, but the tea was good. We were locked in. 'Good night, dear,' though I was sure it could only be about four o'clock. I ate little, but I read and my headache grew worse, if that were possible. The evening dragged on. From somewhere I could hear carols being sung, presumably by the prison choir; later we had *Sunday Half-Hour* on the wireless. (Goodness, was it only that time?) At some time we had cocoa, still unsweetened and with no milk. Then someone came around and, standing outside the cell door, said 'Good night' to each prisoner individually. Her voice could be heard echoing round the prison for what seemed to be about fifteen minutes: 'Good night, good night, good night.' And so the hours passed by.

The next morning, two of the four went out, their fines having been paid by outsiders. I wept. The governor sent for me. Would I pay my fine? The twelve shillings I had on me when arrested would be deducted, and I should get six days less. If I paid more I should be home in time for Christmas. Would I pay? No? I saw the chaplain. I was visited by a lady not in uniform, a prison visitor, perhaps. Would I consider paying my fine? No?

Out for exercise, into the workroom putting the strings on carrier bags. We were with, but separate from, the other prisoners. How young most of them were. There was an ugly scuffle and one prisoner was removed. I tied hundreds of knots in string. It was quite soothing, almost like knitting. And I could speak quietly to my one friend who was left. Back to our rooms. Water. Toilet. It still wouldn't flush, so I put my pail of water down it. Now I had to fill my bucket again, and I think I was frowned upon, though kindly. Tea, still stodge to eat. 'Good night', though it was surely not dark yet. Thomas Hardy, I'd read 400 pages and at last I had my reading glasses. I could now look at the *Bible* with its smaller print. Another sleepless night, but I felt better, and I had drunk my cocoa and water. I'd get used to it.

The next morning the same routine, more knots in string. Then I was summoned, by my surname only, of course. Some anonymous person had paid my fine. I could go. Indeed, I must go: I had no option. But absurdly enough, I wept. I relinquished my prison clothes. After all, I needn't have washed the prison bloomers the night before and put them to dry under my mattress, for now I had back my own black nylon panties. I was given my twelve shillings and four shillings fare and subsistence. I was free. Bewildered, I looked at the big outside world. Was it Tuesday? What time was it? But I had only been inside four days, I mustn't feel like this. I nearly wept again, but pulled myself together and went in search of a taxi and my husband.

TAKING PAINS WITH PINTER

—

John Gale

Observer
10 June 1962

After being trounced by the critics when his first play, The Birthday Party, *opened to much confusion in the West End in 1957, Harold Pinter won almost universal acclaim for* The Caretaker *in 1958. By 1962 his reputation for puzzling his audiences had already become a subject of popular good humour.*

Harold Pinter was last week rehearsing his play, *The Collection*, directing with Peter Hall. Pinter, strong black hair, gleaming spectacles, dark suit, well-polished black shoes, was, superficially, more solid than one might have expected from his work. At first glance you might have taken him for a person who enjoyed discussing fast cars in pubs. He directed with confidence, his actor's voice authoritative. It was when he took off his glasses and twirled them that you noticed the dark eyes and sensitive face that looked as though it had its worries.

Nuance and timing meant a great deal to Pinter: 'I'm probably complicating things,' he said to John Ronane, a young actor, 'but it's worth complicating. We haven't really ever quite examined this speech, have we? Until we find out what it means to you, there can't be any real . . . You know?' Pinter coughed and took off his glasses. 'We have to find . . . Don't be worried.'

'I'm not worried,' said Ronane. 'I'm just completely – lost.'

'I'm not really getting the way you were committed to yourself,' said Pinter, 'and to what you were committed. I feel you must be committed to a possibility, d'you know what I mean?'

In a break, while the cast of four drank tea and coffee out of YMCA cups, Pinter sat down and took pains to discuss exactly what he wanted from an actor.

'The thing is, Harold's plays take such bloody concentration,' Kenneth Haigh said to Barbara Murray. She was playing with a small white kitten that had quite a large part. A man in a white coat brought in a tray of red sawdust for the kitten's WC. Miss Murray liked the kitten, but it was troublesome. 'Bloody cats,' she said to it kindly. 'It'll have to be sedated.'

While the rehearsals went on, Pinter walked round, smoking, threw his lighter in the air and caught it. At times he lay back in a chair, feet up, hand to mouth, frowning. There was a YMCA flag pinned to his dark vest-like jersey.

'John, I think this . . . Since it's quite clear, I think, that the thunder . . . And when you say, *"not again"*. For Christ's sake! And the more you go on with this . . . If you want to know what you feel about women and all that . . .' Pinter snapped his fingers. 'Make it a clean start, as it were.' Fingers clicked. 'Switch in.'

'I should think that *olives* is the word. Whereas, as the change of concentration is very clear, your, slight, thing . . . it's a change at the silence, the change is there.' Several times people, presumably lost, opened the door of the rehearsal room in the YMCA, hesitated, apologized, went out. Pinter looked cross.

Oh, by the way, I've seen your wife [said one of the characters]. *What a beautiful kitten she has! You should see it, Bill, it's all white.*

If I were you, I'd go home and knock her over the head with a saucepan and tell her not to make up such stories.

'Okay. Michael, let's go from *"What about another drink".'*

In the shadows of the Aldwych, Pinter leapt on to the stage, stood there with his hands in pockets, spectacles gleaming. He walked with his arm round Barbara Murray.

She: 'What's *his* attitude?'

Pinter: 'What's *your* attitude?'

'I think we've done, I think it's essential to get this scene, er . . .' Pinter's hands spun like a mouse's exercise wheel. 'Right. When you're ready, let's get on.' He lit a cigarette. 'Okay, John. We're off.' Pointed and snapped fingers. 'Well, let's go, let's go, please, John.' Stands on stage, lies on stage, crouches on stage, sits on stage, flicking ash into a huge shining cylindrical tin that he carries about with him. Makes a gesture of easing collar, as though it were tight. Does this several times. 'Right, right.'

Oh, what a beautiful kitten! What a really beautiful kitten.

'In a sense it's too, rather . . . what's the word?' Fingers click, 'It was a bit too fishwifery.'

Oh what a beautiful lamp!

'Michael, you see, it's not good taste at all. The whole thing's horrible.'

'No, let's try. We've got that bloody Scarlatti. What the hell happened to it?'

Hungry? I've got some olives. Like one? Don't like olives? What on earth have you got against olives?

'Right. Good. Yes. You're there. Okay. Yeah, Let's just go back to the beginning. The whole speech, John. I find it a little elaborate. You're not swinging it.'

What on earth have you got against olives? 'I think this a qualification. You are, at the moment, shoving away, while . . .'

I've come to a decision. I'm going to see him.

Who? What for?

John Gale wrote for the Observer *for more than twenty years, first as a reporter, covering the Suez crisis and the war in Algeria, and later writing many profiles. He also published three books, including an autobiography,* Clean Young Englishman. *He died in 1974, aged 48.*

TRISTAN DA CUNHA: LITTLE WORLD LOST

——

Michael Moynihan
Sunday Times Magazine
19 August 1962

In October 1961, the tiny, remote South Atlantic island of Tristan da Cunha was overrun by a volcanic eruption necessitating the evacuation of the entire population of just over 250. For a people who had been left behind by the modern world home suddenly became a former RAF camp at Calshot near Southampton.

'Home, sweet home, it is to us. All the time we prays to be back. Our homes, our little church that our husbands build with the sweat from their brows, toiling in the heat of the sun, all that left behind . . .'

It is Martha Rogers, sixty-three-year-old headwoman of Tristan da Cunha, speaking. A weathered, wise face, expressive but wary. The vehement spate of strangely pronounced words ('hoam,' 'swayat') is sometimes barely intelligible. Its implication is crystal-clear. After nearly a year in England she is consumingly homesick for a volcanic island in the South Atlantic, seven miles across, 1,200 miles from anywhere.

Life there, as she recalls it, was free and uncomplicated. It revolved around the windswept plots that produced potatoes and other vegetables; the surrounding sea where the stronger men fished from their longboats; the cattle, donkeys and sheep that provided pulling-power, milk, meat, leather and wool; the canning-factory where money could be earned to buy imported goods; the school, church and club; above all the long, low cottages, built of volcanic tuff and thatched with flax, where birth, marriage and death rang the changes on only seven family names – Rogers, Repetto, Glass, Green, Swain, Hagan, Lavarello.

'We was like brothers and sisters,' says Martha. 'We done never had any crimes. Each mother bring her children up at her knee in the way that they must go. They is taught right from wrong and the true God.'

Martha is holding forth in the sitting room of the terrace house she was allotted last January when the 263 islanders were moved from their first camp in Surrey to the former married quarters of a disused Coastal Command base at Calshot, overlooking Southampton Water. It is a house with modern furniture, electric light and cooker, hot and cold water, stairs.

The only things she points out with pride and pleasure are a framed photograph of her Tristan home – high up apart from the others, backed by the rugged slopes that soar to the volcano's 6,760-foot-high cone, facing across to the limitless sea: and another of herself, stern in her Sunday dress, at the side of 'that good man', Prince Philip.

Curled on a divan, Martha's pretty, dark-eyed granddaughter, Jane, listens and watches. An hour ago, boarding the double-decker bus from the infants' school with English children, she was a good deal less demure. Now, asked why her Tristan school was nicer, she answers in a whisper.

But Martha pounces on it with a quick smile of approval. 'She was let hout free, she say.' And what that meant on the island, that Paradise lost, is evoked in a torrent of nostalgia.

Hout from school to the bare grass slopes in the sun and the salt breeze, to the bumpy ox-tracks where the only hazard is a kick from a pannier-laden donkey, to the shallow streams sparkling down to the sea, to rock-pools on beaches grey from lava that poured from an eruption unknown centuries ago. Hout to the freedom of forty-five square miles of the earth that had no name until a Portuguese admiral in 1506 sighted it and gave it his; no human tenant until a Massachusetts American (soon to be drowned) landed and claimed it in 1810 – 'far removed from the reach of chicanery and ordinary misfortune'; no community until the Scotsman Corporal Glass, his coloured wife and a few others stayed behind when a British garrison was withdrawn in 1817.

Hout to Deep Gulch and Seal Bay, Hottentot Point and Pike's Mouse, Ridge-Where-The-Goat-Jump-Off and Down-Where-The-Minister-Land-His-Things.

Now Jane, out from an English village school, is a virtual prisoner behind the camp's high fences. For there are worse dangers even than the double-decker hurtling to Southampton, the cars and lorries that stream in and out of the sprawling oil refinery, the frisky New Forest ponies that (to no Tristan's special surprise) have the freedom of the roads. What happened to Gordon Glass still hangs over the camp like a shadow of evil from the world outside.

It was not long after they came to Calshot. One-armed Gordon, a grave, dignified patriarch of sixty-two, who used to superintend the building of the longboats, had taken a job as a night-watchman, tending the red lamps around a road reconstruction. One dark night he was sitting outside his hut when two young thugs crept up. They jumped on him, clawed at his pockets, found nothing. The only valuable he carried was his watch. One of them wrenched it from him, hurled it to the road and ground it with his heel. Then they made off into the night.

Since then the Tristans have read in the papers of barbarities more shocking than that. For a community that dotes on its children they are scarcely to be thought about.

There is a heavy tread on the path outside and Jane jumps, with sudden animation, from the divan. 'Can I go with Uncle Chief?' From the doorway Willie Repetto, sixty-year-old headman of Tristan, glances heavily from his sister to the stranger. He is back from work and has come to collect the key to number six.

'Dear brother, there at the right,' says Martha. 'We done never need any keys at home, does we? The doors was always open, we was all like brothers and sisters.'

Bachelor Willie – long, solemn, furrowed face and gravel voice – begs to be excused from talking. He is tired out after a day's trench-digging.

Jane tilts her chin as Martha ties the ribbon to her 'kappie,' a sun-bonnet old-fashioned as Kate Greenaway ('just like I had when I was a girl'), and is soon jigging beside her great-uncle as he strides away from more interrogation.

Since they fled from the lava-streams to safety and civilization the Tristans have been blinking in a constant spotlight. And not only from press, radio and television. A London University professor has trapped their voices on tape – a unique dialect, with echoes of Dickensian cockney, Australian, Afrikaans, American, that most have so far preserved unsullied. The British Medical Research Council have recorded their blood pressure and circulation, examined teeth and samples of ear-wax and saliva. The detrimental effects of 150 years of close inbreeding on eyesight have been established. The long-term consequences of transplanting a community hitherto largely free of germs and viruses is being studied.

Aptitude tests have been made of many of the thirty-six children attending the local infants', junior and secondary schools. A Norwegian professor from an American university, who spent four months on Tristan in 1938, is making a close study of their adaptation to civilization (noting, among other things, that none of the men here wear their socks outside their trousers, but that a number of women still wear the knee-length woollen stockings in preference to nylons and that none as yet use make-up or smoke cigarettes).

The Tristans do not turn their backs on all this. They present a communal face (however split between withdrawn smile and outright scowl) that says firmly: 'We want to go home.' But do they all?

Jane is asleep (dreaming of which school?) when the record-player gets revving in a nearby hut where RAF corporals used to unwind and now Tristan young flings itself with some abandon into the twist. There is a soft-drinks bar, billiards, table-tennis, darts, cards. It is not all that different from the Prince Philip Club back home – except that there are new faces around: teenagers from the modern houses across the road where the families of RAF men serving abroad live in similar impermanence; Teddies from neighbouring villages lounging near the entrance, looking tough.

Recently Sgt. Reginald Davies, the RAF's sole representative at the camp, just stopped a firebrand Tristan stirring things up with the Teddies. A kindly middle-aged bachelor, he plays marathon games of cricket with the children in the evenings and, apart from the Rev. Noel Brewster, Rector of Fawley, has probably gained the Tristans' confidence more than anyone else. Since January he has seen a change.

Visible things are the five motorbikes and the gadgety bicycles that have become new status symbols around the camp; the darts-playing with locals and visiting merchant-seamen in the public bar of the Falcon at Fawley; the bubblegum chewed by a Tristan boy in jeans in unison with a village girl; the uninhibited merry-making at a travelling funfair.

Less perceptibly, awe and acquiescence have given place to a sense of adventure and competitiveness. 'In front of their elders or to any stranger they'd think they were letting the side down if they said they didn't want to go home,' says Sgt. Davies. 'I'd say there might be a good third of the Tristans – including older ones I've talked to – who wouldn't be heartbroken living on in England.'

One of the few openly to admit it is twenty-nine-year-old Basil Lavarello, shortly off on his second trip with the Antarctic survey ship Shackleton, who now sees the world as his oyster. He straddles the powerful motorbike he has just finished paying for from high wages as a marine engineer at a Lymington yacht-builder's.

A dashingly handsome figure, impervious to the persistent attentions of a lipsticked English girl, he says he has no thought yet of marriage or engagement. Since coming to England he has flown to Manchester and Canada (he mentions both in an unboasting breath). His brother is working as a deck-hand on the *Athlone Castle* to Cape Town. Neither of them wants to creep back into the shell that is Tristan.

'Of course it will always be a part of me,' he says. 'But I don't see how any of us could live there happily unless the Government says it is all right and gives us an Administrator again and a doctor and the others.'

To Martha the Government is 'him' (or 'heeam') – a shadowy super-Administrator who has made himself a bit scarce lately but will see that everything is all right in the end. To Mary Swain – 'Big Mary', Tristan's exuberant midwife, mother of seven, grandmother of twenty-two, great-grandmother of three – there is no doubt at all that this is anything more than an unfortunate interlude in real existence.

To Willie Repetto, brooding over a cigarette and a cup of tea under the framed documents from Buckingham Palace, the present is purgatory. He hates working for any boss – let alone a series of bosses – has no interest in life around him in the Mother Country that has so much enchantment at a distance. Things have fallen apart. He is no longer the central figure.

Only on Sundays is there some feeling of the old togetherness. Holy Communion in the camp chapel at 8.30 is regularly attended by over seventy of the islanders. Altar-cloth, cross and candlesticks are from the corrugated-iron-roofed church on Tristan. Hymns are emotionally sung to the harmonium the Queen gave to replace an outworn gift of Queen Mary's. At evensong at Fawley's Norman church, there are more Tristans than locals. But it is mostly the older generation. An alien world beckons the young.

'At home you'd hear the church bell wherever you is. We was all God-fearing . . . like brothers and sisters . . .' Behind the plain-chant of nostalgia what discords lie concealed? No feuding, no fighting, no unpleasantness?

In the Calshot houses as the elders talk there are sidelong glances between the silent young, a twitch of lips, a sudden outright guffaw from a grim-faced, baby-rocking mother. Curtains twitch as you walk along the paths and gnarled, shut-in faces withdraw.

'Anyone who lived on Tristan less than ten months or so knew little about the islanders,' says the Rev. Philip Bell, who was their chaplain for six years. 'Up to then they would seem just a simple, happy-go-lucky community. After that you began to find they were not so uncomplicated.'

There were the high-spirited Christmas festivities when sheep were roasted, drink flowed and the mummers went from house to house, masked, gloved, strangely dressed up, talking in high-pitched voices – challenging recognition. There were also, on occasion, hints of something nasty in the potato-shed.

'Public opinion was what greatly mattered,' says Mr. Bell. 'If an islander had been offended in any way he would not rest until he had done something to show he could not be pushed around.'

His wife and two of his four children sit in the study of his rectory at Crawley, near Winchester, absorbed all over again as he runs through some of the colour films he took on Tristan.

The longboats heaving on the sparkling sea, men scrambling to the rocks of

Nightingale Island to collect penguin guana for the potato fields, the sports day, the shooting match, the Dedication service ('We love the place, O God'), the trundling ox-carts and frisky calves, Big Mary billowing and beaming down a windy slope. Many faces stare into the camera.

No more now than then can camera or interrogator really penetrate the mask of this unique, proud, secretive, entangled people. There have been births, marriages and deaths in England – but there is still no addition to the seven family names.

Civilization – the roar of a motor-bike engine, the throb of the twist, the gun-duels on the telly – may be inexorably claiming some. Most remain unwilling outcasts from what its first inhabitants called 'The Island of Refreshment'.

In 1963, all but five of the 153 Tristans over 21 voted by secret ballot to return to Tristan da Cunha. But when, eight years later, Michael Moynihan paid them a visit he discovered that their innocence had gone. For a people who had had little concept of money before the eruption, cash had become all important. Some families had purchased cars, while homes now had fitted carpets and paraffin refrigerators. There had even been a strike by Tristan fishermen working for the South African-owned canning factory.

Michael Moynihan retired from journalism in 1981 after writing for the Sunday Times *for nineteen years. The youngest British war correspondent (he had been declared unfit for national service in 1939), he wrote about his war experiences in his memoir* War Correspondent *published in 1994.*

REVIEW OF LAWRENCE OF ARABIA

—

Dilys Powell
Sunday Times
9 December 1962

Lawrence of Arabia *was to become one of the most celebrated British films ever,*
winning seven Oscars at the 1963 Academy Awards.

Enigmatic subject, legendary hero, historical background and a sense of magnitude
– not simply the magnitude of the huge Technicolor landscapes on the huge Super
Panavision-70 screen, but a size of purpose: *Lawrence of Arabia* is uncompromisingly
serious.

The screenplay, which Robert Bolt has written and which, with Sam Spiegel as
producer, Fred Young as director of photography and John Box as designer, David
Lean has directed, is in two parts: with its interval the film runs for nearly four hours,
and this time four hours is not too much. The first part is about a man in relation to
a country and its people: Lawrence in the desert, Lawrence and the Arabs: a story of
victory, though with hints of risks to come. The second part, though on the face of it
full of explosions, ambushes, tortures and deaths, is about a man in relation to
himself: Lawrence recognizing his own misjudgements, discovering his own flaws: a
story of defeat.

At the outset, though the prologue to the film shows the stubbornly private death
and the solemn public obsequies, the life on the screen looks gaily insubordinate:
the young lieutenant in Cairo breaking the rules of good form, exasperating his
superior officers, acting against orders. But neither Robert Bolt's finely carpentered
and often subtle screenplay, nor David Lean's commanding and imaginative
direction, nor the superbly bold and creative playing of Peter O'Toole leaves us for
long in any doubt of the singularity, the solitariness of Lawrence, his conviction of
being a chosen man.

He is chosen at first for, or perhaps by, the desert. Especially among Englishmen,
I think, one meets this surrender to a foreign country, an alien climate; the film gives
force both to Lawrence's Englishness – the fair slender northern looks, and the
mixture of withdrawn reflectiveness and laconic assurance so well conveyed by Mr.
O'Toole – and to its contrast with the fiery wilderness in which he was to find his
purpose. Then, as the man moves farther away from his own kind – talking with
Feisal, conceiving the attack on Aqaba, leading the expedition across the uncrossable

– it gives force also to his self-identification with the Arab cause, with the Arabs themselves. But that comes later: first comes the desert.

Romantic landscapes, august landscapes – one has seen those often enough on the screen. This is something else. The sun rising on the rim of blood-orange sand; dust-storms like the smoke-trails of a *djin*; the shapes of infinity, the colours of heat – I think it is the first time for the cinema to communicate ecstasy. *Lawrence of Arabia* is full of beauties, and I can't refrain from singling out the ambush of the train load of horses and the capture in particular of one proud milk-white creature – a passage which might be out of Homer. But it is in the immensity of the desert, an immensity interrupted by tiny specks which move, which are men, which are camels, that the film most splendidly uses the powers of its medium.

Self-identification with an alien people has both its exhilarations and its dangers, and Mr. Bolt's Lawrence shows tragically how the dangers follow an excess of the exhilarations. I say Mr. Bolt's Lawrence: no two writers have presented the same character, and certainly there will be objections to this portrait (for instance to the rendering of the crucial arrest by the Turks, an incident from which this Lawrence emerges broken by the realization that under torture he could have readily betrayed his friends).

Euphemisms and evasions no doubt there must be in a film concerning people, some still alive, some recently dead but with living relatives: there is a sprinkling of fictitious names. Enough of the historical figures, though, to give the narrative a proper solidity: for instance a self-contained, calculating Feisal (Alec Guinness) and a shrewdly persuasive Allenby (Jack Hawkins) – both notable portraits. I must mention other performances, too: by Arthur Kennedy, Anthony Quayle, Claude Rains, by Anthony Quinn and the personable Egyptian actor Omar Sharif as Arab leaders; by Jose Ferrer, memorable as the Turkish Bey – whom Mr. Bolt has endowed with intellectual sensibilities not mentioned in *Seven Pillars of Wisdom*.

But naturally Lawrence is at the heart, and round him the other characters circle, worshipping or deceiving. In the end he is powerless to give his Arab followers what he has promised them, not only because their own quarrels prevent it but also because the politicians (this is a painfully English story) have been too smart for him. For ultimately he is confused within himself: a poser, but deluded by his own pose; compassionate, but capable of breaking out in a rage of hideous savagery.

The confusions are the real subject of Part Two, which they make more difficult and perhaps less successful going than Part One. But *Lawrence of Arabia* taken as a whole is a genuine, sometimes even a profound interpretation of character. And that alone, even without the great aesthetic beauties, would make the film unique in the cinema of historical reconstruction.

Dilys Powell was the doyenne of London film critics for over fifty years. She died in 1995.

FLOODLIT FRONTIER

—

Richard West
The Sunday Times Magazine
February 1963

In 1963, following the Bay of Pigs fiasco and with Fidel Castro soon to allow the Soviet Union to station missiles in Cuba, the Cold War was at its height.

It is seventeen years since Churchill announced in his Fulton speech that an 'iron curtain' had fallen across Europe. This was less than a year after the end of the grand alliance with Stalin's Russia. But already the West had begun to lose hope of co-existence with Communism.

Russian soldiers had seen in Europe luxuries and advances beyond their Soviet dreams. Stalin was determined that Russians in peacetime should not go abroad and risk getting dangerous ideas.

The Russian-supported governments which were gaining control in Poland, Hungary, Rumania, Bulgaria, Yugoslavia and Albania, had already begun to harass Western visitors and to stop anti-Communists from leaving. The Soviet Zone of Germany had already begun to grow into a separate state.

The Iron Curtain in Europe had settled by 1949. The Czechs had joined the Russian herd. The Yugoslavs had kicked their way out of the stable. Except for the rioting in Berlin and Poznan and a brave attempt at revolution in the autumn of 1956 by Hungary, the Iron Curtain has remained in place ever since. Indeed it has grown from a metaphor to a physical fact. Barbed wire, electric fence or minefields run along much of its length. The Hungarians have begun to replace their wooden watchtowers with shining constructions of steel.

Even the Communists now talk of an iron curtain, although of course they say that the West put it up. They also say, with more justification, that Goebbels rather than Churchill invented the phrase.

But what does the Iron Curtain mean to the people who live beside it? How does it vary from country to country along the way? Is there any sign anywhere of its slow disappearance?

In search of the answer to questions like these, we made a 3,850-mile trip through seven countries; from Kirkenes in the extreme north of Norway to Kirklareli in Turkey; from mid-Arctic to Near East. Everywhere we found how much the Iron Curtain had changed, both for good and bad, since Churchill's historic speech.

Our first impression of the Iron Curtain was deceptively calm. The Norwegian-Russian frontier on the edge of the Barents Sea is the coldest stretch of the Iron Curtain; but by far the most friendly. When the dividing River Pasvik freezes over in winter, almost anybody can cross the ice to Capitalism or Communism.

There is not even a proper reindeer fence between the two countries, as there is between Finland and Norway. Ten years ago Norwegian farmers collected thousands of kroners in compensation by claiming that their animals had crossed into Soviet territory and had not been returned. These claims stopped when the inland revenue pointed out that the farmers seemed to have lost more reindeer in Russia than they had registered on their tax forms.

Although the Norwegian frontiersmen can no longer shop across the Pasvik, as they could before the war when the opposite bank belonged to Finland, their relationship with the Russians is quite genial. The towering border commissioner, Commodore Andreas Rygg, often goes for a drink or a spot of fishing with Colonel Tsukanov, his chubby Soviet opposite number.

'There are few incidents,' said Commodore Rygg, 'and we think the Soviet authorities deal quickly and justly with cases that arise. Relations are very good at the moment. In the past when people strayed over the border they were arrested and it was a great job getting them back again.'

The Russians have let the Norwegians build a dam on Soviet soil across the Pasvik from Skogfoss; and a Norwegian firm is building a hydro-electric station in the Russian town of Boris Gleb. I met the chief engineer Finn Lorange:

'When we started in 1960, it seemed a bit strange crossing the frontier to work,' he said, 'but now it's no more troubling than five minutes a day at a checkpoint. We were very surprised when Mr. Khrushchev came up in July. We never expected him in such a small place. He seemed very happy with what was happening and all the workers thought him a jolly good fellow. He knew just what to say to everybody and how to draw them out.'

There is no sense of menace along this Arctic frontier. At the tiny hamlet of Stenbak we talked to Nils Bedari, a farmer, whose house lies fifty yards from the USSR. 'The soil is good here,' he said. 'We moved because we found the next village too crowded.' It had fifty inhabitants.

From a NATO point of view, many Norwegians along this frontier are a darn sight too well disposed towards Russia. Left-wing Finns escaped to this part of Norway from the White Russian armies after the Revolution; there is a militant wing among the iron workers. The Communists get twenty-five per cent of the votes in local elections in this Sor-Varanger district of Finnmark, and are the biggest party after the Socialists.

Soviet spies have found this region easy to penetrate. There have been three big spy trials up here since the war, and the Norwegian authorities look glum if anyone talks of security.

The Finns to the south suffer their Soviet neighbour in sorrow and silence. They are the only western country to have bordered on Communism before 1945; and in the short, brave Winter War of December 1939 they lost all trust in the friendly designs of the USSR. Rashly, but understandably, they joined Hitler's attack on Russia in 1941 with the aim of recouping their losses. As a result they lost even more. Their Arctic port of Petsamo and their second city of Viipuri are now in the USSR.

Few humans move among the immense forests where eastern Finland meets the USSR. The Kolt, or Russian-speaking Lapps, have moved across from the USSR in the last few years to settle in Finland. The puritanical Communists did not admire the Kolt way of life, summed up as, 'In summer we fish and make love, but in winter we don't fish.'

The Finns claim that thousands of wolves come across the border in winter because there is not enough to eat in the USSR. 'In central Finland,' I was told in all seriousness, 'there are so many wolves that the schoolchildren have to go to school under an armed escort.' The story is probably false, but it sums up their attitude to the Russians.

When the Russians annexed Southern Karelia, they closed the Saima Canal, which had once joined the great lakes of south Finland to the Baltic. The Russians have now agreed to let the Finns repair and reopen this great canal through the curtain. The Finnish President Kekkonen probably sees it as part of his task as mediator between East and West.

Most Finns have grown too wary for optimism. 'Oh, yes, we'd be glad to see the canal open again,' said Viljo Salonen at Kansola, who was one of its lock-keepers before the war. 'There used to be forty barges a day. Before I worked on the canal, I lived in the Soviet Union working in the fish canneries there. I used to like the Russians . . . that is until the Winter War.'

The Iron Curtain in Germany has a Teutonic violence and thoroughness. Everybody knows of the Berlin Wall. Some forget the older, just as deadly barricade of barbed wire, minefields and double row of white posts that divides Western and Communist Germany. It runs, like a grotesque racetrack, from the Baltic to Czechoslovakia.

At Priwall, in the north, you can see the two systems displayed on the beach. On the west are bathing huts, beach balls and bikinis. On the east is a long stretch of desolate no-man's-land before a collective farm – which the East Germans call a *Landwirtschaftlichesproduktiongenossenschaft*.

Near Hof, in the south, you can see how the same iron curtain of wire continues between the German Democratic Republic and the Peoples' Republic of Czechoslovakia. They seem to distrust each other as much as they distrust us.

The West German authorities encourage visitors to the frontier. Schools, factories and offices send out regular coachloads to gaze at the iniquities of Herr Ulbricht and to kindle the yearning for union. But propaganda is mixed with genuine tragedy. The Iron Curtain, which lies along certain old county borders of Germany, has severed thirty-five railway lines, three autobahns, twenty-nine main and 130 subsidiary roads, innumerable bridges, canals and families.

The border is most depressing where it cuts a village in two. Zicherie, in the old province of Hanover, was to all intents and purposes one with Bockwitz, in Prussia. 'When Hanover was at war with Prussia in 1866,' said Fritz Lange, a Zicherle farmer, 'the children from this village continued to go to school in Bockwitz. Now nobody goes across even though we are at peace. Politics have become quite inhuman since then.'

Fritz Lange's fields border an East German minefield. 'Hares, deer, dogs and cats are often blown up there. We've got used to the noise,' he said. 'But my grandchildren are over there and I'd love to see them again. It wasn't so bad when the Russians were there. One officer I knew used to exchange gifts with me at Christmas.'

Several West Germans said they had preferred the Russians to Ulbricht's men. 'They were friendly and often came to my house for a smoke,' said a woodcutter in Bavaria. 'But the Vopos never utter a word.'

The Vopos, short for Volkspolizei, lurk across the wire at Zicherie. They often skulk in the grass or behind buildings, and take aim with their tommy-guns at inquisitive visitors such as myself. A West German frontier guard said, 'They often camouflage themselves and stay put for hours. Sometimes when I spot one I creep up close and give a piercing whistle to make him jump in the air. The old ones stay put, but the youngsters always jump.'

Near Zicherie, as on much of the East German border, the frontier is not clearly marked. A West German journalist, Kurt Lichtenstein, was shot in the stomach by East German police near here, and dragged into East Germany where he died the same evening. A British border official said, 'He probably went over about a metre inadvertently. He knew what the border meant and there was no reason why he should suddenly have wanted to cross over.' But many West Germans said that Lichtenstein was a Communist sympathizer who had crossed to greet his comrades. I asked the Mayor of Zicherie, Heinrich Reinecke, if there was any evidence for this rumour. 'That Lichtenstein had been a Communist is certain,' he said, 'he was of Jewish blood and all Jews are Communists.'

The West German customs men who patrol the border are able, liberal and intelligent. I could not say the same for the British border patrol we met in Zicherie. The troops stood on the bars of a fence just in front of the barbed wire and shouted jokes and insults across at a group of senior Warsaw Pact officers. One man swigged a bottle of pop, another gave the two-finger sign and a third invited the Communists to buy 'feelthy pictures'. What a pity the cold war cannot be won as easily as a brawl in a Minden bar just before closing time.

Near these troops, a Mrs. Annelise Boving was digging her garden. The soil she dug was two yards from the frontier and only ten yards from the site of her former house in Bockwitz, now East Germany. She had lived across the frontier until 1952 when the East German authorities evacuated (their word) her family to the interior. She escaped through West Berlin and returned to Zicherie – only a few yards away, but divided by four barbed wire fences, a minefield and a fanatic system of politics.

The Hungarian frontier is grimmer than any along the Iron Curtain. It is the only one to have been pierced and freed since the conquest of Communism. Those few days of freedom in the autumn of 1956 allowed everybody to see the reality of the fence between East and West. On the one side lay the free society of neutral Austria; on the other side a prison.

One story sums up the frontier between Austria and Hungary. A Hungarian refugee went from Vienna for the day to stare across the barbed wire into his homeland. In some fantasy of patriotism he decided to put one foot across the border line on to Hungarian soil. He stepped on a mine and was blown to bits.

Nowhere is the cruelty of Communism better demonstrated. At Morbisch, in 1961, a Hungarian woman tried to escape with her daughter and son, aged fifteen and thirteen. A few yards from Austria she and her daughter stepped on mines and each lost a leg. Austrian police wanted to give them medical help, but the Hungarians warned them off at machine-gun-point. The son, who had reached Austrian territory, had to watch his mother and sister screaming in agony for more than three hours as they lay unattended. They were then hauled back to a Hungarian hospital.

By an oddity of the frontier, one line of the Austrian railway runs through an outcrop of Hungarian territory, and the train stops at the big Hungarian town of Sopron. Austrians are free to travel this route. And two Hungarian refugee brothers use it to keep in touch with home. They write their parents to be on Sopron platform on a certain day, and when the train halts they stand in the window discussing their news. Mother and father go through the same charade on the platform.

We went to Andau, where the last thousands of refugees piled in at the end of the 1956 uprising. It has reverted to a sleepy village of Austria's Burgenland. Just outside, by the very barbed wire of the frontier, a party of German and Austrian high society folk went off for a morning's shooting.

But the refugees have gone, and with them all hope of a free Hungary. Nothing remains but Hungarian watchtowers, barbed wire and Austrian partridges.

Nobody would dispute that Yugoslavia lies on the Iron Curtain. But on which side? It is a Communist country and once more friendly with the Soviet Union. In most arguments it takes sides with the 'Socialist Camp'.

But no Iron Curtain separates Yugoslavia from its capitalist neighbours. There are no barbed-wire barricades or heavy patrols along the frontiers of Austria, Italy and Greece; yet Yugoslavia was very nearly at war with the last two countries in 1948. Now peasants can cross on shopping trips or to visit neighbours. Anybody who hates the Communist system finds it easy to make an escape. Only ten years ago refugees faced trigger-happy border patrols. The Albanian frontier is, for doctrinal reasons, bloody and loud with shots. More surprisingly there is no contact whatever with Hungary, Rumania and Bulgaria. 'The frontiers are hermetically sealed,' said one Yugoslav Communist.

The big Romanian minority around Vrsac, on the Romanian frontier, is cut off from its kinfolk a few miles away. 'I live two kilometres from the border,' said a thickly-mustachioed peasant, 'but haven't been across since 1948. It's impossible.' Tito's quarrel with Stalin was in 1948.

Yet peasant women travel from Vrsac to Belgrade and from there to Trieste. They go to sell butter and cheese and buy gaudy Italian clothes.

One woman admitted that she could buy the clothes just as cheaply in Belgrade and without the expense of travel. 'But when my daughter marries,' she said, 'I want her husband to be able to say that his mother-in-law has been abroad.' She lives only an hour's ride by ox cart from Romania. But thanks to the Iron Curtain she is obliged to go to the opposite end of Yugoslavia to be 'abroad'.

In Macedonian Greece the atmosphere of the Iron Curtain underwent a sudden and rather comic change. Gone was the high ideological purpose, the clash between Communism and a Free Society. This was just another Balkan quarrel, another round in the long feud between Greeks and Bulgarians. In this part of Europe most neighbouring nations loathe each other and frighten the children with tales of Turkish/Greek/Albanian/Bulgarian rape, impalement and babies skewered on bayonets.

Near Promahon, one of the five mountain passes joining Greece with Bulgaria, a Greek Army intelligence officer pointed out a monument to 'Basil the Slayer of Bulgars', a Byzantine Greek king who won a battle here in 1014. 'After this battle,' said the officer, 'he blinded 10,000 Bulgarian prisoners and sent them back to Ohrid, the Bulgarian capital, led by a man with one eye. When the Bulgarian king saw his army he dropped dead with a heart attack. For a long time we were not troubled by the Bulgarians.' Near the field of battle, some 943 years later, the Bulgarians shot down an unarmed airliner of El Al which had accidentally strayed across the border.

'The Bulgarians have no culture, they are almost savage,' I was told by Miss Athens Makri who teaches at a craft school in Promahon. 'All the children love my Greece, my Queen, my King.' As if to prove the point, she got them to dance and sing an ancient battle hymn. The words, I gathered, threatened all kinds of doom for the Bulgarians.

At Mikron Verion, on the eastern end of the Greek-Bulgarian frontier, the priest Gost Janakopolos said, 'Bulgarian and Communist – it's all the same thing. All they change is the shoulder tab. Here Communist means Bulgarian and Bulgarian means Communist.'

However, both anti-Communist Bulgarians and Communist Greeks have preyed on this village during the last twenty years. In the Greek civil war, Communist troops killed the priest and kidnapped 140 children.

These hills have the smell of danger – like 'Indian country' in Western films. All the able-bodied men do part-time guard and patrol work along the frontier. Their status was summed up by an officer in a phrase that rings true to conscripts throughout the world: 'They are not volunteers but they are paid as volunteers', i.e. nothing.

The Iron Curtain in Europe ends on the Black Sea. The Turks, who hate their Greek NATO allies, have no racial dislike of Bulgarians. One of the village elders at Derekoy, on the frontier, said, 'We don't blame the Bulgarians for their government. It was imposed on them by the Russians. But nobody is a bigger enemy of Communism than we Turks.'

This is probably true. The Turks are much the devoutest nation along the Iron Curtain. The Mullahs may not actually call for a holy war against Communism but they preach against it with fury. As a result the Turks use religious arguments against Communism.

And that, when you come to think of it, is a little odd. Because less than a hundred years ago Turkey itself was the infidel outcast of Europe; and Russia preached Holy War. The Turks now lead the Christian Crusade.

Is there any way that the West can help to get rid of the Iron Curtain? Certainly we should give no ground for charges of provocation. Those of us who dislike the dictatorship of Ulbricht and would like to see his subjects reunited with free West Germany, are sometimes embarrassed by the attitude of the West German Government. It is right to claim East Germany. But what we call East Germany the West Germans call Middle Germany. What they call East Germany lies in Poland, Czechoslovakia and USSR. The West German Government should pull down those propaganda posters of 'Germany Divided in Three' which are found everywhere on the border of East Germany. It should pull down those ridiculous signposts to Memel, Lwow and Danzig. Until it renounces these impossible claims, there is always some shred of justification for Ulbricht.

But the West plays it cool along the whole frontier. It is the other side that puts up the wire, lays the mines and shoots down harmless civilians. Nor is there any evidence that a show of Western pacifism reduces tension along the Communist frontier. Neutral Austria has the cruellest stretch of the whole Iron Curtain. NATO Norway gets on quite well with the Russians.

These two examples prove another point: that the Iron Curtain is worst where the regime on the other side is most unpopular. The Russians within the USSR have some degree of freedom and self-government. They are proud of their country whatever its faults; probably few want to escape. The revolt in Hungary proved that nine-tenths of the country loathes its alien government. The same is true of East Germany.

The example of Yugoslavia shows that a Communist country which achieves independence and some degree of liberalism can tear down its former Iron Curtain against the West without much damage to its security. And Yugoslavia's stretch of the Iron Curtain was until 1948 perhaps the worst of all.

This journey was not in the end so depressing. The Iron Curtain proves that a free society is stronger than a dictatorship. The watchtowers, mines and barbed wire are a confession of fear and weakness. They are used not to keep out enemies but to keep in their own people.

Except in Russia, the frontier guards whom we saw across the frontier looked shifty, ashamed and sullen. Only one returned my wave. It was in Austria on a misty day. There were two Hungarian soldiers marching parallel to the wire on the other side of the frontier. When I waved, the man in front scowled and pretended to lift his carbine. But the soldier behind, who could not be seen by his comrades, gave a wag of the hand and a furtive smile.

Richard West is the author of Tito and the Rise and Fall of Yugoslavia *and* War and Peace in Vietnam.

THE LAST DAYS OF MACMILIAN

—

Christopher Booker

Private Eye
5 April 1963

By the spring of 1963 London was giggling with gossip about a major political scandal which was said to be threatening Harold Macmillan's government, but which had not, as yet, appeared in any detail in the newspapers. Only by reading Private Eye, *and examining in detail the clues in Timothy Birdsall's brilliant cartoons, could some inkling of what was soon to be known as the Profumo Affair be glimpsed.*

By the early days of the year 1963, the twilight of the British Empire provided a sorry spectacle of collapse and decay on every hand.

It is evident from history that there is no nation which, having extended its sinews and vigour in the conquest and administration of empire, can then, on relinquishing that empire, maintain its previous standards of morality and efficiency in the prosecution of its remaining activities.

A strange mood walked abroad in Britain of that year, the eighth of the reign of the Emperor Macmilian. The ability and desire of the Emperor and his advisers to undertake the proper responsibilities of government seemed to have quite evaporated.

Vast tracts of the Northern provinces had fallen into desuetude. Along the great rivers of Tyne, Clyde and Mersey, the hammers of the shipyards were stilled. The busy workshops that had once provided the sinews of imperial prosperity were silent. The people moved in uneasy groups through the streets, deprived of bread, craving in vain for circuses, sensitive to that stirring of the instincts of the mob that finally erupted in open rioting outside the Senate at Westminster.

Throughout the country the broad roads went unpaved. The iron roads that had once been the proud arteries of a brilliant civilization were uprooted to give way once again to the weeds of the forest.

Even in the furthest reaches of the Empire unrest was slowly ripening into bitter contempt for the symbols of authority that had for so long held sway. When Macmilian's consul, the horse Elizabetha, made a progress through the province of Australia, few bothered even to stop in the streets to observe the passing of the tattered imperial standards. Among the placid farms and latifundia of Rhodesia, black rebellion was brewing up in the hearts of the African slaves, exacerbated by the iron rule of the Governor Winstonius Ager, and unassuaged by the smooth ambivalence of Macmilian's proconsular envoy Butlerius Africanus.

the last days of MACMILIAN

But it was in Britain itself, and in Londinium, that the air was heavy with the smell of indulgence and decay, with searchings after strange Gods, with rumour and counter-rumour and with a drifting sense of doom.

The old faiths of the Republic had lost their hold. Even the High Priests no longer proclaimed the existence of the Gods. The legions had abandoned their once fierce bull-worship almost entirely. Only Son-Worship still flourished, in outlying regions of Suffolk.

In place of religion, there came at this time a great spate of omens. An outbreak of the plague among travellers, one of the first for many years. Rumours of strange cults and black magic practised in ruined temples spread through the land. On the coast of the province of Sussex, a woman was attacked by a grey squirrel. Even the harshness of the winter, one of the coldest and most prolonged for hundreds of years, merely added ominous misery and bewilderment to the fears of the people.

But it was in Londinium, at the very heart of the Empire, that rumour, distrust and corruption had finally broken out into the open. After years of an uneasy indulgence, the people were restless and dissatisfied – a spirit which reached into all quarters of society. Even the flower of the legions, the Praetorian Guard, were in mutinous mood at their camp at Pirbrittius.

After his final defeat in the Gallic campaign, after the prolonged and tiring battle of Brussels upon which all his ambitions had been centred, the Emperor Macmilian himself lounged increasingly powerless at the heart of this drift and decay. His Ministers fought and intrigued over the succession, no longer mindful of the great perils that lay without. While the proper administration of the country languished utterly.

Wild rumours flew nightly through the capital. Of strange and wild happenings in country villas out in the country. Of orgies and philanderings involving some of the richest and most powerful men in the land. In the private diaries of a well-known courtesan of the times, we can read the names of many leading members of imperial society – ranged in order of sexual prowess.

But while natural debauchery became the small talk of a capital long sated with public offerings of vice and harlotry of every description, among the clerks and eunuchs of the administration the old standards of the Republic had vanished altogether. Men proclaimed their love not for their wives, but for each other and the strange loyalties thus formed, stretching up into some of the highest places in the land, allowed laxity, indulgence and even treason to flourish unchecked.

At this time too, the Chief of the Praetorian Guard, Sextus Profano, came under widespread suspicion for his admission in the Senate that he had been acquainted with Christina, a beautiful girl known well to many of the great figures of society despite her lowly origins, and whose lover, a negro slave, had been sentenced to seven years in the sulphur mines for threatening to kill her in a fit of jealous revenge. It was a sign of the times that few expressed surprise at such an admission.

All these happenings brought the capital into a frenzy of speculation that was far from healthy for the continued reign of Macmilian, and the scribes and pamphleteers were only the leaders and articulators of the widespread hostility and contempt aroused by the Government in the hearts of the great mass of the people.

But it was finally the sight of one of Macmilian's more despised advisers, Henricius Domus Secretarius, making himself a private triumph through the streets, leading from his chariot the proud and chained figure of a great African chief Enobarbo, that drove a weary people into deciding that the Emperor's tyranny and disregard for any sentiments but the cheap, the opportunist and the ignoble must be put aside for ever. And that these small men who had disgraced all the noble and glorious history of the British Empire with their petty deeds should be humiliated and forgotten.

Christopher Booker still writes for Private Eye *as well as the* Daily Mail *and the* Daily Telegraph. *He has published several books, including* The Neophiliacs, *a study of the revolution in English life in the Fifties and Sixties. Cartoonist Timothy Birdsall died of leukaemia in June 1963, at the age of twenty-four.*

MAC THE MAN

—

Jocelyn Stevens
Queen
May 1963

Beloved of cartoonists for his almost music-hall, Edwardian airs, Harold Macmillan, an astute, far-sighted Prime Minister, was at heart a lonely man. At a time, when Prime Ministers were not given to chatting to young magazine editors, this was an exceptionally revealing piece.

'He won't like this much,' said Harold Evans, the Prime Minister's Press Secretary, when he looked through the list of questions I had sent to the Right Honourable Harold Macmillan, MP.

Three days later I was ushered into the Cabinet Room at Admiralty House. Mr. Macmillan was seated halfway along the huge square-ended oval Cabinet table. Behind him, over the fireplace, a portrait of Robert Walpole. Before him on a large sheet of yellow blotting-paper, the inevitable telephone, its green handle betraying its importance, the ultimate weapon of diplomacy. His handshake was unimportant. He pulled out a chair next to him.

His is a marvellous face. An Identi-kit designed by Vicky for a Conservative prime minister (Edwardian model). Now its familiarity gave me that false confidence that leads people to greet television faces as old friends. 'Come and sit down,' he said. For a moment we sat beside each other looking across the wide table. I pushed my chair back. 'I particularly asked if I could see you, Prime Minister, because to me and so many of my generation you are a remote figure, growing more remote.' His eyebrows depressed. I began:

'Why did you go into politics?' The Prime Minister picked up his pipe and a box of matches from the blotter in front of him and walked away from me towards two long windows overlooking Horse Guards Parade. For an awful moment I thought he was leaving. Then, at last, he turned like a bowler at the beginning of his run.

'It seemed at the time the only possible thing I could do. On the one hand I could see all the misery and suffering of the slump and on the other, the apparent incapacity of our economic society to do anything about it.'

In 1923 Mr. Macmillan was defeated by seventy-three votes in his first election. His constituency, Stockton-on-Tees. In 1924 he was elected.

'My father was a Christian Socialist, which was regarded in those days as being almost subversive. I was brought up in a strong radical tradition. England was governed at that time by an upper-middle-class intelligentsia. My family were scholars. I was a scholar. My family moved in a literary circle with such men as Morley and Asquith.' He elaborated at length about his early literary days.

'I was twenty when the First World War broke out. In those days they used to sell newspapers all through the night. I was on my way back from a party in London and I remember the newsboys shouting 'Archduke Murdered'. It didn't seem important at the time. Three weeks later we were at war. I had been at Oxford for two years.'

Mr. Macmillan was a scholar at Eton. (Nineteen of Britain's forty-four prime ministers have been Etonians, but only Macmillan and Walpole were scholars.) He won an 'exhibition' to Balliol.

'I always ran second to my brother Daniel. You see, he got a scholarship to Balliol. It would be hard for you to understand that there was a great divide between the intelligentsia and, for example, the Services. The war dissolved all that. A whole generation was submerged.'

The Prime Minister was once again in his chair, his pipe unlighted on the blotter in front of him. He turned away and looked out of the window. A long pause. 'I managed to fix myself up in the Grenadier Guards and got to know men I would never otherwise have met. I shall never forget the suffering. Seventy thousand men killed in one day on the Somme.' He told a story of one of his corporals. 'One of the finest men I ever knew.' Another long pause as he stared out of the window. 'I was lucky to survive.'

Mr. Macmillan was wounded three times – the third time seriously. A story is told of this incident that he rolled into the bottom of a shell crater where he feigned death as the Germans counter-attacked over him. Twelve hours later his sergeant-major found him, half-conscious, reading a copy of Aeschylus he had had in his pocket. He was in hospital for two years.

'I worried as I lay in hospital. I felt that I must get something done. Soldiering had been quite new to me. Why not politics? Oliver Stanley, Duff Cooper, Anthony Eden and a few other friends got together. They called us the YMCA.'

The Prime Minister stopped. 'It's rather cold in here.' He got up, turned on an electric switch by the fireplace and sat down again. Harold Evans came round the table, put the plug in and returned noiselessly to his place across the table.

'Where was I? Oh yes. Well, things went along. One tried but there was very little one could do in those years.'

In fact, Mr. Macmillan ceaselessly harried the complacent Tories with a passion and an impetuosity sharpened by Balliol and tempered by the suffering which he had seen in the war and the misery of the poverty at Stockton. In an early speech in the Commons, he called the Front Bench of his own party 'a few disused slag-heaps which might well be tidied up'. Although a rebel he was swept out of his constituency by the Socialist landslide in 1929 only to be re-elected in 1931, still a vehement critic of his own party.

'Then along came Munich. It was inevitable the way things were going.'

At the time Mr. Macmillan described Chamberlain's agreement at Munich as hypocrisy and when the House of Commons cheered the Prime Minister he was one of the few MPs who protested.

'When the Second World War started, Winston sent for me. I can remember him saying, 'There's one thing you can say for Hitler. He's made me a Prime Minister and you an Under-Secretary of State!'

'There are two kinds of politics – policy and things. At the Ministry of Supply I was dealing with things. When I was sent to North Africa as Minister Resident I had to deal with policy. Two people turned the job down before me. I wasn't too sure about it myself. Winston wanted me to go in uniform but I didn't feel that a Grenadier Captain on the Reserve would carry much weight in General Eisenhower's headquarters. I explained this to Winston who replied, 'I quite understand. You mean that there's no place between the Baton and the Bowler.' I enjoyed that job tremendously. One met everybody.'

In 1945 his constituents rejected Mr. Macmillan again and he lost his seat by 8,644 votes. However, in a by-election at Bromley the same year he was once again returned to the House of Commons.

'Winston asked me if I could build 300,000 houses in a year and if so, would I be a Minister of Housing. I agreed on condition I could run it my way. We ran it, in fact, like a war department. You see, I'd learnt a thing or two at the Ministry of Supply working with the tycoons. Then I was made Foreign Secretary but Anthony didn't want me there so I became Chancellor of the Exchequer. I was rather sad about that because I enjoyed the Foreign Office.

'I never had any feeling about becoming Prime Minister. I took things as they came and I still do.

'Power? It's like a dead sea fruit. When you achieve it there's nothing there. The art of government is mixing the thinkers and the doers. When we're having a Cabinet Meeting, Lord Home sitting over there,' he pointed across the table (suddenly he was Peter Cook), 'will say "What about . . .?" We discuss it. "Will So-and-So fall?" (pause). "Will they move in?" (pause). "What will he do?" (pause). We think about it.

'Then someone else,' another wave of the hand, 'will say, "What about the railways?" Now Dr. Beeching is a doer.'

Then as suddenly as he had come 'on the air' he was off – reflecting on the historical role of the Prime Minister.

'Pitt had to deal with the Closet first and then Parliament. Then it became Parliament first and then Closet. Then Parliament and People. Now it's People and Parliament.

'I've been accused of caring too much for the material well-being of the people. I don't think that you can care too much about the well-being of the people. You would agree with me if you had seen what I saw in the First World War and the 1920s. People who criticize me on that score are the first to leap to their feet when we have two per cent unemployment.

'Yes, I am sensitive to criticism. One has to be. There are moments when I loathe everybody and then I retire and read Gibbon for a few hours. Don't I, Harold?' Meaningful assent from across the table.

The strain of being Prime Minister? 'I'm a Highlander. That's why I'm so pale. People often think I'm ill. They're wrong. It's true, I get a bit tired but soon pop up again. Isn't that right, Harold?'

Nodded assent from Harold Evans across the table. In six and a half years as Prime Minister Mr. Macmillan has not missed a day's work.

'My clothes Edwardian? I thought that cardigans were rather smart at the moment. My grandchildren gave me this one.' He plucked at his black cardigan. 'Suits? I always wear the same suit. When it wears out I tell my tailor to send another one round. I've got three shooting suits. I rather like them.

'What do I dislike? Questions in the House of Commons. I can't bear them. What else? Things that have no purpose – formalities – like the function I'm going to this evening. Now I enjoyed Princess Alexandra's wedding. That was very pretty.

'What do I like? Most of all being with Dorothy and my family. They are my chief interest. As I get older, I find that I am more tolerant. I like people more. My father was very shy. I learnt books before people. But what I really like to do is to go off with Dorothy in the car, alone, to Scotland. I love Scotland. Where the hedges cease there is real freedom.'

A Private Secretary came in, reminded the Prime Minister that he was due to look in on an exhibition in a few minutes.

'What do I have to do? Just walk round. Oh, that's all right.'

The Prime Minister pulled out a pair of what appeared to be very old horn-rimmed spectacles, and peered owlishly at the list of his day's engagements which was propped up in front of him like a menu.

The Private Secretary withdrew.

'Let's have a little whisky. It's a bit early but never mind.'

He pressed a bell. A messenger brought three glasses of whisky on a silvery tray. No ice.

'My work centres round the box. I'm rather good at doing the box. In fact, I'm very good at doing the box. Aren't I, Harold?'

Ready assent.

The 'box' is the Prime Minister's Despatch Box. Every evening the mass of papers he has to read are placed in it.

'I only require six hours' sleep a night and I normally do the box when I get home in the evening, whatever time it is. In fact, I have two boxes. Into one I place everything that I can decide upon at the time and into the other all matters that require further consideration. If I don't do the box in the evening, then I do it as soon as I wake in the morning. Anyway, it's always done. The only difficulty arises at times like Easter or Whitsun when all the other government departments, in a rush to clear their boxes, fill my box with all sorts of problems that they have been meaning to deal with for ages. But we're putting an end to that. Aren't we, Harold?' Heavy assent.

'No, I don't get enough exercise, although yesterday I had a four-hour walk through the woods. I went to see my gamekeeper. He wasn't too hopeful about next season's prospects.'

The Prime Minister is a hard and fast worker and when his work is done he appears to be able to relax and forget it. Every day he reads for at least two hours. His conversation is laced with quotations and literary references. He sleeps easily. 'It's the quality of sleep that counts, not the quantity.' He likes forestry, shooting and being out-of-doors. He goes to church every Sunday and reads the lesson, enjoys theatre and ballet, is not particularly interested in food or drink. When trapped into a choice, he is said to ask for cold meat and salad. He appears to have the constitution of an ox. 'I was weak as a child but have grown stronger and stronger.' 'Do I find my position lonely? No, if you mean the number of people I meet. Yes, if you mean whom can one ask for advice. That's quite a different story.'

The Private Secretary reappeared. The same dialogue was repeated.

The Prime Minister rose and walked to the door. Seventy minutes had passed in five. Outside the Cabinet Room we shook hands again, 'I hope I've been some help to you,' he said, and disappeared into a black Humber, leaving me with the distinct impression that Britain and Macmillan would go into the Seventies together.

Later to become managing director of the Evening Standard, *Jocelyn Stevens was rector of the Royal College of Art from 1984 to 1992, and is now chairman of English Heritage.*

ANTIC ANTIQUE

—

Arthur Hopcraft
Guardian
Cup Final Day 1963

Manchester United beat Leicester City 3-1.

That massive, devious and ingratiating conspiracy which works without rest to transfix us as its creature, obedient and untroublesome, has some notable battle honours on its hygienic, plastic banner. It has convinced us that our armpits smell, that blotting-paper is chicken, and that a box is a building; that a tent on a hillside is a public outrage and a green belt a noble penance. The Docility Plot numbs where it smooths and stills the doubts with flattery.

But let not the plotters underestimate their task. There is more to decharacterizing a Briton than tearing down his brown-framed portraits of uncles at the wars and ordering a compulsory purchase of those plaster ducks that must fly his wall in symmetrical diminution. He may dutifully follow the national treasure hunt, ticking off on his acquisition progress chart his car, his fridge, his daughter's riding lessons and his fibreglass boat, and square the council rent collector for letting him berth it on the verge. Even yet he is not quite a slave to the cause.

Still he flies his pigeons and rears his hens in defiance of the housing manager, refuses to vote, votes illogically, picnics on motorways, fights the county council for the mosaics round his bay windows, and drags out long-hidden ballads to embarrass the golf club on a Saturday night. And, most outrageously of all, he keeps British football alive.

This is surely the greatest of all challenges to the forces of gloss and identity-repression. It should, by the logic of things, have sunk deep under the seas of social change years ago; British football, that is, the whole grim, sweaty, thump and hack and glory and discomfort of it; not football, the international sport, which is not the same thing at all.

Anyone with half an eye for dramatic movement can see that football, the game, will last as long as men and boys have feet; but the survival of British football, the institution, is a marvel of the modern world, a bulwark against the creeping plague of tinsel, a great, gap-toothed belly laugh at the world of the smart and the sweet.

It is, of course, a group exercise in conserving roots. For all that the crowds at so many grounds in the Football League get smaller and that the future is glum for more than a few of the smaller clubs, the old curmudgeon keeps grinding on, mumbling curses and accusations at all the slick, upstart competitors in the entertainment industry who have pinched some of his customers. He grumbles, but makes not a single concession that might suggest he values that public which loves him so dearly but will surely tell him soon that he must trim his beard and wipe his nose or all is over.

With very few exceptions in British professional football, the sensation of being moved back in time a generation or two starts with the physical setting of the grounds. Usually they are buried deep in a maze of those crouching terraces that shameless villains erected as a gaol for the necessary, but over-demanding, workers. The shoving crowds take on a sudden coarseness which the same people do not show elsewhere.

There may be wooden seats for a quarter of them, but probably less. The rest will stand, in heat, rain, frost, and snow, sometimes lifted off their feet, if the teams are crowd-drawers, and carried in a slithering, whooping mass three or four steps down the greasy terrace, before the crisis lifts and back up they stumble, to gasp and laugh and set their teeth until the next time.

What possible place does all this simple, ugly pleasure, made for the underprivileged, have in Macmillan's lotus land of all the comforts? It is a weekly dose of heritage, and the need for it is part of the peopleness of people. Do not tell the man on the terraces that with his car and his overtime pay he could be driving his family to a wondrous dawn with the oyster-catchers on some murmuring Scottish shore. He was not born to that.

He kicked a ball when very young against the row of lavatories behind his house, stood on the corner outside the pub, later, in a crowd visibly trembling with anxiety as it waited for the Saturday night Sports Pink (or Green, or Buff) to give it the results of the game it could not afford to go to; and later still he organized his friends in a savings group to pay for the bus trip and the entrance money for two hours of frenzy every other Saturday.

Do not ask him now why he sweats and sways and shivers and swears on his square foot of concrete, while the team below mocks his faithfulness and loses to those dandelions from down the road. He is there because he is made of flesh of a particular vintage, and also of fears, and he clings to what once was all he had.

So today there will be real tears at Wembley, as the hymns are dredged through a haze of sentiment and last night's booze before the Cup Final starts. Next year it will be the same, and the year after. But not for ever. Younger men are on the terraces only under sufferance because the seats are full, and they will not bear with the old gasworks atmosphere much longer. They do not cry. The players have long since changed their playing kit from British warm to Continental strip. The castle is being stormed, for a start, from within.

After an impressive career as a journalist, Arthur Hopcraft moved successfully into novel-writing (The Football Man) *and television drama, winning prizes for his adaptations of* Tinker, Tailor, Soldier, Spy *and* Bleak House.

THE FOUR PHASES OF THE PROFUMO AFFAIR

—

Insight
Sunday Times
9 June 1963

No public scandal in modern times caught the imagination like the Profumo Affair. At the end of the day the government survived, but there were casualties. John Profumo retired from political life and osteopath Stephen Ward died from a drugs overdose while on trial for living off immoral earnings – charges he strenuously denied.

There are four phases to the Profumo Affair. The first, the dormant stage, began when the Minister met Christine Keeler in July, 1961.

The weather was hot, and Lord Astor had invited his own weekend guests to use the open-air swimming pool on his Cliveden estate in Buckinghamshire. The pool was also being used by other acquaintances and neighbours. Mr. Profumo, with his wife, Valerie Hobson, was a personal guest of Lord Astor; Miss Keeler was also spending the day at Cliveden, but as a guest of Dr. Stephen Ward, who was at that time a tenant of one of the small cottages that are scattered around the estate (he now no longer lives there). They encountered each other at the pool, walled, overlooked by flats of the Cliveden staff above nearby stables, and thronging with people.

Few of their fellow guests remember much about the meeting. There was a continual flow of people to and from Cliveden. Apart from Lord Astor's many dinner and house parties, Dr. Ward also entertained at his cottage. Among his guests was Eugene Ivanov, of the Russian Embassy.

At the time the casual conversation between the model and the Minister seemed innocuous. But they continued to see each other on a number of occasions during the late summer and autumn. Their meetings ceased at the end of 1961.

The second phase began on 14 December last year. Keeler was in the flat at Wimpole Mews, Marylebone, with a friend, Marilyn [Mandy] Rice-Davies. A previous lover of Keeler's, a West Indian called John Arthur Edgecombe, arrived outside the flat with a gun. He fired five shots at the locks of the flat door, and two shots at Keeler (both missed) when she looked out of a window.

On 15 December Edgecombe appeared at Marlborough Street magistrates court, accused of shooting at Keeler with intent to murder her. Edgecombe was remanded in custody until 22 December. (When the case eventually came up at the Old Bailey the charge was of possessing a firearm with intent to endanger life.)

For Keeler the threshold between nonentity and notoriety had been crossed. Before 15 December her name had never appeared in national newspapers. In the six months since then the file on her has become as bulky as that of the man whose career crumbled last week.

This was the incubation phase. At this period Fleet Street and Westminster were preoccupied with the Vassall case.

But at Westminster the word began to get around that another affair was brewing which would make the Vassall case very tame. James Margach, the *Sunday Times* political correspondent, in common with other lobby correspondents, had heard the gossip, but says that it was not until early in 1963 that Mr. Profumo's name was introduced.

The conditions for the growth of rumour were as ideal as those of a hothouse designed to rear tropical plants.

Newspapers which felt that for a girl of barely twenty-one Keeler already had an eventful biography sought stories about her life and her friends. Both Mr. Profumo and Ivanov were mentioned.

There was a report that in the middle of February the security services passed on some aspects of the case to the Government. The newspapers suddenly had a story that was too hot to print.

One MP who became particularly interested was Colonel George Wigg, the Labour member for Dudley. Colonel Wigg is an authority on defence, and his interest was aroused by possible security implications, not scandal-mongering. His enquiries led him to believe that MI5 had had Ivanov under surveillance and had been led by him to Wimpole Mews, Miss Keeler and Mr. Profumo.

By this time Ivanov had returned to Russia. The fact that Profumo and Ivanov were directly linked with Keeler (but not with each other) built up the speculation at Westminster.

Lord Lambton, Tory MP for Berwick, who has often criticized the Prime Minister, was worried about the rumours – particularly as they had spread to Washington. Writing in last week's *Evening Standard* Lambton said he conveyed his doubts 'to an authority in the Conservative Party, who refused to entertain them seriously'. In fact, the authority was Mr. Martin Redmayne, Tory Chief Whip.

Lobby correspondents, of course, still had nothing that they could print. Then, on Thursday, 14 March, Mr. Alastair Morton, prosecuting in the Edgecombe case at the Old Bailey, told the jury that Keeler, who was due to be called as a witness, had disappeared.

The newspapers then began to develop a kind of code: nonsense to the majority of their readers, but meaningful to those on the grapevine. The first step was taken by the *Daily Express*. The morning after the announcement of Keeler's disappearance, that paper's main story by Ian Aitken, its political correspondent, said that Mr. Profumo had offered his resignation to Mr. Macmillan for 'personal reasons'. Aitken said that the Prime Minister had asked him to stay on.

One column away from this story was a large picture of Christine Keeler, and the story of her disappearance. This was as near as Mr. Profumo's name was to get to Keeler's in print for a week.

When, just before midnight on 14 March, the other newspapers got copies of the *Express* they sent reporters to find Mr. Profumo. At 1.05 a.m. on 15 March he arrived at his house at Regent's Park with his wife. He had been at the House of Commons. Asked about the *Express* report, he said, 'There is no truth in this story at all – I have not seen the Prime Minister. I have been working on the Army Estimates.'

On 20 March the *Daily Mail* carried on its front page the report of a Commons question about Keeler's disappearance and, three columns away, a story by its political correspondent, Walter Terry, headlined 'MPs, rumour and Mr. Profumo'. After recalling rumours about Mr. Profumo's resignation, Terry concluded, in a remarkably disingenuous paragraph, 'Continuous speculation about possible resignation is always irritating for a Government, and naturally embarrassing for the Minister concerned.'

The next day, 21 March, the story passed dramatically from the incubation phase to the open phase. The Commons was debating the case of the two journalists gaoled for refusing to disclose their sources to the Vassall Tribunal. Feelings about the Vassall case ran high.

But nobody was prepared for what Colonel Wigg had to say when he got on his feet late in the evening. He said that there was not a member who had not heard rumour upon rumour involving a member of the Government front bench. He was using the privilege of the House to ask the Home Secretary, who knew about the rumours, to answer them at the dispatch box. Colonel Wigg's request was supported by Mr. Richard Crossman and Mrs. Barbara Castle. Mr. Wilson had not been consulted on this beforehand. Mr. Profumo's name was not mentioned.

While the House was getting its breath back the stoic Mr. Henry Brooke replied, 'I do not propose to comment on the rumours that have been raised under the cloak of privilege and safe from any action of the law.' Mr. Wigg and Mrs. Castle should seek other means of making these insinuations if they were prepared to substantiate them.

The production of the skeleton from the cupboard came as a shock to the Government. Mr. Macleod, the Leader of the House, and the Government's Chief Whip, Mr. Martin Redmayne, sent for Mr. Profumo, who had to be got out of bed.

Between midnight and 1.30 a.m. they went over with Mr. Profumo the allegations implicit in the Commons speeches. Sir John Hobson, the Attorney General, was there. Mr. Profumo was accompanied by his legal adviser. He strenuously denied the allegations. By 2 a.m. on 22 March a statement was drafted which Mr. Profumo was to make in the House when it assembled at 11 a.m.

Friday mornings are usually anti-climatic in the Commons. This one was historic. Flanked by Mr. Macmillan and Mr. Macleod, Mr. Profumo rose to speak. He was pale and taut, self-controlled but obviously under high emotional tension. He spoke slowly and deliberately.

It soon became clear that far from fighting for political survival, he was asserting himself with a challenging defiance.

He and his wife, he said, had met Miss Keeler and he had been on 'friendly terms' with her, but there was 'no impropriety whatever'. He last saw her in December 1961. He denied that he had anything to do with her disappearance from the Old Bailey trial and, as a final shot across the bows, he said, 'I shall not hesitate to issue writs for libel and slander if scandalous allegations are made or repeated outside this House.'

According to tradition, a personal statement is not debated. Mr. Profumo left the chamber immediately and was joined by his wife, who had been sitting in the public gallery. Later in the afternoon they fulfilled an engagement arranged some time previously to join the Queen Mother at Sandown Park races. Later they went to a Conservative dance at Hatch End.

Mr. Profumo's statement seemed effectively to stifle the rumours.

All this time, of course, Miss Keeler had been missing. Several national newspapers had despatched posses of reporters and photographers to the Continent to track her down, and on 26 March, the *Daily Express* found her – in Madrid.

By now established as a goddess of sensuality, she was photographed in the clothes for the role: calf-length black boots, a short, tight skirt and sweater. She told the *Express*, who paid her several hundred pounds for the interview, that she had left Britain on 7 March in a red Jaguar driven by a boyfriend. A blonde called Kim Proctor was with them.

Late on 28 March when she returned to Britain she had a police escort to help her through London Airport. A television reporter who had interviewed her in Madrid after the *Daily Express* had been told by her that she had been Mr. Profumo's mistress.

In view of Mr. Profumo's personal statement in the Commons, and his libel warning, the newspapers were warned by their legal advisers that in spite of what Keeler might say, her unsubstantiated word could not stand up against Mr. Profumo's and publication could not be risked.

But Continental newspapers and magazines, particularly in Italy – where parallels were drawn between the Keeler milieu and Rome's own *'dolce vita'* – had been less inhibited. In the High Court, on 11 April, Mr. Profumo was awarded agreed damages of £50 against the English distributors of the Italian magazine *Tempo Illustrato*, which had repeated an unfounded rumour that Mr. Profumo had in some way been involved in Miss Keeler's failure to appear as a witness. It was also said that the article 'contained suggestions that Mr. Profumo had been, or might have been, in some improper relationship with her'.

The defendants, Continental Publishers and Distributors Ltd., said that they recognized that all such allegations were unjustifiable, and agreed to pay Mr. Profumo's legal costs, in addition to the damages (which he gave to an Army charity).

This distributor – the main British importer of foreign magazines – altogether withheld thirty-two periodicals from publication in Britain, for fear of further proceedings. They have now referred back the *Tempo Illustrato* case to their lawyers for further consideration.

Throughout the rest of April the affair seemed to be flickering out, although Keeler got back into the headlines when she was assaulted by 'Lucky' Gordon. But beneath the surface several things were happening.

Ever since the shooting incident, the police had been collecting information about the whole background of the case. Marilyn [Mandy] Rice-Davies, arrested for a motoring offence, had been interviewed in Holloway Gaol.

Two policemen were leading the inquiry, Chief Inspector Samuel Herbert and Det. Sgt. John Burrows. They worked from Marylebone Lane Police Station. Scores of people were seen in this inquiry.

Later Chief Inspector Herbert's dossiers were sent to the Director of Public Prosecutions, to decide whether a prosecution could be instituted. The DPP sent the dossiers back, asking for more information.

On 21 May Dr. Ward issued a statement to newspapers, which they did not then publish because of the libel inhibition. This said: 'I have placed before the Home Secretary certain facts of the relationship between Miss Keeler and Mr. Profumo, since it is obvious now that my efforts to conceal these facts in the interests of Mr. Profumo and the Government have made it appear that I myself have something to hide – which I do not.

'The result has been that I have been persecuted in a number of ways, causing damage not only to myself but to my friends and patients – a state of affairs which I propose to tolerate no longer.'

Dr. Ward asked for an interview at Admiralty House, where he made a statement to the Prime Minister's Principal Private Secretary, Mr. Bligh, who reported to Mr. Macmillan.

Immediately afterwards Mr. Profumo was summoned to Admiralty House where he strenuously insisted that his statement in the House was accurate.

On 23 May Mr. Ben Parkin, Labour MP for Paddington N., notified a question to the Home Secretary, asking him 'what conclusions he has reached about information supplied to him by Dr. Stephen Ward and what action he proposes to take following recent Metropolitan Police enquiries to prevent the increase of expensive call-girl organizations'.

On 24 May Mr. Parkin withdrew his question. Mr. Wilson had asked him to do so, because he did not want Labour to appear to be joining a public witch-hunt.

On 29 May Mr. Wilson himself decided to approach the Prime Minister direct, taking a file of information contributed by Labour MPs who had been interested in the case. The Labour Shadow Cabinet had approved Mr. Wilson's direct approach to the Prime Minister.

But on 30 May another question was put down by Mr. Chuter Ede, a former Labour Home Secretary (who set up the Lynskey Tribunal in the Stanley case). He asked of the Home Secretary 'What information he has received from Dr. Stephen Ward in connection with enquiries carried out by the Metropolitan Police and what action he proposes to take.' Mr. Parkin then renewed his withdrawn question.

The fact that Mr. Ede, known for his strong feelings about maintaining the highest standards in Parliamentary and public life, had raised the issue in such a direct way was a formidable warning.

On the surface, the principals remained phlegmatic. Parliament broke up for Whitsun. On 30 May Mr. Profumo requested an interview with the Prime Minister, but Mr. Macmillan had left for a holiday in Scotland. The next morning the Profumos, too, went on holiday to Venice.

They returned on Whit Monday, on the *Golden Arrow*.

On 4 June Mr. Profumo saw Mr. Redmayne and Mr. Bligh, making his confession. This was translated into a letter of resignation to the Prime Minister.

Mr. Bligh telephoned Mr. Macmillan in Perthshire and told him the terms of the letter of resignation. On Wednesday the Prime Minister dictated his curt reply, omitting any word of thanks for past services, by saying 'this is a great tragedy for you, your family and your friends'. The protocol had been observed. The final, crisis phase had begun.

NIGHTMARE REPUBLIC

—

Graham Greene
Sunday Telegraph
29 September 1963

In May 1963 'Papa Doc' François Duvalier declared martial law after protests against his dictatorial rule in Haiti. A year later he made himself President for life.

After the drum-beats which continued for an hour or more, after the saints' banners and the chanting and the Latin prayers, came the priest swinging his censer. But the censer was a live cock, and after the priest had incensed the congregation, he put the head in his mouth and crunched through the neck. Then, using the neck like a tube of red-brown paint, he made his mystic designs upon the earth-floor.

I remember this ceremony from nine years ago, and the long service which followed: the novices borne in like mummies wrapped in white sheets with only a hand protruding, a hand which was held in a live flame by the attendants while the drums beat to cover the cries; the arrival of the god of war, Ogoun Ferraille, who took possession of one of the peasants and sent him careering around the temple with a naked sword. You find the ceremonies reflected in many Haitian paintings, especially in those of Hector Hyppolite, who was a Voodoo priest. Even around the mural of the Marriage at Cana in the Episcopalian Cathedral the drummers play and a dead pig has the appearance of a ritual slaughter.

Some strange curse descended on the liberated slaves of Hispaniola. The unconscious of this people is filled with nightmares; they live in the world of Hieronymus Bosch. Perhaps it is wrong to speak of the unconscious, for here the Ego and the Id seem joined in unholy matrimony. Baron Samedi, in his top hat and tails, who haunts the cemeteries smoking a cigar and wearing dark glasses, spends the days, so some believe, in the Presidential Palace, and his other name is Dr. Duvalier.

A reign of terror has often about it the atmosphere of farce. The irresponsible is in control. The banana-skin is a deadly one, but it remains a banana-skin. From the moment you land from an aeroplane in Port-au-Prince – that city of ruined elegance where the houses belong to the world of Charles Addams and the door may well be opened to you by a Boris Karloff – you are in the hands of the unpredictable.

You reach your hotel, symbolically enough, in darkness, for the plane touches down around 5.30, and between 6.30 and 7.30, and again from 8.30 to 9.30, the lights are all out. In the hotel you may find yourself the only guest (the tourists fled last spring and never returned). There were three others in my hotel and the owner calculated with wry insouciance that he could break even with five of us (his wages bill used to be $1,500 a month and is now $100).

While you wait for the lights to go on, you sit around oil-lamps exchanging rumours – the rebels are only twenty-four hours from Port-au-Prince, one optimist declares; the army has suffered a hundred casualties (it is always a hundred when an optimist speaks); a military plane has been shot down. Someone has heard on the *Voice of America* . . . On the way to the hotel one night when I was stopped at a road-block, the man who searched me for arms, patting the hips, the thighs, laying a hand under the testicles, asked my companion in Creole, 'Is there any news?'

But there is no such thing as news any more. (The stories which appear in the *New York Times* or the *New York Herald Tribune* as a rule have a Santo Domingo dateline and reflect the hopes of the exiles.) The President's daughter is said to be on hunger-strike to induce her father to leave; the President's wife has abandoned him and is in America . . . The Spanish Ambassador came home the other night to find a black dog in the Embassy, but none of his staff would touch it because it might house the spirit of Clement Barbot, the President's deadly enemy, shot down a few weeks back on the edge of Port-au-Prince by the Tontons Macoute, the evil militia founded by himself. The Ambassador (the story grows and grows) had to put the dog in his car himself and drive it away. He tried to turn it out in the great square by the Presidential Palace, but it refused to move – the dog was too close to Dr. Duvalier. Only when he reached the cathedral did he consent to budge, trotting off into the dark to seek another sanctuary. Of course there was no truth in the story, but it seemed probable enough in this city without news and, between certain hours, without light.

A few minutes from the hotel one can see the blackened ruins of Benoit's house. Benoit, one of Haiti's prize marksmen, was suspected of having been concerned in the attempted kidnapping of the President's children earlier in the year. He took refuge in an embassy and his house was set ablaze with petrol by the Tontons Macoute, who machine-gunned the flames. Mme. Benoit escaped, but no one knows whether her child is alive, nor how many servants were shot or burnt to death.

Anything may happen, any time, anywhere. One night a man came running up the steps of the hotel, under the impression that it was an embassy, seeking refuge. He was probably a madman, for surely everyone knows for his own safety the position of each embassy, but what dark experience had driven him mad? Was he one of the sixty-two army officers who were so suddenly dismissed this year? Some have disappeared, some have taken sanctuary; the Chief of Staff who signed their dismissal walked next day into a South American embassy for refuge. The British *charge* finds his car abandoned on a street – the chauffeur taken to the police station to be interrogated about his master's movements, and there is no redress.

The diplomats have watched the slow disintegration of the American Military Aid Mission, after the head of the mission objected to the arms for the army going to the Tontons. In the last weeks of its existence pilots were not allowed to visit their planes, even to service them, and marines were separated from their ship. No one makes a stand. It is as though the diplomatic missions – with the honourable exception of the British Ambassador – had been hypnotized by the dark glasses of Baron Samedi (they are the uniform also of the Tontons Macoute).

In the cathedral, on the national day, when the excommunicated President puts in his one appearance at Mass, the Tontons arrive armed with sub-machine-guns and search, even behind the altar. Then they take up their position in the cathedral with their guns covering the diplomatic corps, while in the choir rifles dominate the congregation. The bishops of Haiti and Conaives have been driven into exile, the Nuncio has departed. (A kind of evil farce enters even into the religious conflict. The Bishop of Gonaives had tried to suppress voodoo and required of his communicants that they should surrender their voodoo charms – he was accused of robbing the country of archaeological treasures.)

There have been many reigns of terror in the course of history. Sometimes they have been prompted by a warped idealism like Robespierre's, sometimes they have been directed fanatically against a class or a race and supported by some twisted philosophy; surely never has terror had so bare and ignoble an object as here – the protection of a few tough men's pockets, the pockets of Gracia Jacques, Colonel Athi, Colonel Desire, the leaders of the Tontons Macoute, of the police and of the presidential guard – and in the centre of the ring, of course, in his black evening suit, his heavy glasses, his halting walk and halting speech, the cruel and absurd Doctor.

Everyone is in some sort a prisoner in Port-au-Prince. The exit visa for a foreigner is twice the price of the entry. For a Haitian a passport costs $100 and the visa (controlled personally by the Doctor) another five. You pay your money, but it is dubious whether you will ever see your passport.

Travel on the island is almost at a standstill. The roads were always a deterrent, but now there are road-blocks round Port-au-Prince to the north and controls at every small town to the south. Within a circuit of a few kilometres from Port-au-Prince I was searched four times, and it took me two days at the police station, where the portrait of the Doctor is flanked by snapshots of the machine-gunned bodies of Barbot and his companions, to gain a two-day permit for the south. The north, because of the raids from the Dominican Republic, was forbidden altogether.

All trade which does not offer a rake-off is at a standstill. A whole nation can die of starvation so long as the Doctor's non-fiscal account is safe. The public revenue of Haiti in a reasonable year should be around $28 million, but the non-fiscal account which is paid directly into the President's pocket amounts to between $8 million and $12 million. On all the main commodities, sugar, flour, oil, tyres, cement, a special tax is levied which never goes into the general account. The export of cement is forbidden because the world price would not admit this extra tax. The export would aid Haiti, but not the ring.

The President has, of course, other less traditional sources of revenue. The British Ambassador was expelled because he protested at the levies which the Tontons Macoute were exacting illegally from all businessmen. An arbitrary figure was named and if the sum were not forthcoming the man would be beaten up in his home by the Tontons Macoute, during the hours of darkness.

Tolls are enforced on all cars between the rich suburb of Petionville and Port-au-Prince. These particular sums go to the only project in Haiti visible to the naked eye. This project is the new town of Duvalierville, forty miles out of Port-au-Prince. The Doctor has obviously read accounts of Brasilia and in the absurd little tourist houses with roofs like wind-wrecked butterflies one can detect Brasilia's influence. There is no beach, and the town, if it is ever finished, is supposed to house 2,000 peasants in little one-roomed houses, so that it is difficult to see why any tourist should stay there. The only building finished in Duvalierville is the cock-fight stadium. In the meanwhile the peasants' homes have been destroyed and they have been driven from the area to live with relatives. Many people believe that the town if finished will become a Tontons garrison.

As with most major constructions in Haiti, since the Emperor Christophe built his fantastic citadel on a mountain-top, the cement used is cruelty and injustice. Labour on the project is controlled by the Tontons Macoute. One young labourer was taken off his job because a Tonton wanted it for another. The labourer tried to appeal to him, 'Please I am hungry. I have no work', and the Tonton promptly shot him through the head, the cheek and the body. He now survives in Port-au-Prince paralysed.

It is impossible to exaggerate the poverty of Haiti. One has the sense that even the machine of tyranny is running down. The levies on businesses have ceased because there is no money to exact. The army has received no pay for two months (but the President has seen to it that the army is powerless), nor have the civil servants nor the priests.

Port-au-Prince has always been a city of beggars who make their headquarters around and in the Post Office, but even they feel the pinch now that the tourists have departed, and there may well be truth in those hollow voices that pursue you even within the grounds of the hotels: 'Master, I'm bad. I'm real bad. I'm hungry.' These are the professionals. Who knows what has happened to the hundreds of workers abandoned by the tourist trade? They are starving invisibly behind the decaying mud walls of the Port-au-Prince slums. Meanwhile an officer of the Tontons Macoute is building a large ice-skating rink up at Kenscoff, the mountain village above Port-au-Prince.

What hopes are there for this poor, beautiful and bedevilled country? Optimists point out that Duvalier has no supporters (apart from the police and the Tontons). Even voodoo is a doubtful ally; the priest, the *houngan*, is a luxury which only the more prosperous parts of the country can afford. Voodoo hardly exists in the poor south, but perhaps the Doctor for one reason may be content to see it wither. He is himself almost certainly a believer (he has declared '*Je suis immateriel*'), but oddly enough it is his excommunication by the Church which prevents him from practising his religion, since a voodoo worshipper must receive Holy Communion if he is to be accepted by the *houngan*.

The shooting of Clement Barbot has taken away the only real threat to Duvalier in the capital. Rebels may make raids in the north, but it hardly affects the inhabitants of Port-au-Prince. A few brave youths the other day attacked the police station at Kenscoff, and slaughtered a couple of Tontons and a couple of policemen. Three of them held out in a cave in the mountains for more than twenty-four hours against several hundred police, and they killed more than twenty of their pursuers ('a hundred' says the optimist) before they were burnt out with flame-throwers.

Did they hope the peasants would rise? That hope was killed for ever after the small Cuban invasion of 1959, when Barbot – then still head of the Tontons – massacred with machine-guns in a town square every peasant of the region where the men had landed. The peasants now will never rise until photographs of the President's dead body are nailed like Barbot's photo on the walls of every police station.

The refugees in Santo Domingo, like the Cubans in Miami, are divided among themselves. The last presidential candidate, Louis Dejoie, plays a vain, loquacious role in the restaurants of Santo Domingo while he denounces the few men who cross the border to fight. Intervention by the Dominican forces is out of the question. Haitians remember Trujillo's slaughter of unarmed Haitian labourers at the frontier-river now called Massacre, and Haitian pride cannot be exaggerated; it is a quality noble and absurd and comforting for the persecutors. Even a man released from the torture chamber under the palace who had been beaten almost to the point of death would not admit that he had been touched. The great-great-grandchild of slaves is never beaten. (A whip hangs on the central pillar of every voodoo temple as a reminder of the past.)

Santo Domingo is fifty minutes from Port-au-Prince by air, but the distance separating the two places must be judged not in miles but in centuries. In Santo Domingo businessmen and politicians feel at home among the fruit-machines and the swimming-pools; on their belt a little leather purse has taken the place of a revolver holster. The talk at the next table in the luxury hotel is all of dollars and percentages, but neither business nor politics has any relevance in Haiti. Haiti produces painters, poets, heroes – and in that spiritual region it is natural to find a devil too. The electric sign which winks out every night across the public garden has a certain truth. JE SUIS LE DRAPEAU HAITIEN, UNI INDIVISIBLE. FRANCOIS DUVALIER.

Graham Greene's visit to Haiti in 1963 provided the background material for his novel The Comedians. *He died in 1991.*

AN AMERICAN TRAGEDY

—

James Cameron

Daily Herald
25 November 1963

On 22 November 1963, President John F. Kennedy was assassinated in Dallas, Texas, almost certainly by Lee Harvey Oswald. Two days later Oswald himself was fatally wounded in the underground car park of Dallas police station while being transferred to the county jail.

Now the American Tragedy is complete. Nothing like it has been seen before. There is room for no more drama. The wheel has come full circle. The American nation is almost tangibly in a state of shock – stunned by the size of its own violence, by the picture of its own excesses.

Two dead men have made this day traumatic. It was electric enough to hear – just as Washington was freezing into immobility for the passing of John Kennedy's body – that the man accused of shooting him had himself been shot. Then, just as Jacqueline Kennedy knelt to kiss the coffin, we learned that Lee Oswald had died in the same hospital as the President. This brought the situation to a pitch of incalculable intensity.

Lynch law has followed assassination. The corruption of high tragedy by the personal vengeance of a Dallas club-owner has brought total fantasy to the American scene.

While Lee Oswald lay dying with a bullet in his belly and as Jack Ruby, the self-appointed executioner, was held in Dallas City Jail, the immense formula of pageantry went on here in Washington. Thousands watching it did not even know how this new mad Texan melodrama had intruded on their grief.

The American people have been spared one terrible legal trial. But there will have to be another, and how does one try a strip-club proprietor for usurping the function of the nation, and doing for his own awful reasons what the State would almost certainly have done for its own?

Meanwhile there is the spectacle of Washington in mourning – a city almost supernaturally silent. Crowds stood blank-faced under a brilliant, bitter sun as Kennedy's coffin was borne from the White House to the Capitol. There, in the Rotunda of the seat of Government, people are filing past the bier all night.

Tomorrow, proclaimed a day of mourning throughout half the world, there will meet in Washington the most immense and solemn gathering of world leaders ever brought together in one place.

It will indeed be the strangest of days that links such men as Charles de Gaulle and Anastas Mikoyan, Sir Alec Douglas-Home and Eamon de Valera, Prince Philip and the high, exotic dignitaries of fifty States – the great and the little. Only one thing could have united them: the common mystery of death.

At first sight the American nation seemed today to be still in a condition of anaesthesia, an almost visible combination of outrage and regret, and a sort of incredulity – *how could this ever happen to us?* It is the reaction of all human beings to a brusque bereavement, multiplied a hundred million times.

Quite suddenly, the United States feels itself simultaneously horrified, guilty and vulnerable. It is a hateful sensation, and there is nothing one can say.

The assassination of the thirty-fifth President of the United States has suspended all values. I was here only a couple of months ago, when the great Negro freedom march was underlining both the good aspects of the Kennedy optimism and its helplessness. My coloured maid today recalled it. 'How much has been wasted,' she said. 'I shall never know why it happened.'

How John Kennedy will rate historically as a president after only two years, ten months and two days – the goodwill, the energy, the image of vigour and the achievements that did not come off – will be argued for years. But not today.

Even at such a time the American sense of drama has heightened everything. This is the first presidential assassination in the television and popular newspaper age, and the impact is numbing – even without the new violence that has followed.

Yet it is perhaps true that even the most authentic emotion is crude. The papers that exploit the haggard misery of relatives, photographed in unwillingly public grief, are themselves grieved.

The circus parade of human sorrow, the day-long keening on television, is America's true trial of mourning. Even when all the big advertisers turn their displays into black-bordered *In Memoria*, it looks less cynical than you might suppose. Every society expresses itself in its own idiom. Public relations lamentation need not necessarily be insincere.

But the other mood is uglier. In Dallas a little while ago we got a glimpse of how ugly. Whoever shot President Kennedy – and unlike the United States Press, we have been trained to await at least a trial – the political theme was bitterly thrust forward today.

'Kennedy slain by Red,' the banners shouted. 'President dies by Commie bullet.' 'Red killer held.' Jack Ruby became the symbol of violent reactions.

The former General Edwin Walker of the John Birch Society, has said Kennedy's death was 'tragic, but not surprising. This internal threat must never be underestimated'.

Lee Oswald's association with the Fair Play for Cuba Committee has pricked that boil again. This morning they dragged the wretched Cuban delegate to the UN on the television and rubbed his nose in it.

'Aren't there Castro-lovers in Cuba who would want Kennedy's death?' they demanded. And he could only cry: 'No, no – for so many reasons, no. You will never understand.'

Today the whole apparatus of United States Government is in abeyance. President Johnson has returned to his home in Spring Valley, to the house that used to be the scene of the hostess Perle Mesta's celebrated parties. Now it is ringed with police and secret servicemen.

The roaring tide of speculation and pressure that will descend on the new President is momentarily held back. It will not be for long.

Today Kennedy's family flew in from Hyannis in Massachusetts – all but his father, crippled with a stroke. Joseph Kennedy, one-time Ambassador in London, is not ordinarily an easy subject for sympathy, but it is impossible not to flinch at the many blows fate has dealt him.

His first son, Joseph, vanished during the war on a bombing flight. His second daughter, Kathleen, married the Marquis of Hartington – killed in Normandy – and herself died in a plane crash. The eldest daughter, Rosemary, is, at forty-four, still in a school for the retarded in Wisconsin. And now this – in the last days of his life.

Tonight the late President's coffin lies in the Rotunda, surrounded by marble statuary and vast ceremonial paintings.

Nine soldiers and sailors – including two Negroes – brought the body in. The official mourners stood around in the bleak empty way of those who must listen to official eulogies. Among them was Jackie Kennedy, two days widowed, looking very erect and slim in black.

She stood there with every smallest change of expression brutally exposed to the zoom lenses of a dozen TV cameras. On one of her hands hung her son John, three years old tomorrow. On the other Caroline, who will be six two days later.

They know of the tragedy. But they cannot know the full drama of the youngest man ever elected President of the United States – and the youngest ever to die.

Now two men lie dead, one in Dallas and the other in the Capitol, for a purpose no one will now ever know.

James Cameron was one of the best reporters Fleet Street ever knew, working for Picture Post, *the* News Chronicle, *and the* Daily Herald *as well as the* New Statesman, *the* Evening Standard *and the BBC. He was a founder member of the Campaign for Nuclear Disarmament. He died in 1985.*

WHAT SONGS THE BEATLES SANG . . .

—

William Mann
The Times
23 December 1963

At the height of Beatlemania no one was quite sure how tongue in cheek William Mann was being when he wrote this review. The reverberations, however, linger to this day. 'Don't ask me about Aeolian cadences,' Paul McCartney said to an interviewer in June 1995, 'I still can't read music.'

The outstanding English composers of 1963 must seem to have been John Lennon and Paul McCartney, the talented young musicians from Liverpool whose songs have been sweeping the country since last Christmas, whether performed by their own group, the Beatles, or by the numerous other teams of English troubadours that they also supply with songs.

I am not concerned here with the social phenomenon of Beatlemania, which finds expression in handbags, balloons and other articles bearing the likenesses of the loved ones, or in the hysterical screaming of young girls whenever the Beatle Quartet performs in public, but with the musical phenomenon. For several decades, in fact since the decline of the music-hall, England has taken her popular songs from the United States, either directly or by mimicry. But the songs of Lennon and McCartney are distinctly indigenous in character, the most imaginative and inventive examples of a style that has been developing on Merseyside during the past few years. And there is a nice, rather flattering irony in the news that the Beatles have now become prime favourites in America, too.

The strength of character in pop songs seems, and quite understandably, to be determined usually by the number of composers involved; when three or four people are required to make the original tunesmith's work publicly presentable it is unlikely to retain much individuality or to wear very well. The virtue of the Beatles' repertory is that, apparently, they do it themselves; three of the four are composers, they are versatile instrumentalists, and when they do borrow a song from another repertory, their treatment is idiosyncratic – as when Paul McCartney sings 'Till There Was You' from *The Music Man*, a cool, easy, tasteful version of this ballad, quite without artificial sentimentality.

Their noisy items are the ones that arouse teenagers' excitement. Glutinous crooning is generally out of fashion these days, and even a song about 'Misery' sounds fundamentally quite cheerful; the slow, sad song about 'This Boy', which features prominently in Beatle programmes, is expressively unusual for its lugubrious music, but harmonically it is one of their most intriguing, with its chains of pandiatonic clusters, and the sentiment is acceptable because voiced cleanly and crisply. But harmonic interest is typical of their quicker songs, too, and one gets the impression that they think simultaneously of harmony and melody, so firmly are the major tonic sevenths and ninths built into their tunes, and the flat submediant key switches, so natural is the Aeolian cadence at the end of 'Not a second time' (the chord progression which ends Mahler's *Song of the Earth*).

Those submediant switches from C major into A flat major, and to a lesser extent mediant ones (e.g. the octave ascent in the famous 'I want to hold your hand') are a trademark of Lennon-McCartney songs – they do not figure much in other pop repertories, or in the Beatles' arrangements of borrowed material – and show signs of becoming a mannerism. The other trademark of their compositions is a firm and purposeful bass line with a musical life of its own; how Lennon and McCartney divide their creative responsibilities I have yet to discover, but it is perhaps significant that Paul is the bass guitarist of the group. It may also be significant that George Harrison's song 'Don't Bother Me' is harmonically a good deal more primitive, though it is nicely enough presented.

I suppose it is the sheer loudness of the music that appeals to Beatle admirers (there is something to be heard even through the squeals) and many parents must have cursed the electric guitar's amplification this Christmas – how fresh and euphonious the ordinary guitars sound in the Beatles' version of 'Till There Was You' – but parents who are still managing to survive the decibels and, after copious repetition over several months, still deriving some musical pleasure from the overhearing, do so because there is a good deal of variety – oh, so welcome in pop music – about what they sing.

The autocratic but not by any means ungrammatical attitude to tonality (closer to, say, Peter Maxwell Davies's carols in *O Magnum Mysterium* than to Gershwin or Loewe or even Lionel Bart); the exhilarating and often quasi-instrumental vocal duetting, sometimes in scat or in falsetto, behind the melodic line; the melismas with altered vowels ('I saw her yesterday-ee-ay') which have not quite become mannered, and the discreet, sometimes subtle, varieties of instrumentation – a suspicion of piano or organ, a few bars of mouth-organ obbligato, an excursion on the claves or maraccas; the translation of African Blues or American western idioms (in 'Baby, It's You', the Magyar 8/8 metre, too) into tough, sensitive Merseyside.

These are some of the qualities that make one wonder with interest what the Beatles, and particularly Lennon and McCartney, will do next, and if America will spoil them or hold on to them, and if their next record will wear as well as the others. They have brought a distinctive and exhilarating flavour into a genre of music that was in danger of ceasing to be music at all.

William Mann was chief music critic at The Times *from 1960 to 1982. He died in 1985.*

REVIEW OF *DR STRANGELOVE*

Dilys Powell
Sunday Times
February 1964

After a career in radio, most notably with The Goon Show, *Peter Sellers was already a successful film actor before he made* Dr Strangelove. *But it was Stanley Kubrick's brilliant black comedy which brought his gifts full international recognition.*

Full title to begin with: *Dr Strangelove or: How I Learned to Stop Worrying and Love the Bomb.* With a name like that it obviously isn't a solemn film, though it deals with a solemn subject. But its origins are not, apparently, in comedy.

Dr Strangelove is based, one is told, on a straightforward thriller about the chance of starting a nuclear war by mistake. The director, Stanley Kubrick, working with the American novelist Terry Southern and Peter George, author of the thriller, has taken the story and turned it into an appalling, and I mean appalling, joke; he calls it a nightmare comedy. I suppose the description is as good as any. I have been searching for a parallel to the film. Nothing really like it in the cinema; political jokes, yes, but not doomsday jokes, and the possibility of blowing the world up offers a theme for which black comedy is a phrase much too bland. Turning to literature, I think vaguely of Swift and his *Modest Proposal* for disposing of inconveniently starving Irish children by serving them up for dinner; the straight face which is so telling in Kubrick's film is there in Swift, and so is the deathly idea. But then you don't get a belly-laugh from reading Swift.

Swift and slapstick: perhaps that would be nearer. But this isn't exactly slapstick. It is a succession of minor mishaps in the Harold Lloyd manner: mis-arrangements, miscalculations, each in itself a major absurdity because of its consequences. A plan devised to guard against human error succeeds only in guarding against the correction of error, in preventing anybody, and that goes for the President of the United States, from countermanding the order to bomb. Everybody, in this safety system, is cut off from everybody else: cut off by design; by the conviction that the other fellow is a Commie (the Pentagon general's word, not mine) who has managed to dress up as an American; and by such incidentals as shortage of change for making a trunk call. You laugh at the mixture of trivial accident and misapplied ingenuity, you laugh at the disproportion between causes and effects, and in a shuddering way you laugh all the more (tragedy often contains a shame-faced element of comedy) because the danger which threatens is universal, horrible and real.

The double-face of the story – serious events broken up into farcical incidents – is expressed in double-face acting of a high order. There is Sterling Hayden as the general in command of the strategic air base who at the start of the film sets the ball, or rather the Bomb, rolling: a portrait of a psychotic fanaticism twisted now and then into the ridiculous by an emphatic braking of pace or a pleased inflection of the voice (and strengthened, I should add, in its ferocity by the use of carefully angled close-ups). There is George C. Scott as the general called on, at the meeting in the Pentagon War Room, to reply to the incredulous expostulations of the President: gleefully glib in his account of the provisions which prevent the recall of the bombers, exploding into maniac suspicion at the sight of the Russian Ambassador – Mr. Scott moves in a blaze of nihilistic idiocy between satire and burlesque.

And there is Peter Sellers; and here one has to drop double-face and, using the phrase in strict accuracy, substitute treble-face. Mr. Sellers plays three roles. He plays the President struggling to convey the news to Russia over the hot telephone (the writing of this monologue is a little masterpiece of comic euphemism). He plays an RAF officer at the American base. And he plays Dr. Strangelove, a scientist from Germany who has changed his name but not his nature.

The last portrait is the least successful of the three because the most extravagant – it is, in any case, involved in the final War Room scene which, deprived of the cross-cutting to the bomber's desperate flight, cross-cutting which gives earlier passages a painful comic tension – drops into a slightly slack, speculative mood. Least successful – but still, with its uncontrollable reversions to Nazi type, successful enough, and I fancy that if anybody else had achieved its diabolic glitter one's reactions would be all-admiring.

The difficulty is that Mr. Sellers is in competition with Mr. Sellers, and the standard can't be set higher. The Sellers President, a decent rational being in a lunatic situation, makes delicate play with the irony of embarrassment. The Sellers RAF type is another reasonable, reliable man beset by the mad and the mulish, but here the portrait, enriched by national traits and class mannerisms – the sloping walk, the voice from the back of the nose, the amiable off-hand approach – adds a particular pleasure which makes the performance my favourite: the pleasure of recognition, I know that Group Captain, and sitting at my typewriter I laugh when I think of him.

The President and the Group Captain are played without caricature and in the context they are all the funnier for it. But farce is essential to the film. Fantastic farce governs the climax; and if you are against that, think of the alternative. For me at any rate farce makes the theme of *Dr. Strangelove* not only more bearable, but also more believable.

After all it is difficult to accept Doomsday unless as a monstrous joke.

WOULD YOU LET YOUR DAUGHTER MARRY A ROLLING STONE?

—

Maureen Cleave

Evening Standard
21 March 1964

From the beginning, the Rolling Stones worked hard to cultivate their anarchic image. Maureen Cleave was not taken in by them.

'But would you like your daughter to marry one?' is what you ask yourself about the Rolling Stones. They've done terrible things to the music scene – set it back, I would say, by about eight years.

Just when we'd got our pop singers looking neat and tidy, and above all, *cheerful*, along come the Rolling Stones, looking like what we used to call beatniks. (I use this démodé word deliberately. I hope you can remember what beatniks looked like.)

The Stones, which is what they are called by intimates, have wrecked the image of the pop singer of the Sixties.

'We're a horrible looking bunch,' they say of themselves, and there is no murmur of dissent. Girls stop to stare and giggle in the street, men shout things that are unrestrainedly rude, the Hilton Hotel shows them the door and so do many provincial pubs.

They do take a bit of getting used to. And certainly no prospective mother-in-law is going to accept them in their present condition.

Their ages range from nineteen to twenty-two. There is Keith Richard, who has a pert face, pert manners and was eating an apple; there is Charlie Watts who is keen on clothes and considered by his manager to have the bone structure of Steve McQueen and therefore a great future in films; there is Brian Jones who has floppy yellow hair and is the one best-liked by me; there is Bill Wyman who bears a marked resemblance to both Charles I and Charles II, an essentially Stuart face; and then there is Mick Jagger who is undescribable.

On television they look curiously appealing with their great heads shaking vaguely, Mick Jagger jerking like a jack-in-a-box but his feet rooted to the spot.

They possess no uniforms. 'We couldn't adapt ourselves to a uniform,' they say. They will walk on to the stage in their everyday outfits, tie or no tie as the case may be. They sell a lot of records. Their *Not Fade Away* is in at number three. Their manager, a young man with red hair called Andrew Loog Oldham, is passionately devoted to their scruffy image.

'Aggressive,' he said with satisfaction. 'They don't wash too much and they aren't all that keen on clothes. And they don't play nice mannered music; it's raw and masculine. I get letters from the kids begging me not to let them appear at the Palladium or go to America and get all tidied up.'

Often he is asked if they are as stupid as they look. 'People,' said Mr. Oldham nonchalantly, 'keep asking me if they're morons.'

Indeed the Stones are not what they seem. You discover that one was a graphic designer, another did engineering, another went to the London School of Economics.

Brian Jones now lives in a village in Berkshire but shortly moves to Belgravia where, he says, he will live next door to Lady Dartmouth. He hires a different make of car each week so as to get used to them all.

Charlie Watts has invested a lot of money in the Rock of Gibraltar which the others think is pretty stupid.

They originally created a stir in the Station Hotel, Richmond. The place held 140 people and on a good night there would be 500 dancing in the street. Sometimes you would find the Salvation Army at one end of the street and the Stones at the other.

'The kids used to hang off the ceiling,' said Brian, 'taking their shirts off and that. They liked the way we raved. In places like Cardiff they kiss us, getting the sweat off our faces on to their faces.'

As the Stones would say, the kids 'reckon' them like mad. They claim to have a disruptive influence on other pop singers, many of whom long to throw away their blue mohair suits and rebel.

And of course their effect on the poor young man in conventional employment is to make him extremely discontented. He is forever confiding in the Stones how he longs to wear his hair down his back only his bosses and teachers won't let him. 'From that quarter,' Mick Jagger said, 'there seems to be some sort of opposition.'

Two weeks ago, they scored a victory over the grown-ups in the north. They appeared on *Scene at 6.30*.

'Get those horrible people off the screen,' cried the adults, switching over to *Top of the Pops*. There, gaping at them from *Top of the Pops* were the Stones.

'We're quite clean really,' Brian Jones says, just for your information. 'What we want to do is bring a lot of pleasure to people. Thereby earning a bomb!'

Maureen Cleave's Evening Standard *profiles of pop stars were innovative for their wit and observation. Still one of the best interviewers in journalism, her articles are to be found mainly in the* Evening Standard *and the* Daily Telegraph.

THE ELECTRIC MAN

Margaret Laing
Sunday Times Magazine
22 March 1964

In the period which followed Harold Macmillan's 1959 election boast, 'You've never had it so good', a new breed of entrepreneur was born, offering consumer goods at more or less affordable prices to the newly affluent. John Bloom was quite simply the pushiest and the flashiest.

A 1964 version of *The Gold Rush* might star, instead of Charlie Chaplin, another East-Ender of Jewish descent who has climbed high. John Bloom.

Like the little man in the film he set out from nothing with grandiose ideas and a complete lack of technical know-how. His enemies have often rejoiced to see him suspended from a slippery lifeline only to meet him on another peak six months later. Four years ago, when he took over Rolls Razor to make washing machines, he had next to nothing. Two years and several mistakes later he was a millionaire.

Parting shots in *The Gold Rush* showed Chaplin with the money and the girl he wanted, sailing as a first-class passenger. In Bloom's case, the boat is his own – the 376-ton yacht *Ariane*, equipped with a cinema, lift and a stately blue and white office. And his wife Anne has been his best investment. An exceptionally pretty and somewhat innocent girl of twenty-four, she nevertheless has a strong practical streak. 'If John ever went bankrupt she could run a business,' says one of their friends. She has to organize her own life entirely around his. She must be ready to pack in an afternoon for a three months' trip. She must be free to entertain the wives of his business contacts.

Their third wedding anniversary was last month. They met about four years ago when she came to a meeting of a charity he was running. She lived in Ealing, and worked as a secretary for the Transworld Features Syndicate Inc. in Fleet Street. 'I think I was the only person who didn't know anything about John Bloom,' she says. 'I didn't know what to make of a different car every time he took me out. We both went out with other people, then I went for a holiday to Majorca and stayed on for an extra week. He telephoned and told me to come back.'

Bloom says he changed quite a lot all of a sudden. 'I got this mania to settle down. Going home to the butler and the cook was all right but I wanted something more.'

Bloom often works better from their flat in Park Lane than from his Regent Street office. It costs £1,000 a year and from the sitting room there is an uninterrupted view of the pedestrian subway. 'We live rather modestly. We don't have ninety-three

Picassos and four Rembrandts,' he says. Most of the pictures are reproduction Canalettos. The furniture is comfortable and upholstered in dark blues and greens chosen by his wife. 'When I moved in it was like a film set, not a home, with white carpets and a scarlet suite,' she says. Two red telephones and one grey one have bare dials – their number is ex-directory, and it is sometimes months before even the closest associates are given it.

Above the mantelpiece hangs a larger-and-brighter than life colour photograph of Bloom. The same sight greets visitors both to Bloom's West End office and the Cricklewood headquarters, and is used in miniature in his advertisements. (Also in the office is a portrait of him done from a photograph by Stephen Ward, a birthday present from his wife, which he considers 'not good enough for home'.) In the photograph he wears a blue suit, shirt with buttoned-down collar, and poised smile. Quite vain, and without much taste, this is his ideal vision of himself – tanned, blue-eyed and beneficent.

In reality his colouring is very pale. In spite of the daily efforts of his personal hairdresser – with whom he spends half-an-hour a day, and without whose help he has been known to refuse to go out – his fine hair and minute beard are hardly dynamic. His slight frame, almost five feet ten but stooped so that it seems much smaller, shrinks to a wisp in the featherweight suits he likes. (Trousers and sleeves are a little short, and sometimes four inches of cuff show.) He buys them by the dozen for about £40 each from a show-business tailor in Shepherd's Bush. His wife buys all his other clothes.

Several wedding-day photographs stand round the room. Gilt cupids support one lamp, gilt dolphins another. A row of coloured glass clowns stand on the sideboard. There are two bedrooms and two bathrooms, a staffroom for the Spanish couple, a dining room, and a bar with an illuminated mural of can-can dancers with glittering garters.

The Blooms go out a lot, mainly to business dinners and first nights. 'I like musicals and Doris Day, and he doesn't,' says Anne. 'He likes more dramatic things – cowboy films, and he liked *The Servant*.' They are now trying to spend two evenings a week at home. They go to bed any time between 9 p.m. and 2 a.m.

Bloom gets up at 8.30 and reads the papers for an hour. Breakfast consists of hot chocolate and toast. He eats rather sparingly, and his favourite dishes are boiled chicken and liver. 'We keep a clean home and don't have milk after the meat for hygienic reasons,' he says, although this is standard Jewish practice. He does not smoke, and drinks very little. He works most Saturdays as well as Sundays, but he does observe some Jewish notable days such as the Passover and the Day of Atonement. He would not have married Anne if she had not been Jewish. 'I've seen some mixed marriages and the way they break up. I don't particularly fancy being ostracized by either side. It's one of the set things I'd made my mind up about,' he says.

Although they both say that the repercussions of his meeting with Christine Holford in the South of France in August 1962, and the subsequent 'Blue Gardenia' trial after her husband shot her, were a great strain, they claim a united front on it. 'My wife knew all about the girl from the start,' says Bloom.

Anne is now very happy with him. She runs her own Mercedes, has shares in the business, and could be independent if she did not prefer to stay with him. 'He's very lovable. When he has time, he's thoughtful,' she says. 'I couldn't imagine being married to anybody different. Everybody else is so dull and tame. He literally never ceases to amaze me. There's nothing he doesn't know about. Yet he's completely unpractical: when I was ill in bed once he spent an hour banging about in the kitchen to make me a cup of tea. Then he came in with hot water and some tea-leaves floating in it.'

Surprisingly, she is probably the only person with a temper to quell Bloom's own. 'We both flare up, and five minutes later it's forgotten,' she says. He claims she stays angry longer than he does, and outsiders confirm that she sometimes puts him in his place. Bloom basks in the slightly hen-pecked aura of his marriage, proudly stating what his wife will or won't let him do. Perhaps it softens the reflection of the work-tyrant in his own eyes.

At about 9.45 Bloom leaves for his office in his Rolls-Royce, the colour of a black tulip. (He looks back in some horror to the figure he cut in his roaring twenties – he is now thirty-two – when he wore cufflinks shaped like washing machines and had a different car every time he called for his girlfriends; now he shudders as he describes one car he remembers as the 'orange monster – a horrible flashy American bit of rubbish. I don't need special features any more'.) And from the moment he arrives until he leaves again, about nine hours later, he is the fighting bantam.

'The little chap's electric,' says a City adviser. 'He treats some of his employers like dirt and they seem to enjoy it.' Chairman of the company is Richard Reader Harris, the Tory MP who introduced him to Christine Holford at Juan-les-Pins. Several of the other directors are in their early thirties ('I don't like old fuddy-duddies, with a few exceptions,' says Bloom), Jewish, and some went to school with him. They give the impression of a slick team of Rolls Razormen, all super-sharp-edged. He has trained replacements for all of them.

His father now works for him. So do two brothers-in-law and one uncle. His sister Noreen ran a shop for him before she married. It was called J. & N. Electrics – for John and Noreen.

In his office, Bloom uses a squeaking quill pen to tot up his millions. Round the walls are Alken hunting pictures. 'I said I liked them and the owner gave them to me,' he says. He issues instructions rapidly and excitedly, often failing to finish his sentences. His boyish, slightly twanging voice, with its adolescent vocabulary, darts straight to words like 'nice' and 'diabolical'. He is often shy of using proper nouns, and talks of things as 'all that nonsense', 'all that rubbish'. The highest term of praise is 'I like that.'

It is not used indiscriminately. 'I have the ideas – they have to make them work,' he says. 'If you make a mistake there's hell to pay,' said one of the directors. Few people care to argue with him, although the fact that there are a few people with whom he has never lost his temper show that, when necessary, he can control it. He will never admit to being wrong. But if he has been given some good advice he will, while appearing to reject it, store it and use it at a later date. He does the same with information. He can listen to three conversations at once without apparent effort – and correct mistakes in all of them.

Though he himself has turned up at board meetings in blue jeans after rushing back from his yacht, he reproves his staff for dressing casually on Saturdays.

'He's a tireless worker. He never walks, he runs – that's the pace at which he lives,' says Sir Charles Colston, the ex-Hoover chairman who makes many of the washing machines at his factory in Aycliffe, near Darlington.

'Bloom is someone who makes decisions instantaneously. I have never heard him talk about anything but business, not with anybody. He has a fantastic brain and will repeat a conversation verbatim weeks after it took place. He works on hunches. If one comes off he flogs it to death. If not, he cuts his losses and is out of it as quickly. That's why he left the dish-washing idea. He expected it to explode and take fire and it went slowly.'

Wherever he is, he broods over the day's sales figures. 'Fifteen months ago he was in Hong Kong when orders from the north dropped off because of unemployment. He cabled instructions to offer free insurance against unemployment so that hire-purchase payments were guaranteed. The drop stopped,' said an associate.

God help anybody, says Bloom, who tries to make a decision on advertising or sales policy without consulting him. He uses four advertising agencies and they work in open competition together at meetings. He gives them his ideas, and the one with the best presentation gets the job and the discount. (Last year he spent about £2 million on advertising, and was the largest individual advertiser in the *Daily Mirror*. This year the appropriation may go up to £3 million.) He runs the advertising almost as if the agencies were his own. He plans all the copy and approves every single line that appears. 'We do things now we didn't think were humanly possible,' says Eric Evans, of Stowe and Bowden, one of the four agencies. Roger Pryer, who has another agency, recalls the day when a full-page advertisement was booked one afternoon – and appeared next morning. I was in this agency when a Rolls proof arrived. A castor was missing from the picture of the machine. 'Get down there and make them change it. Tell them your job's in the balance. It is,' Pryer shouted.

The sales force is run on lines laid down by Bloom, although day-to-day administration is in the hands of Jack Jacobs, the sales director. There are 400 salesmen, self-employed, who live entirely on their commission – £2 for the 39-guinea model, £3 10s. for the 59-guinea one. 'I tell applicants they must be prepared to work twice as hard as in any other job and then they will be paid three times as much,' says Jack Jacobs.

They get an average of £3,000. Not all their commission goes straight to them. Some of it is put in a retention account. If they then transgress in some way – miss a branch meeting, forget to put the burglar alarm on their van and have a machine stolen, are in a crash which is judged to be their fault, or fail to demonstrate the machine properly – they are fined. A second transgression probably brings the sack.

'I'm the hatchet man,' says Mr. Jacobs. He is glad that John Bloom no longer works from the administrative headquarters in Cricklewood, as he claims that sacked salesmen used to burst into his office and come out again with their jobs back. (Bloom dislikes getting the blame for anything. He wants to be liked.)

Even so Bloom, who is reputed to know all his salesmen by name, has a pretty good idea of what happens to them. If all other sources of information fail, there is the company's weekly newsletter. This is sent to the salesmen's home addresses, Mr. Jacobs explains, so that wives can see how their husbands are doing and act as the company's sub-manageresses.

Three January issues tell one short story. In the first, London West are announced fourth (out of twelve branches) in the Cup of the Month competition. A week later their place has dropped to tenth, and Jacobs comments, 'I have had my say with – [official named] and will refrain from further publicity at this time.' In the next issue we read, '– is no longer with us and we wish him great success in whatever field he now chooses to venture into.' Now, it seems, the man is back with the organization – but he has been demoted.

The flavour of Mr. Jacob's exhortations comes over best, perhaps, in a paragraph addressed to two other branch managers. 'The advice I have given these gentlemen has varied from a suggestion that they wear tight shoes, and thus be forced to dispense with some of their inherent good nature – to establishing the whereabouts of the nearest Labour Exchange.'

With this modified *Inferno* backdrop in their minds, it is hardly surprising that the salesmen are extremely well-informed about the merits of their machines. When Mrs. Kathleen Weldon of Talbot Road, W2, changed her mind about buying the expensive model over three years the morning after it was delivered, her husband had to spend two hours arguing before it was taken back. There was of course no legal obligation on Rolls to accept the machine at all: they could themselves have taken legal action to enforce more payment. 'I would rather have gone to court than paid. We've bought £600 worth of furniture on HP and never been charged such high rates,' says Mrs. Weldon.

I asked Bloom if the interest rates were not rather high. (They average almost thirteen per cent per annum, or nearly forty per cent over three years.) Over three years, the 59-guinea model costs £83 1s. The deposit is £8 19s. and there are 156 weekly payments of 9s. 6d. Yes, he said, but H.P. insurance was included. Rolls Razor got less than three per cent of the interest, in the form of commission paid to them by Sir Isaac Wolfson's General Guarantee Corporation which lends him money for the £10 million H.P. debt. (Many finance houses charge ten per cent a year, and some big stores charge only five per cent.)

Bloom also believes that the fact that the deposit on both his models is the same – it comes to over twenty per cent of the cheaper one, but that of course leaves a smaller balance to pay interest on – persuades three out of four customers to choose the expensive model. The higher commission paid to salesmen must be a help, I suggested. It was no secret, he replied, that they would rather sell the higher-priced model. But salesmen caught switch-selling were sacked – several were last year. Anyway, he said, 'The public help them with it at the front door, don't they?'

In this statement lies the real reason for his success. When someone sends in a coupon asking for details of the washing machine, a model is already half-sold. (The conversion rate of replies into sales varies between about fifty and seventy per cent.) And had he not stumbled on this method of selling, Bloom might well have ended up no richer than he began.

He was born on 8 November 1931, in the City of London Hospital. A typical Scorpio, says one of his stockbrokers. The first home he moved to was in Nelson Street, Stepney. His father, Samuel, a Polish-born tailor who was then about as old as John Bloom is now, was eking out a narrow income with his in-laws. Of his father, Bloom says, 'He's no genius.' He remembers his mother as being more influential at home. 'Everything I did was right.'

The family moved fairly frequently, and when John was nine went to 20 St Kilda's Road in Stoke Newington. The house was rented – he has still never owned a house, or lived in one that belonged to his family. From the outside, it now looks a solid little house, a gabled end-of-terrace Victorian cottage. 'There were two families living there

– my uncle and aunt were there too. I had to sleep in a bedroom-cum-dining room, so you see it wasn't exactly brilliant,' he says now. His parents could hardly afford to give him any pocket money. He remembers that most of it came from his uncle – who now works for him.

He got into the Hackney Downs Grammar School. Bernard Conway, managing director of a company Bloom took over eight years ago, was at school with him. 'The rest of us came from vaguely middle-class homes,' says Mr. Conway. 'We felt sorry for him because he came from such a poor background, but we always admired him. He was determined at the age of thirteen that he was going to alter his circumstances and go into business. He was very single-minded and determined, and always planning some sort of business activity on his own.'

The activities included selling comics, chewing-gum and fireworks to the other boys. 'I was like the discount store of the school,' says Bloom. 'He would do anything to make a halfpenny,' says his father.

At about this time another interest had him in its grip. Never any good at games himself, he became an ardent fan of the Arsenal Football Club nearby. One day he and another boy went down to the ground with an empty camera and asked if they could take some photographs for the school magazine. They got in.

In spite of his excellent memory and quick grasp, he did not shine at school, and left when he was just sixteen, before taking the school certificate. His father would have liked him to stay on but the headmaster told him it was useless to try to change his son's mind. John's leaving report said that 'He has shown interest and ability in English subjects, with considerable powers of expression, has some aptitude in languages and practical subjects. He is quick and practical in calculations . . . possesses initiative and resource, is alert and energetic and mixes well with others.'

At about this time (he claimed in the letter he was sixteen and a half, but may have been younger) John had his first taste of the mail-order appetite. He wrote to an American students' magazine asking for a penfriend. Wishful thinking shines through his list of interests: 'tennis, swimming, boxing, dancing and swing music' – but the effect was magical. 'They had to have special people to handle the letters,' says his father. 'Chewing gum arrived in tons and ties in bundles.' He showed less imagination when it came to getting his first job in the interval before National Service; he eventually started in the hardware department at Selfridges. The job lasted only about three months. It was followed by what he calls a weird collection of jobs as office boy and general run-about.

His financial rewards were hardly spectacular, but they were put to immediate use. He bought one of the first tape-recorders. He went on a week's holiday to Brighton. For £35 he bought an old Austin 7. He had to push it over the kerb and park it in the front garden. But it took him on his first Continental holiday, and won him a congratulatory letter from Austin's. Later he sold it for £30.

He was never short of girlfriends. The boyish effervescence and unpretentiousness that he still has must almost always have made women like him.

For his National Service he went into the RAF. He was posted to three stations and started running a cheap charabanc service for his mates. A prosecution was dismissed because the judge said, 'It's no sin to make a profit.' He was then posted to the Air Ministry to train as a teleprinter operator. The official attitude to him was, he thinks, 'You're an idiot. Your IQ isn't good enough for anything else.' He says it gleefully.

On leaving the RAF he thought first of carrying on as a teleprinter operator. He applied for a job at the US Embassy because he knew they paid well. He did not get the job – nor hundreds of others that he applied for at this time. 'I spent about five whole days writing letters. One day I applied for every job in the *Daily Telegraph*. For about 99.9 per cent of them I didn't get an interview. They didn't even bother to reply.'

After short spells in various clerking jobs he started in the transport department of Eastwood's brick company, and liked it so much that he decided to become a transport tycoon. Two notably unsuccessful transport ventures followed ('We were under-capitalized. We spent two years trying to stave off the creditors'). The same thing happened when he tried to sell paraffin, and has since happened with several other schemes – like the spray-on shoe polish which was supposed to last for a week but split the leather instead. Like a man with the digits of the number SUCCESS in his head but with no idea of the correct combination, John Bloom could have gone on dialling one wrong number after another.

But at the beginning of 1958, he began selling washing machines. He started off on a door-to-door basis, without any particular success. Then, in April, his mother died. Bloom admits that he has always been more influenced by women – his mother, sister and wife – than by men. To fill the gap he started to work harder, and on a trip to Holland he found a twin-tub machine that he felt would have more success. On 24 September 1958 he spent £424 on a back-page advertisement in the *Daily Mirror*. He had about 7000 inquiries, nearly all of them from women. Bloom now realized exactly how his market could best be approached and his own efforts halved – with coupon replies, he was half-way home. Only the successful follow-up was needed.

The success of this method at this particular time was partly due to the economic structure of the country, partly to psychological reasons. From 1945 until 1958 manufacturers were enjoying a sellers' market. There was a shortage of consumer goods. Then, gradually, production began to overhaul demand; 1959, the year of Heathcoat Amory's election-winning budget, was also the peak year for the sale of consumer goods. After that, selling became more important, and the producer with the most aggressive sales force stood to benefit.

The washing machine market had been prepared. Public demand was whetted by the advertisements of traditional manufacturers. More wives were working, so they had less time to do washing and more money to spend on a machine to do it for them. But for many families price was still a huge drawback. In 1960, the year when Bloom took over Rolls Razor and began to make his own machines, the average family's weekly expenditure on durable household goods was 21 shillings. Most washing machines would therefore swallow up considerably more than a year's expenditure.

Bloom's machines were considerably cheaper than most. He also approached the slightly more affluent, but still very unsure, customer at home. 'Most people are very shy. I remember when I was young I was afraid to go into a shop and ask for anything. In their own home it's different,' says Bloom. As for quality, he says that his machine is good (and it has improved over the years) but he makes no exorbitant claims for it. 'My market is the mass market, not the A1.'

He was also helped by a stroke of luck. Until he started making his own machines, he was cutting right down on storage costs by having the Dutch machines flown over by a charter company; and because of a miscalculation a bill for carriage and duty which should have come much earlier did not arrive until September 1959. By this time Bloom owed them £19,000. 'If the mistake hadn't been made, there would be no business today,' he says.

Nor would there have been if he had not shown his usual powers of salesmanship in persuading his creditors not to close down the company. He said he would pay them back gradually, and he claims he did it in less than a year. Thus his empire really stood, at one time, on the shoulders of two debts, his own, and that of his customers.

What is the picture now? The financial problems of Rolls Razor, which had been weak and impoverished for some time when Bloom took it over, were routed by the end of 1961. There had been some bad moments when supplies of the machines from Holland stopped before the Cricklewood factory had been adapted to make them. But a mixture of obduracy and the enthusiasm he has always been able to inspire in people – so that when necessary they hand-built machines through the night – carried him through. (He is, both he and others agree, at his best when things look bad.)

He became a millionaire as recently as June 1962. 'Until then I didn't consider myself really established. People can say that you are a millionaire, but it doesn't mean you are,' he says. Since then the million has mushroomed until he has become a millionaire several times over.

'I shouldn't like to be poor again, and I have taken all the precautions to see that I shan't be,' he says. Whether this will last depends crucially on the success of the financial structure which he has set up for his various interests. Essentially this takes the form of two inverted pyramids, one standing upon the other.

The lower pyramid consists of Rolls Razor and this company is now valued on the stock exchange at £9.5 million. This value, however, rests on the price of the publicly-held shares in Rolls, which are in relatively short supply, representing as they do only between one third and one half of the total ordinary capital. The price the public are prepared to pay for them depends only partly on the profit record; a major element represents the faith placed in Bloom's future ability to earn more and pay bigger dividends.

Poised above is a second pyramid, represented by a company called English and Overseas Investments – stock market valuation £3 million. E. & O.'s dominant asset is a holding in Rolls Razor – some 1,400,000 shares – but of the £3 million only about half is represented by the value of Rolls shares (allowing for various complicated conversion rights). The other £1.5 million represents a further instalment of faith in Bloom.

This is a classic form of financial structure which in the past has produced both triumphant successes (as with Sir Isaac Wolfson's Great Universal Stores and Drage's companies) and some sensational failures (of which the best known are probably the Insull crash in the United States and Mr. Clarence Hatry's various empires in the 1920s and 1930s). The ultimate stability of Bloom's structure has yet to be conclusively proved. It will require, first, continued profitable expansion on the part of Rolls Razor, secondly, the injection of large and profitable new activities into English and Overseas.

At the moment Bloom is juggling happily with at least three newish projects – trading stamps, Bulgarian holidays, television rentals – and when I saw him he was contemplating the balance sheet of British Lion. If he decided to go into films, he said, he would do so just as he went into washing machines. He would concern himself with promotion, and leave the technical side to those trained for it.

Whatever he decides, Sir Isaac Wolfson's advice will probably be required. 'I am so similar to what he was thirty years ago – he's said it and other people have said it – and I therefore look to him for advice. I wouldn't make a business decision without consulting him,' says Bloom.

What does he want to do now? 'I don't want to end up with £335 million. I like the challenge of work,' he says. Lately another thought is beginning to glimmer – that there might be other ways of enjoying himself. He likes mainly American literature, particularly books which portray big business, political machinations, and the internal workings of bodies like the U.N. There is no bookcase in Park Lane, but he has just put one into the *Ariane*. Books he's bought in the past – his wife says he can read one in an hour – have been left piled high in planes or hotels.

'I don't think I'll ever become the greatest culture lover in the world. I'll accept it, but that's all. The most I've ever paid for a painting was £25 for a reproduction of the *Mona Lisa*,' he says. He would not like to have more education. 'I look around me and I see people with fantastic educations coming for jobs here and I see what they're doing in the world – nothing. The people who are getting on in the world are people who are prepared to work themselves and persevere.'

He would send his own children (he would like to have some now) probably first to the *Lycée* in Kensington, so that they would be bi-lingual, and then to a finishing school in Switzerland. He is against the English public school system, because 'it leads to the breeding of the Establishment, which I think is diabolical'.

I asked him if he would like a knighthood. 'Not at the moment, but I might when I'm forty,' he said. As part of his very gradual campaign to avoid working all the time he is trying to make more friends outside work. He now has several friends in show business, including Bernard Bresslaw, Adam Faith and the Beatles. 'I like the Beatles because I think I'm the top of one sphere and they're the top of another. There are a lot of similarities.'

He would also like to be a director of Arsenal Football Club. One of the greatest personal shocks he has had was when he failed to get the chairmanship of Queen's Park Rangers in a paper ballot of shareholders. This was also an encounter that shook the foundations of the club. It has still to recover both financially and on the field itself from projects envisaged then. In 1961 and 1962 they finished third and fourth in the third division. Last season they slid to thirteenth place.

'He chose the wrong approach because he was wrongly advised. He was very welcome when he arrived. If he had taken his time he would eventually have been chairman,' says Alec Stock, the manager. He thinks that the impression given by Bloom's assistants tipped the scale against him.

'When it comes to choosing people, I am terrible,' Bloom admits. Now, he says, his wife is trying to keep him on the straight and narrow path of people he can rely on – 'I trust everybody.'

She has also vetoed three books which people want to write on him. I asked him why he had refused. 'My wife didn't like the contracts,' he said.

He is pleased with himself, his wife and his life. He likes being rich, because it means he gets the best tables in restaurants, goes to first nights, has his boat and lives in Park Lane. He once thought he would like a house, but not now. 'You can't have a house in the middle of Park Lane and that's where I like to live. It's very central. If I want to go to the films or anything it's round the corner.' He is going to have another flat built a few hundred yards from his present one. It will be entirely planned by Anne.

He likes helping his family. His father, who has remarried, now lives with his wife Lily in another Park Lane flat.

But most of all Bloom has enjoyed proving people wrong. He has enjoyed surviving against the odds, and being a thorn in the flesh of traditional manufacturers. He enjoyed facing Bernard Levin when people told him to leave the country for the weekend rather than appear on *TW3*. 'I liked that; it was my thing of the year, that was. A television programme could never be worse. I go in and frighten the interviewer now – it's lovely.'

He served a writ on ATV because, he says, Edgar Lustgarten implied that he dared not appear in a programme with him. 'I wouldn't be afraid to go on a programme with Adolf Hitler. If Edgar Lustgarten was standing there with a machine-gun he couldn't frighten me.'

Bloom has been known to miss appointments, to invite people somewhere and fail to turn up himself, to put the phone down half-way through a conversation, and leave important letters unanswered. He lacks tact. And there is one employee that, with a staff of 1,250 (apart from self-employed salesmen) he still lacks – a secretary. He has gone through them in the past like tissue paper. 'At the moment I'm sharing with everybody,' he says. 'Eventually I want someone who can take shorthand at 200 words a minute or something ridiculous, and put up with my temper and shouting and screaming and getting over it.'

But there is scant danger that his rivals will catch this particular business man unawares. If it is important, Bloom will remember a whisper in a crowded room ten years later. 'If it's business,' he says, 'I'll turn up at midnight in Iceland.'

John Bloom was too candid for his own good. Within three months of this article appearing Rolls Razor was in the hands of the liquidators. John Bloom then decamped to Los Angeles and opened a night-club.

Margaret Laing is now a successful biographer, her subjects including Robert F. Kennedy, Edward Heath and the Shah of Persia.

THE FUNERAL OF WINSTON CHURCHILL

Patrick O'Donovan

Observer
31 January 1965

Sir Winston Churchill died on 24 January 1965, at the age of ninety. He was buried in a village churchyard near his family's ancestral home at Blenheim Palace, Oxfordshire.

The procession took that most ancient road that runs from the Palace of Westminster to the steps of the Cathedral of St. Paul. It is a road that half the history of England seems to have taken, on its way to a crowning or to a public and ignoble death, to murder or be murdered, to raise revolt, to seek a fortune, or to be buried. The route was lined with young soldiers, their heads bowed over their automatic rifles in ceremonious grief. The bands played old and slow tunes. The drums were draped in black. The staffs of the drum-majors were veiled. They moved slowly, steadily, at a curiously inexorable pace, and it looked as if nothing could ever stop them. They moved through a tangible silence and the great crowd watched with an eloquent and absolute silence.

It was beautiful in the way that great works of art are beautiful. It obeyed secret rules. There was the Earl Marshal walking alone and worried in the centre of a great space like any man lost in a high street, but carrying a gilded sceptre. There was Lord Mountbatten pacing behind the Chiefs of Staff carefully manipulating his sword and, like any trooper, trying to keep pace with the band. There were the officers with their trays of Churchill's medals, held out like ware for sale. There were the heraldic banners of the Cinque Ports and the Spencer-Churchills, too stiff to wave in any wind, carried like trophies before the coffin. And there were the marshals with their batons held on their hips in a baroque gesture that Marlborough would have known.

There was the family looking lost and human and trying to keep up. But the central, the overwhelming fact was the dead body in a box made of oak. It was trundled into the City on a huge and impractical gun-carriage. It was pulled by a great phalanx of lusty young men. It moved, huge and red with the Union flag, past the hotels and the steamy restaurants and the newspaper offices and the pubs, surrounded by this extraordinary silence that could not be broken even by the bands and the rhythmic feet. It was a silence, not of grief but of respect. In fact the City was stopped and was turned into a theatre and it was all performed as a drama that all men understand.

This was the last time that such a thing could happen. This was the last time that London would be the capital of the world. This was an act of mourning for the Imperial past. This marked the final act in Britain's greatness. This was a great gesture of self-pity and after this the coldness of reality and the status of Scandinavia.

But really this was a celebration. And however painful, most funerals are just that. When a man is buried, those who are still alive crave some gesture of respect that cannot help the cadaver. And this gesture is made over and over again by Christians and Communists and humanists and the unconcerned. It is a proud half-conscious assertion that man is not an animal that dies alone in a hole. It is almost a gesture of contempt to the face of death. And once or twice in a generation a dead monarch or hero is chosen to epitomize a whole nation's assertion of continuity and dignity. And because Churchill at a certain time and in a special way was, for all public purposes, Britain and more than Britain, this assertion was unbelievably eloquent over this corpse.

This was a celebration, then, of our humanity and of the fact of Britain. The ritual, performed to music like a masque for the edification of a king, said things that cannot quite be put into words. The whole country watched the agonized care of the eight guardsmen who carried the box. And vicariously shared their anxious pain. But perhaps most marvellous was the slow move up the turgid Thames. There were things like the gantries of cranes dipping in salute and the music of a host of pipers. There were generals in improbable uniforms and what looked like all the rulers of the world standing on the steps of St. Paul's as if this were a family burial. A whole city looking in on itself as a dead body went by.

It was a triumph. It was a celebration of a great thing that we did in the past. It was an act of gratitude to a man whom we can no longer help or please. The many Heads of State there were appropriate but not important. We were not sad. We knew for whom these bells tolled. We knew the man whose body we removed in such unimaginable splendour. And we did not weep – that is not fitting for great old men – but we saw him off and because he was us at our best, we gave him a requiem that rejected death and was almost a rejoicing.

Patrick O'Donovan joined the Observer *after the Second World War. In the late 1940s he covered China, followed by Africa, the Korean War and Washington in the Kennedy years. In the 1970s he wrote books on Catholicism. He died in 1981.*

LONDON, THE MOST EXCITING CITY IN THE WORLD

—

John Crosby
Weekend Telegraph
16 April 1965

Although history gives Time Magazine the credit for inventing the phrase 'Swinging London', they were actually a full year – 15 April 1966 – behind American journalist John Crosby in noticing what was going on.

> *'Fly me to the moon and let me play among the stars*
> *Let me know what spring is like on Jupiter and Mars.'*

An American girl from Natchez, Mississippi, singing at the new Cool Elephant. Blue walls. Cigarette smoke. The gleam of a trombone through the nightclub blackness.

At Annabel's in Berkeley Square are the elegant crowd – the Duchess of Northumberland, Frank Sinatra when he's in town, King Constantine dancing with his young queen, Anne-Marie, Aristotle Onassis, a sprinkling of Saudi Arabians, perhaps Princess Margaret. In Soho, at the Ad Lib, the hottest and swingingest spot in town the noise is deafening, the beat group is pounding out *I Just Don't Know What to Do with Myself*, on the floor, under the red and green and blue lights, a frenzy of the prettiest legs in the whole world belonging to models, au pair girls or just ordinary English girls, a gleam of pure joy on their pretty faces, dancing with the young bloods, the scruffy very hotshot photographers like David Bailey or Terry Donovan, or a new pop singer – all vibrating with youth. At the corner table more or less permanently reserved for the Beatles (you'll always find at least one of them there when they're in town) Ringo proposes to Maureen (that's where he did it).

These are for the rich and famous. But London's throbbing nightlife has room for everyone. At the Marquee, a jazz club, non-alcoholic, on Wardour Street, you'll find the young kids from the offices. The Scene on Great Windmill Street brings in the Mods. Ronnie Scott's in Soho is a classless place – the sons of dukes and working men rubbing elbows in mutual appreciation of jazz; the Flamingo, a beat spot, caters to the West Indians.

Diana Vreeland, who as editor of *Vogue* is almost supreme arbiter of taste in America, has said simply, 'London is the most swinging city in the world at the moment' – putting into words what a lot of us Americans living here have long felt. The young bloods from Madrid and Rome – for reasons they only dimly understand

– suddenly converge on London. London is where the action is, as New York and then Paris were right after the war, as Rome was in the mid-Fifties. Now it's London – the gayest, most uninhibited, and – in a wholly new, very modern sense – most wholly elegant city in the world. It seems to me that the last people to find it out are the Londoners themselves, under whose nose these changes in mood and tone have taken place, almost imperceptibly over the past four or five years.

'Fill my heart with song, let me sing for ever more
You are all I long for, all I worship and adore'

There's a quality of eager innocence in that old song and that's exactly the tone of London's nightlife. In an English girl's eyes is a starry innocence only possible in an island that has not been invaded for 1,000 years. Behind the dark-eyed invitation in a French girl, a Spanish girl, an Italian girl, there always lies a hint of wariness, a tiny veil of distrust, the ancient memory of ancient rapes, forgotten pillage.

I asked Leslie Linder, proprietor of those Elephants, The White Elephant (restaurant), and the Crazy and Cool Elephants, both night-clubs, what made London a swinging town. He answered simply and immediately, 'It's the girls. Italian and Spanish men are kinky for English girls. When I opened The White Elephant we had the prettiest girls I ever saw.'

Mark Birley, the immensely tall and coolly elegant owner of the coolly elegant Anabel's says the same thing. 'The girls are prettier here than anywhere else – much more so than in Rome or Paris.'

They're more than pretty; they're young, appreciative, sharp-tongued, glowingly alive. Even the sex orgies among the sex-and-pot set in Chelsea and Kensington have youth and eagerness and, in a strange way, a quality of innocence about them. In Rome and Paris, the sex orgies are for the old, the jaded, the disgusting and disgusted. Young English girls take to sex as if it's candy and it's delicious.

England, in fact, is getting something of a corner on all the pretty girls who are flying in from all the other capitals of Europe. 'The au pair girls started all that,' says Leslie Linder. 'All these pretty young chicks from Sweden and Denmark. London is getting very Continental. We've got all these French chicks, Spanish chicks, German chicks. Of course, Rome has a lot of foreign chicks, too, but it seems to me the girls are nicer here and more natural. In Rome, all the chicks are grabbing – they want to be film stars or they want to marry a millionaire. Here, they're just students or au pair girls. They don't want anything except to be girls. It's a healthier atmosphere than either Rome or Paris.'

The deluge of pretty girls is on all levels. Betty Kenward, who writes the social column under the name of Jennifer for *Queen* magazine, points out, 'The young King and Queen of Greece may fly in for a ball and that brings in all those young princesses from Holland or Denmark. Then there are so many international marriages. Tina Onassis, a Greek, married to the Marquess of Blandford. Lord Bessborough is married to a chic American girl. So is Kenneth Keith. Young David Montagu has a charming young French wife. We have charming young Italian wives, charming Spanish wives – and they all bring in their friends from their countries of birth.'

The nightlife is just a symptom, the outer and visible froth, of an inner, far deeper turbulence that boiled up in Britain around – if we must date it – 1958, though some say as late as 1960. In that period, youth captured this ancient island and took command in a country where youth had always before been kept properly in its place. Suddenly, the young own the town. Brian Morris, who runs the Ad Lib Club and who is himself only thirty, says, 'This is a young people's town. In the old days, the middle-aged dominated the night-clubs. [His father owned one.] The young went to the night-clubs then, it's true, but they were there on sufferance. It wasn't their place. Now . . .' he looked out at the jam-packed floor of the Ad Lib where Edwina Carroll, a dazzlingly pretty Eurasian model, half Burmese, half Irish, was twirling near by her close friend Tsai Chin, Chinese actress and singer . . . 'this place is owned by the young. The middle-aged come here but they're on sufferance. It belongs to the young people. We get all the young ones, young designers like Mary Quant or Jean Muir, the young actresses like Hayley Mills or Julie Christie, the Beatles. Well, I'm pretty young myself.

'A kid of twenty-three or twenty-four isn't a kid any more. Twenty years ago he'd have thought himself one. Not today. The young work harder and they make a lot of money. Twenty years ago, ambition itself was unfashionable. Now it isn't.'

It certainly isn't. Behind the swing and the gaiety, there's a steady pulse of serious purpose in these young ones. In Chelsea young Mary Quant and a bunch of other pretty Chelsea birds, fed up with the stuffy and expensive dresses in the shops began stitching their own dresses – simple, dashing, clean-limbed clothes more suited to their good looks and youth and their marvellous clean-limbed way of walking (English girls walk like huntresses, like Dianas) and they didn't give a damn what anyone else thought about them. It so happened that the rest of the world adored them. Today Mary Quant has shops in New York and Australia as well as London. English dresses are invading the world market. A short time ago, a group of young English girl designers, all in their twenties, invaded New York with their clothes and the London Look swept New York.

One of this group was Caroline Charles, who started designing clothes a year and three months ago, now designs dresses for Cilla Black, Barbra Streisand, Ringo's new wife Maureen, and four way-out suits for Ringo himself, and does forty per cent of her business in America. 'I'm rich,' she admits. She's twenty-two.

She has only scorn for the pessimists who say England is finished as a great nation. 'I think the young generation between eighteen and thirty in England is the most forward-moving set of people in the world in all fields – even at running grocery stores.'

There's the same explosion of creativeness and uniquely English dash in the young men's clothing game. Young John Stephen – he's twenty-eight but looks more like seventeen – came down from Glasgow to open his first shop in Soho in 1957. Now he practically owns Carnaby Street which is dotted with his little shops sporting names like His, Mod Male, Domino Male and Male W.1. On any twilight evening when the day's work is done, Carnaby Street pulses with slender young men in black tight pants that fit on the hips like ski pants, their tulip-like girlfriends on their arms, peering into the garishly lit windows at the burgundy coloured suede jackets with the slanted, pleated pockets – very hot stuff with the Mods right now.

'England leads the world in young people's fashions both female and male,' says young Stephen in his rolling Glasgow burr which has a strong Cockney beat underneath. 'Buyers from American department stores come here and are absolutely astounded at what is happening. Why – they say – is this happening here and not in America, and they go right home and start young men's shops in their own stores.'

There's a revolution in men's clothes here that is very much part of the London swinging scene, partly because it's adding so much dash and colour and glamour to the London street scene, but also as a sign of deeper social turmoil that is transforming England, especially among the young. English men's clothes were once almost uniform: staid, sober and, above all, correct, advertising your precise rung on the social ladder and even your bank account. Today the working-class boys – many of them fresh out of the Army or Navy and in full revolt against conformity of dress – their pockets full of money, are splurging on suede jackets, skin-like tweed trousers, double-breasted pin-striped suits (the very latest mode) with two buttons – or perhaps six. The impact of Carnaby Street is becoming worldwide. Tony Curtis wears Carnaby Street clothes. So do Peter Sellers and the Beatles.

The same thing on a different social and income level can be seen at Blades in Dover Street where the custom-made suits cost £52. At Blades the clothes have an elegance and a sort of look-at-me dash not seen since Edwardian times. On the racks I found, just as an example of what goes on there, a jet black velvet dinner jacket – trousers the same material – with a mandarin collar and buttons that I would never have the courage to wear.

A typical customer of Blades is Hercules Bellville, not long out of Oxford, who swathes himself in brown corduroy of velvety texture, long skirted, with waspish pants, which he tops with a short fur-collared coat. Fully assembled, with his flowing blond hair and almost classical good English looks, Hercules looks like something straight out of Max Beerbohm.

The proprietor of Blades is Rupert Lycett-Green, and both he and Bellville typify the revolt of the upper-class young. Bellville toiled in advertising a while, a socially acceptable occupation, then threw the whole thing up to get into movie-making. He's an assistant-assistant director now, frequently out of work, but he's doing what he wants.

Lycett-Green worked for a bit in the family engineering firm in the north of France. Two years ago, he quit and started Blades with his own money. After a shaky start it is doing quite well.

'Twenty-five years ago,' says Lycett-Green, 'young people would be almost afraid to speak out and do something like this with their money. They'd have followed their fathers into the City, or estate management. Now the young people want to see what they can do on their own. Some of my friends have started their own insurance companies, their own restaurants or their own nightclubs. They're all doing what they want to do, not what's expected of them.'

Another case is Noel Picarda, another Oxonian, who comes from a long line of lawyers. His father and brothers are barristers and they wanted Noel in the law firm, too. But he's in love with show business and he's performing at the Establishment, writing and appearing in sketches at the Poor Millionaire and has started a talent agency.

Richard de la Mare, grandson of Walter de la Mare, declined a nice safe job in the publishing house of Faber & Faber, where his father is chairman, to undertake the extremely precarious and not at all lucrative task of making *avant garde* films like *Carousella* about the life of stripteasers.

The caste system, in short, is breaking down at both ends. The working-class young are busting out of the lower depths and invading fields where they can make more money and the upper-class is breaking down walls to get into the lower levels where they can have more fun. Caroline Charles says: 'Here they're so much more democratic than America – everybody mixes!' It's the bounce and vitality of these youngsters, both upper and lower class, that contributes most of the fizz to London.

De La Mare observed also, 'My mother told me that, after she and my father were married for about five years, they settled down. But she says that my wife and I have been married five years and haven't settled down. By settling down, they mean moving to the country, playing golf and raising roses and children. The young marrieds don't settle down like that any more. They keep right on swinging right here in London.'

This has changed the nature of their entertaining much for the better, according to *Queen's* Mrs. Kenward. English upper-class dinner parties used to be renowned for the quantities of servants and the tastelessness of the food. Now, the servants have disappeared and the food is much better. Mrs. Kenward credits the late Constance Spry who taught many of the young brides how to cook. 'Cooking is much better than it was,' she said. 'Young married couples know how to entertain much better – without staff or with temporary staff.'

Much of the stuffiness, in fact, has been knocked out of the Royal entertaining. The Queen's party for Princess Alexandra and Angus Ogilvy was a really swinging affair that went on to the wee hours, my American friends who attended it told me. Those used to be dreary affairs. Not long ago, Prince Charles and Princess Anne gave a twist and shake party for their young friends at Windsor Castle. Princess Margaret is usually found with actors, writers or painters rather than Guards officers.

London, says Leslie Linder – and everyone else – has lost its reputation as a bad food city. Largely, I suspect, because the English are travelling abroad more, they are demanding and getting better food in the restaurants. The young swingers prefer the little restaurants – places like Trattoria Terrazza in Soho, Pavillon or Au Pere de Nico in Chelsea, or Chanterelle on Old Brompton Road – rather than the stuffier big places like the Savoy Grill which used to get the play. The White Tower on Percy Street has magnificent food and superb wines for the well-heeled. Tiberio's Italian food is marvellous. Even the penniless young ones eat better – at Buzzy's Bistro under the footpath on King's Road, Chelsea, or at Hades in Exhibition Road, South Kensington, where the girls are beautiful, the prices rock bottom and the food not at all bad.

The most astonishing change of all to me is the muscular virility of England's writers and dramatists and actors and artists – this from an island we'd mostly thought of in terms of Noel Coward and drawing-room comedy. English plays used to be jaded, fey, rococo – and so were the actors. Now, it's all anger, sweat and the working classes, and expresses the vitality and energy and virility among the young people I meet.

Vitality was the keynote of *Tom Jones* which made a fortune (for the Americans because the British film companies didn't have the sense to invest in it) and was also one of the principal ingredients of the James Bond film *Goldfinger* which has already earned £7,800,000 and of *Lawrence of Arabia* and the Beatles film – all British-written, directed and acted. (And all of them American-owned. Why haven't you British any faith in your own writers and directors and actors?)

Talent is getting to be Britain's greatest export commodity. Not long ago, the New York film critics made their nominations for the year's best acting and every last actor was English (and two of the actresses were English, too.) In Paris, at New Jimmy's or at Kastel's, they dance now to the records of the Beatles or Cilla Black or the Rolling Stones where only a year ago the music came from Frank Sinatra, Tony Bennett and Dean Martin – all Americans.

The new National Theatre has presented almost casually one masterpiece after another, from *Uncle Vanya*, which was described as the supreme achievement of the English stage, to *Othello*, a somewhat more controversial masterpiece. To a theatre-goer, the variety to pick from is sumptuous. And in that great pile of red plush and crystal chandeliered elegance, Covent Garden, Kenneth Macmillan has unveiled a wholly new, very renaissance, very masculine version of Prokofiev's *Romeo and Juliet*. The theatres themselves with their nineteenth-century opulence and curves and charm are a perennial lure to visitors.

This explosion of creative vitality, a sort of English renaissance, has occurred on the very highest levels, as well as the more frivolous ones. On the topmost sphere of pure thought, Fred Hoyle, the Cambridge astronomer, has just advanced a theory about the physical nature of the universe as sweeping in its implications as those of Copernicus, Newton or Einstein.

Several theories have been suggested as to why all this is happening, where all this explosion of creative energy came from. It has been suggested that England, shorn of its world-wide responsibilities for keeping the peace, has turned its energies, previously dissipated in running the colonies, inward toward personal self-expression.

I think this is quite true but there's another factor. The English, I think, had a long Dark Age which started in the depression of the Thirties, continued through the long and terrible war and culminated in a long period of austerity, much longer than anyone else's. Longer even than Germany's, that didn't end really until about 1958. After any prolonged darkness, the Middle Ages, or the Napoleonic Wars, there's a renaissance, a flowering, a release of pent-up energy – and London is right in the middle of it.

Or perhaps just at the beginning. Most of these kids, who are starting dress shops or writing songs or making films, are in their twenties or early thirties. The best years, several decades of them, might well lie ahead when these talents mature.

THE CASE OF THE SATIRICAL PERSONALS

—

Auberon Waugh

Nova
June 1965

Then, as now, the Private Eye *small ads were never less than diverting.*

A mystery that has been intriguing and amazing connoisseurs in Fleet Street and elsewhere is the uninhibited wording of the small ads in the satirical fortnightly *Private Eye*. Were the ads satirical too, or could they be serious? To settle this fascinating mystery, I turned private-eye myself. Armed only with valour and a righteous heart, I pondered such promising evidence as:

> **Married executive (28) wishes London telephone number of young nymph with own flat**
> **Young Gent requires complement**
> **Girls, models, fresh types sought, v. buxom, travel opportunity**
> **100s of Continental girls seek friends**
> **Mistress urgently sought**
> **Young girl seeks friendship of another. Similar tastes.**
> **Striptease wanted for private parties. Offers?**

Some of the ground had already been covered by a few newspapers, renowned for their strict moral attitudes, who made enquiries and reported censoriously. *The People* exposed that couples advertising themselves as 'sociable' and in search of friends were in fact trying to introduce the ancient Welsh practice of wife-swapping. These advertisements were stopped. The *News of the World* exposed a man who advertised for girlfriends and took on fifty. These advertisements continue. But for the most part, journalists have steered clear, partly through their newspapers' reluctance to give free publicity to a rag which has chosen to be rude about nearly all the newspaper proprietors, partly through fear that the advertisements might turn out to be an elaborate hoax.

Clearly, the assignment was one to treat cautiously. There was the additional risk, too, that if I ran foul of *Private Eye* editors, they might reply with one of their famous pen-portraits: 'Auberon Waugh is a stink-nosed bum who can't write like his father and has to take it out on us . . . *Private Eye* says, Creep off, Mr. Waugh.' But that is one of the hazards of life in this satirical age.

Appealing for help in my enquiries, I sought out Mr. Peter Usborne, the business manager and brains behind the column. He is a gentle, soft-spoken, balding young man who seems genuinely concerned that so much vice should be thought to flourish under his aegis. 'We are making a continuous effort to clean it up. On the average, about one new thing is banned every month. But it's impossible to keep abreast of all the latest kinky words until it's too late.' He showed me a list of currently banned words:

Pussy
Social couples
Man seeks man
Nymph
Lessons (of any sort)
Bizarre
Interesting . . .

'We always investigate anything which describes itself as interesting. If it's above board, of course, we let it through.'

American couples . . .

'I think there's something odd about the use of that word "American".'

Married men
Leather ware
Rubber ware

'Apparently there are these fetishes on:'

Mackintosh
Blue photos
Bachelor
Lonely

'Both these last words have to be investigated. They may mean homosexual.'

Mr. Usborne sank his head in his hands. 'I can't tell you how I detest these kinky things. Life is a constant struggle to keep any suggestion of prostitution out. We refuse advertisements from girls advertising for boyfriends, because you can never know. I hate the whole business. What I'd like would be to turn the Personal Column into a genuine Lonely Hearts medium, for people who are too shy to go to a marriage bureau. All the Continental newspapers carry them. It would be extremely profitable, too.'

At the mention of that dirty word 'Continental' my ears pricked up. But no, Mr. Usborne was being genuine. I showed him an advertisement: 'Be kinky once a fortnight. Buy *Private Eye*.' How did that fit in with his campaign to attract lonely governesses and shy but pure young company directors?

'Obviously, that was written tongue in cheek. I think everyone realized that.' This advertisement, apparently, was satirical. What Mr. Usborne loathes and detests are those which are not. 'As a matter of editorial policy, we don't wish to encourage perverted sex relations or prostitution.'

There is a new editorial directive forbidding adultery, too. But this is a question of improving the 'image' (useful word, that) so as to prepare the field for serious advertisers wishing to take a full page at £120.

I asked about the legal position. Strangely enough, *Private Eye* employs no lawyers until after the event. 'I think there is something called corrupting the public morals,' he said vaguely.

He told me of his own traumatic experiences after advertising in *Private Eye*. Among all the kinky and obscure phraseology of the other insertions, he put in a straightforward offer of a motorbike for sale. Soon, his telephone started ringing. Was there any leather equipment for sale with the motorbike? Was Mr. Usborne prepared to wear it in front of the purchaser? Was he prepared to watch while the purchaser tried it on? 'I loathe and detest them all,' said Mr. Usborne, who is a happily married man with no problems.

He started going through the newly arrived batch of advertisements. *'Two-way spy mirror*, OUT, *Discreet photographer*, OUT. *Bachelor seeking part-time evening work*, under consideration. Here's a funny one. *'Propagate Servum ad Crucem. Young initiate wants practical experience. Anything considered. Travel no problem. Genuine.'* What on earth can that mean?' Mr. Usborne wrote DUB (dubious) and passed on. *'Registered Manipulative Therapist.'* Don't like it. Better check up on that one.'

He put down the sheaf of papers, suddenly looking tired and impressively mature: 'One day, we honestly hope we will get real advertisements. It doesn't help if you have a small-ad page looking like a nightclub in Caracas.'

Never having been to a nightclub in Caracas, I don't know how the parallel stands up. My own investigations into some of the advertisements revealed nothing that was remotely illegal. Many, despite their glamorous appearance, turned out to be completely respectable – a kind of postal clip-joint service.

Thus, among advertisements offering *'fads and fancies available in glamour photos'*, there was one which simply said: *Remarkable life-size photographs 6'0"x 2'0" 2/6 PO (returnable) for Details. Box no. 2981.*

But those who applied, crazy with anticipation, received this answer, I found:

Dear Sir,

Thank you for your inquiry regarding life-size photographs. The current prints are of the Beatles. Please say which Beatle you require. The price is 10/- each less 2/6 already paid.

On the other hand, advertisements for *'Handsome young scooter kid in leather'* produced, among others, a colour photograph taken from behind of a mature male scooter kid completely nude. The attached literature might rank among the classics:

Grace, good looks, brimming vitality, skill and experience in posing and clear lighting combine to present Larry's lovely sun-tanned classical body almost 'in the flesh' – a must for all serious collectors of the male nude . . .

There is again an exceptionally wide variety of subjects, including split-second action poses, whip-poses, acrobatic and balancing, buttocks studies, crutch-tight blue jeans, black leather, yellow skin-suit poses, close-ups and many others . . .

Among the captions supplied are:

A Man's Man
Curves of Youth
Boy Sacrifice
Slave Driver
Mate in 2 Moves

The female nude photographs which arrived through my post like an April shower included nothing more indecent than can be bought at any W.H. Smith bookstall. Incidentally, W.H. Smith refuse to handle *Private Eye*; this is the source of much dissatisfaction and satirical pen portraiture ('W.H. Smug').

One set offered *'glamour girls in rainwear, Directoire, Booted, also Dunking photos'*. I asked Peter Usborne what Dunking meant. 'Probably sexual intercourse,' he said gloomily. Another advertiser answered: 'For set of risk photos, send £1 to £5 to *Private Eye*. Box no . . . 22 Greek Street, W.1.' Usborne looked uncomfortable at that, but the samples were no worse than you can buy on any railway platform.

All the enticing advertisements for Friendship/Marriage enterprises, which I painstakingly investigated, turned out to be entirely respectable. They thanked Mr. Hugo Robinson (my *nom de plume*) for his enquiry, but regretted to inform him they did not cater for married men. One advertised 'Interesting new friends. Trial free.' The interesting new friends on free trial turned out to live respectively in Chicago, Malaya, Indonesia, Formosa, Hungary, New York and India.

Less exotic was the outcome of an advertisement inviting men with homosexual problems to write to an address in Bradford, Yorks. The literature that came back included an advertisement for cut-price contraceptives, an application form to a personal friendship club, and a mimeographed letter remarkable for its illiteracy as much as for its lewdness. Here is the first paragraph:

During the past few years, I think our problem has developed tremendously. Unfortunately the laws of this land do not enable us to have any outlets, therefor I am organizing the club under my own initials . . . MH . . . to try to bring some sort of – um – relief to our feelings.

Writing under the name of Phyllis Chulmleigh, I volunteered my services to the advertiser who offered *'girls, models, fresh types, v. buxom'* the opportunity of travel. Phyllis said that if it was only photographic modelling that was required, she was still interested, but hoped it was something more modern, and which earned more money. She received no reply.

Nor did Hugo Robinson, when he asked about a sociable group among whom orgies were a speciality. Poor Hugo, having posed as a male homosexual, a connoisseur of orgies, a leather enthusiast, someone with a special taste in reading and a collector of glamorous photographs, eventually had recourse to an advertisement of his own:

Young man desperately seeks female, London. Write Box no . . .

He did not receive a single answer. When I taxed Peter Usborne, he looked sympathetic. 'Can't understand it. Lots of people get answers. What frightens us is the prostitutes. God, I detest this whole business.'

Finally, Hugo wrote to the Pic Friendship Club, which advertised *'hundreds of Continental girls seek friends'*. The combination of three dirty words – *'Continental'*, *'girl'* and *'friends'* – could not fail to produce results. In due course, and after payment of £1 membership fee, a list of Continental girls in London seeking friends arrived at Hugo's address in South Kensington. Also a set of rules, e.g.:

(1) On no account whatsoever may any member call at the address of another unless by prior, written, mutual arrangement.

(2) All the lady members are of high educational standard and good family. Members are requested to be respectful and courteous in their correspondence . . .

(4) It is recommended that members begin their letters 'As a member of a correspondence club, I wish to introduce myself' . . .

Abandoning the persona of Hugo Robinson, I wrote to about six of the girls explaining that I was a journalist writing an article about these advertisements. The answers came back soon enough. Pic Friendship also operates under another name, Improve Your English Club. Au pair girls are liable to get a letter out of the blue telling them they have been granted free membership of the Improve Your English Club. Few demur. The next thing they know is when 20 to 40 letters arrive, all from men suggesting they should send a photograph or meet them in London.

One Norwegian girl showed me a selection of the letters she had received. One was from a young physical training instructor in Southampton, another from a Saudi Arabian in Glasgow. Another, from an eighteen-year-old in Streatham Hill, announced he was 'Vaguely interested in languages' and hoped to meet her.

The most effusive was from a twenty-two-year-old Ghanaian law student in Golders Green:

Until I hear from you, it is tons of greetings for your unprecedented, amicable and kind generosity in making your address available to me. I hope to do my best to make you enjoy my company when we become familiar with each other, and also to be able to tell you more about life in Ghana. Until then, Bye for now and look after yourself well.

The tragedy is that none of these letters to the Norwegian girl was answered. Nor were about twenty letters to a Finnish girl, who contacted me. But an attractive, twenty-one-year-old Austrian girl, Miss Dorle Marning, told me she answered twelve of her letters, actually agreeing to meet two of her correspondents – 'and the experience was awful'.

My curiosity was not sufficient to send £50 for a chastity belt, even though I could have had many ornamental refinements at small extra cost – imitation precious stones, sequins, etc. The literature assured me that *'the belt is so designed and constructed as to cause the minimum of discomfort to the wearer under day-to-day conditions and, with the minimum of inconvenience, all the natural toilet functions are possible'.* That was the only thing that worried me.

Perhaps Mr. Usborne really hopes to make the advertisements respectable. Until he succeeds, they provide a fascinating insight into England's sexual twilight. When his noble mission is accomplished, he might move on and clean up *The Times*, where this notice appeared recently:

Young man seeks post as manservant/companion to bachelor. Write Box . . .

By the strict new standards of *Private Eye*, this advertisement would be dubious.

Auberon Waugh is the editor of the Literary Review.

COME WITH FLOWERS

—

Norman Shrapnel
Guardian
12 June 1965

The Poets of the World readings at London's Royal Albert Hall – alternatively titled 'Cosmic Poetry Visitation Accidentally Happening Carnally' – can now be seen to have been the ignition point for the London 'underground'. That a parliamentary correspondent should have been sent to cover a psychedelic circus shows a keen sense of humour all around at the Guardian.

'Come in fancy dress', said the invitation to the International Poetry Conference in London last night. 'Come with flowers,' it added enticingly. 'Come.'

Well, they certainly came – thousands of them. There seemed little fancy dress around, unless you counted numerous striped sweatshirts and some astonishing figures looking as though they had been tarred and feathered with the torn leaves of books and newspapers. But the Albert Hall was full to the brim. People were actually clamouring to get in. This is not what publishers usually think about the drawing power of poets.

The biggest poetry-reading meeting in the English-speaking world, they were calling it. Knowledgeable Americans – and there were many in the audience – questioned this but were impressed by the boast. 'I am almost as surprised to see you here as you are surprised to see us,' said Alexander Trocchi. He called it 'a very spontaneous happening'. They were trying to find out what happened 'when we put 5,000 people in a hall with a few poets trying to be natural'.

Natural was the word. Four-letter words boomed pompously round the great dome of the hall. Queen Victoria would not have been amused if this language could have been echoed back at her out of the dome of the future when she opened the great hall a century ago. Would she even have heard of such words? But the audience were amused – perhaps by the poetical surprise of finding rude words in the dome of Prince Albert. Perhaps the poets thought they should have been more shocked. Some of the poets were hard to hear; others were highly articulate. Some stood, some sat, some bowed, some lifted their arms like successful wrestlers at the end of their pieces.

The audience was predominantly young, though a future grey beard bristled among the black ones, and some of the poets must have found them depressingly well-behaved. Yet they were a largely cosmopolitan crowd and many of them had probably heard mass poetry readings before, in countries where they grow more naturally.

After a preliminary incantation by Allen Ginsberg, some poems were read by Simon Vinkenoog, introduced as 'the grand old young man of Dutch letters'. Then Laurence Ferlinghetti, from San Francisco, told us of all the things he is waiting for, and they drew quite a lot of appreciative laughs.

Michael Horovitz did some action poems, and these were followed by the resonant voice – but not the presence – of William Burroughs. Adrian Mitchell came over well with a poem about Hell and Alabama and another one about Vietnam. They encored him.

'When do we get the naked ladies,' somebody shouted from the audience, but he was on his own.

For seventeen years Norman Shrapnel was the Guardian's *parliamentary sketch writer. Now retired, his books include* The Seventies *and* The Performers, *a study of the thearte of parliament.*

P.J. PROBY

—

Francis Wyndham
Sunday Times Magazine
26 June 1965

By the mid-Sixties the British public had become extraordinarily obsessed with popular music. Noting this, unsuccessful American singer P.J. Proby moved to London where he had a short-lived notoriety based largely on his penchant for splitting his trousers while on stage. As it happened, he could sing, albeit in a melodramatic fashion, but he never let that get in the way of his career as an exhibitionist.

'I feel kind of blue today,' said P.J. Proby. 'Blue and hungover. I spent last night drinking with a friend of mine. He was very depressed and talking about suicide. I cheered him up and depressed myself! He was worried that he wasn't a *star*, that his *marriage* was unhappy, all that. Everyone's problems are so alike, his reminded me of the ones I'd only just got over.'

Proby was dressed from head to foot in baby blue. 'I don't do any two-tone bullshit,' he said. 'Everything's the same with me – coat, pants, shoes and the bow in my hair. This is the last of the goddam suits – the fans have torn all the others to bits. I'll have to go over to France for some more. It's a special stretched velvet you can only get over there – there's no demand for it in England. These pants are so damned tight, it's unreal. But they're made for the stage – you can do *anything* in them. See this loose jacket? Hides my beer belly!' He took a noisy swig of Scotch, camouflaged in a Coca-Cola bottle. Proby is supposed not to drink spirits, which might harm his voice. 'But wine drives you out of your mind! I tell you, I'm losing my mind on wine . . .'

Proby is a tough-looking Texan of twenty-seven, six feet tall, with a deep, fruity speaking-voice. On the stage he adopts effeminate mannerisms and blatantly sexual gestures which have little to do with his personality in real life. His long hair and velvet suit were therefore more disconcerting off the stage, where they seemed pointless and almost embarrassing, as if he had mistakenly gone out of doors in his pyjamas.

'Shape of my head look okay?' he asked as he posed for some photographs. 'Be sure you blot out my double chin when my face is at this angle. Anything under *here*' (tapping chin) 'I want out of that picture. Why, even Prince Philip would look like an idiot if you gave him a double chin. I guess you want me kind of lackadaisical in this one? I got two profiles, you know, one good and one bad. I'm quite a different person one side of my face to the other. This is my worst side, so take that goddam hump out of my nose if you can, with shadow or something. Give me an *aquiline* nose. Want me to wear my bracelet? A girl just gave me this. It's sterling silver. I told her, I prefer gold.' He examined it. 'Christ, I believe it's *brass*!'

Proby is unusually old for a pop star. After an undistinguished career in American showbusiness, he came to England last year where his extravagant appearance and bizarre, suggestive style of singing soon became popular with a very young audience. Increasing complaints from adults, however, have recently limited his appearances. 'But I've got an Australian tour coming up in August. And before that I go back to Los Angeles for three TV shows.

'My whole act is made up from different girls I've been with. I took the walk from a girl in Hollywood, the body movements from a dancer in *The Ed Sullivan Show*, and the pout from Chrissie Shrimpton. Now I see on TV that Tom Jones is copying the pouting bit. But I don't think that it will work with him, because when he pouts he looks like a basset hound.

'The Tom Jones bow was my own idea. I've always lived in a fantasy world, so I decided to wear my hair in a ponytail, like they did in the olden times. I've learned a lot about hair. Every man had long hair till the First World War – short hair only came in for the troops, for hygienic reasons. But this year I'm going to cut it all off and go for the adult market. I want to move from the *hysteria* stage to the *applause* stage, and you only get hysteria from the kids. I'm hoping to star in a movie, too – *The Greatest Story Never Told*. About a pop star who goes off his head and believes he's Jesus Christ. Then I want to make a whole series playing a sort of a Bond-type character. That's what I want – to play *characters*. I've been playing P.J. Proby so long I'm getting tired of myself.

'The kids will forgive me when I cut off my hair. It will be done in such a way that they won't mind. If you're *truthful* to them, the fans will take anything, even if it's bullshit. I tell them some tall Texan story and they know I'm not serious. But it's got to be *truthful* bullshit.

'That's what I deal in – raw truth. In England they don't like the raw truth. Know what I think when some Lady Hereford or somewhere says I'm disgusting and obscene? I pity her. I come over here and I do *more* than the English boys, I go further. They don't trust foreigners so they make me feel like a nigger must feel in Alabama. They can't take the *raw truth*.'

Cars were thickly parked outside the California Ballroom, a bright, gimcrack building perched on a windy hill near Dunstable. On the evening of Proby's appearance there, it was cynically supervised by a cordon of police. A nearby bungalow – home of the Ballroom's manageress, Mrs. King – served as the pop star's dressing room. He slouched on a chair in the daintily decorated sitting room, surrounded by statuettes of crinolined ladies, his hair in metal grips sticking out all round his head like Medusa's. Barry, his personal assistant, was engaged on the long and complicated ceremony of Proby's coiffure – an intricate ritual of back-combing and pinning, involving a tool-kit as extensive as a garage mechanic's. An odd little man, with spectacles mended by Elastoplast and a look of Peter Lorre, sat on a sofa reading a paperback on vampires: Bongo Wolf, Proby's best friend. A dark girl, Lesley, was paying vague attention to a budgie in a cage. Terry, Proby's bodyguard, stood stiff in a corner. The pop star held forth.

'I left Houston when I was seventeen because there was no show business there. Had to choose between two places – New York and Hollywood. I chose wrong. I'd been singing with Tommy Sands at the Hitching Post in Houston, and he was dating my sister, so I followed Tommy to Hollywood. Now in New York there is competition, maybe 200 people after the same job, but if you're talented you have a chance of getting it. In Hollywood there's a clique – if you're not in the clique, you don't work. For years I bashed my ass against a brick wall. You only make it if you stick it out and don't give up. Some of the ones who leave are even more talented than you are. But you're *there*. I worked in B movies of the hot-rod era, things like *Dragstrip*. And I did the demos for Elvis movies. I'd record all the numbers sounding just like Elvis, so that when he got through acting he could come and learn the songs straight off my demos. I've known Elvis since I was fourteen – he used to go with my sister. But Elvis won't talk to me now. While he was in the army I became quite involved with one of his girlfriends, is the reason. Though I hear that since I've made it over here in Britain, Elvis wants to have me round to the house again. What he minded was his girl being balled by a nobody. Funny thing, you really get to know a guy when you date his girl. Mick Jagger has forbidden all of the Stones to speak to me because I went out with Chrissie Shrimpton. But all she did was talk of Mick all the time. Mick's a very sensitive kid. I really got to know the inside of that boy, but I guess he'll never know it.'

Jimmy Henny, Proby's road manager, entered the room: a nervous man with a manner at the same time distracted and brash. He fussily told Proby that he was due on stage. After a disapproving pause, Proby cleared his throat and noisily spat several yards beyond the electric fire and straight into the grate. He hadn't seen Henny since their return from Denmark, when there had been a mix-up at London Airport – the road manager had failed to lay on a car and the fans had got out of control. 'Next time I won't get off the ramp till there's a car to meet me like there is with the Beatles and the Stones. Understand?' Henny began to defend himself, rather hysterically, but the animosity in the room was too strong, and he left it.

'But Denmark was unreal,' said Proby. 'No pop star ever had such an ovation. Here it's the girls who surge forward just to touch me, but there it was boys rushed on to the stage to shake my hand. I didn't get it at first – I thought they were hostile, and began punching them! The ones at the back would make themselves stiff, like arrows, and be passed forward over the heads of the others. We had a ball in Denmark, didn't we, Bongo?'

'Yeah,' said Bongo. 'I brought back some artistic mementoes.' He produced a packet of nude photographs.

Lesley, who has a reputation for being psychic, suddenly looked at Barry and said: 'I get Ethel. Do you know an Ethel?' He shook his head. 'You will,' said Lesley.

The metal pins were now out of Proby's hair and fastened to Barry's jacket. As he manipulated the stiff black mass, Barry clicked his tongue in wonder: 'Lesley's fantastic. She told me I'd meet a lovely blonde girl in Denmark, and I did. The other day she got through to my dead gran who told her something about a blue and green sweater. It meant nothing to me. So I rang my mother, and she said yes, your Gran *did* knit you a blue and green sweater when you were small.'

'Unreal,' said Proby. 'Bongo's a warlock, aren't you, Bongo?' He saw that Bongo was stroking Mrs. King's cat, which had jumped on to his lap. Proby startled the room by suddenly bellowing: 'Leave that cat alone!' Then, softer but still sternly: 'You frighten animals. You touch them too hard.'

Proby explained about Bongo. 'That's not his real name. His real name is Donald Grollman, but he loves to play the bongos and he's interested in werewolves, so we call him Bongo Wolf. We've been buddies five years now. Bongo seems to be mentally deranged but that isn't true and he's the kindest guy in the world. Although he's thirty-three years of age he still lives with his parents in Hollywood. My father was rich and when I first came to Hollywood I kept a lot of people, but after he cut me off I went round all these former friends asking for handouts and none were giving any. Except Bongo. When my wife and I were nearly starving, he'd throw us trays of frozen TV dinners out of the window, we'd grab 'em up and run off home. I swore then that if I ever made it I'd show Bongo the world, and that's what I'm doing. Something he'd never be able to do without me. I may seem to be cruel to him sometimes, but it's for his own good – for his health.'

'Maybe,' said Bongo. 'But I wish you and the boys would lay off teasing me, making out like I'm a faggot. It's a joke, but it gets boring.'

Henny returned, more agitated than ever. Proby was now *very* overdue. But he wouldn't be hurried – 'Let them wait.' At last Barry produced, and carefully folded, a white satin coat with the Texas flag on it in red and blue. 'I wear this at the end of my act,' said Proby. 'When my trousers split.' Henny winced. Bongo said, 'You've *got* to be joking!'

Protected by his entourage, Proby was swiftly smuggled across a dark courtyard to the ballroom, which was now unhealthily full of impatient fans. Henny approached a police officer at the door. 'I'm P.J. Proby's manager,' he announced, and held out his hand. Surprisedly shaking it, the policeman replied; 'Well, good luck to you then. I'm Inspector Lambert – *his* manager' – and pointed to another policeman, with an irony which Henny missed.

The stage was guarded by an impressive group of chuckers-out. Proby crouched in the wings. He took a last, long pull at the Coca-Cola bottle and asked for a mirror. A panic-stricken whisper was repeated, 'Is there a mirror in the office?' Eventually a small powder compact was produced and urgently passed down the line of policemen and chuckers-out. 'Jesus Christ, I'm getting a beard under my eyes,' said Proby; then, extending his arms in an ineffably camp gesture, he tripped daintily on to the stage. The roars of the audience drowned his theme song, 'Somewhere'.

Proby claims that if one fan in the audience stops screaming, he hears it and acts accordingly. His performance takes forty-five minutes, but can be much longer if he ad-libs: it depends on the audience reaction. On this occasion, there was a steady roar – stimulated less by his voice and the music, which could hardly be heard, then by his voluptuous massaging of his buttocks and groin, his queenly gestures and mincing gait. The blue velvet, dangerously stretched, gleamed in the spotlight. 'Am I clean?' he called out. 'Don't you want to touch *me*? Am I clean?' 'Yes! Yes!' they yelled back, and arms stretched out to him – but a line of bodyguards in front of the stage prevented any physical contact. Mrs. King had been over-cautious in protecting her ballroom – physical contact is the *point* of Proby's act. Stinging drops of sweat flew from his body to land on the grim faces of the guards below, punishing them with temporary blindness.

After the show, his uniform limp and stained with sweat, Proby lay for a while unconscious in Mrs. King's bungalow. 'He could get fabulous crumpet at some of these concerts,' said Barry. 'See all those birds go wild? But he always passes out. The strain is terrible.'

When he came to, Proby said that the performance had been a disaster. 'No audience participation. That line of chuckers-out stopped the fans from getting anywhere near me. That's the last time I work in a ballroom. From now on it's genuine *concerts*, like in Denmark, or I don't work.' He began to change into street clothes: black velvet trousers, open white shirt, white sweater, white socks, black buckled shoes. His hair was allowed to hang loose in a long dark bob, between which his jutting, grinning, handsome features had a fleeting look of Mary McCarthy.

Proby and his entourage were sedately conducted back to London in a chauffeur-driven Rolls. The car was delayed in a traffic block beside a Post Office van, driven by a woman in a postman's uniform. Proby, who had been silent, shook his head and spoke in rich, elegiac tones: 'It's just terrible to see a woman working like a man, and dressing like a man, and looking like a man, and everything. There's no excuse for it.'

Proby's house in Chelsea is filled with firearms of every size; the drawing-room walls are hung with antlers. A pretty girl was waiting there; she was introduced as Sarah, and poured out drinks. 'All these cannons fire,' he said. 'Most of these objects I owe on still. Can't afford the Portobello Road at the moment. You like good music, don't you? I'll play you my new LP. This is not commercial, it's the classics. Standards from shows like *Carousel* and *Oklahoma*. You see, I'm old enough to remember the Forties singers – Sinatra, Dick Haymes. These younger boys were only exposed to the Fifties and rock 'n' roll, so they don't have any standards. Just listen to this. When all the teenage shit is over, I'll have this to fall back on.' A slow, syrupy version of 'If I Loved You' was listened to in reverent silence. 'I wish we had mission bells there, goddam it,' Proby muttered at the end.

A basset hound lumbered into the room: Mister President, a gift from the President of the P.J. Proby fan club. 'I'm crazy about animals. I have a cat too, called Marmaduke. And Japanese goldfish – they're so beautiful! I love to walk in the park and watch people and their dogs. Have you ever noticed how people get to look like their pets? Dachshunds – they're so individual, it's unreal. Trotting on, ignoring their masters, like they said 'I think I'll just go take a walk by myself'. One thing I have to have, a Saint Bernard. Maybe when Mister President is a little older, so he won't get jealous.'

Mister President jumped on to the drawing-room sofa. After a shocked pause, Proby bellowed at Sarah; 'GET HIM OFF!' The dog jumped down, alarmed, and Sarah began; 'I thought . . .' 'Don't think!' Proby shouted. 'Act!'

The telephone rang, barely audible above Proby's singing on the gramophone. Sarah went to answer it. 'If it's a fan, hang up. I'm not interested. Tell her if she comes round I'll punch the hell out of her. Women come round here when *I* want them.' Sarah hung up. Proby patted her face. 'She'd be all right if she wasn't so fat,' he said. 'Good little cheekbones and nose, but all round here will have to go.'

'That's puppy fat,' said Sarah. 'I'm not eighteen yet, am I?'

'My type is the petite type.' Proby went on. 'I don't mean I couldn't ball Sophia Loren, but in the perspective of like marriage, and living with a woman all your life, I don't like them too big. Marriage! I'm kind of cynical about marriage. I divorced my wife for one reason – cheating. I never cheated on her till she implanted in my mind the idea that she was cheating on me. So I left for England a year ago and haven't seen her since. One good thing, we didn't have any kids. I've several illegitimate ones, and if I don't have any real ones, some day when I'm very old I might leave something to the ones I have. But only if I don't have any real ones. If my wife had had children, and she'd got custody of them after the divorce, I'd have shot her. Then she'd be dead, I'd go to the electric chair, and they'd be put in military school which wouldn't do any harm. I was made a ward of court myself at twelve, and had a military upbringing, and I'm in favour of the discipline. All I've done in the world I owe to that military discipline.'

The entourage began to drift away. 'I think I'll go to the Ad Lib tonight,' said Proby. 'I don't feel like sitting around alone.'

'But you're not alone,' said Sarah.

'Yes, I am too alone,' said the pop star. 'When you're dealing with yourself, you're alone.'

After being features editor of Queen *magazine, Francis Wyndham became the chief profile writer on the* Sunday Times Magazine. *He has published several anthologies of his profiles.*

JOAN HUNTER DUNN

—

Peter Crookston
Sunday Times Magazine
1965

John Betjeman's cantering poem, 'The Subaltern's Love Song', written during World War II, became a favourite of school English literature classes during the Sixties. Joan Hunter Dunn epitomized the wholesome, open-air, middle-class English girl. What few realized was that there was actually a real life Joan Hunter Dunn.

> *Miss J. Hunter Dunn, Miss J. Hunter Dunn,*
> *Furnish'd and burnish'd by Aldershot sun,*
> *What strenuous singles we played after tea,*
> *We in the tournament – you against me!*

Joan Hunter Dunn is a widow now, with three sons all at boarding schools. She lives in a whitewashed house deep in the Home Counties with pine trees in the drive and croquet hoops on the lawn.

She is forty-nine, a handsome, brisk woman, with grey hair, brown eyes and sturdy tennis-girl legs. The absolute Englishness of her character, which inspired Betjeman to write his classic of suburban folk lore, runs so deep that her whole life seems to be a continuation of the poem. In her home, one almost expects to see pictures of Egypt on the walls and it's no surprise to find that, in fact, there are prints of China. Framed photographs of her children and her late husband stand on the occasional tables. On the mantelpiece are invitations to two 'at homes', a wedding and a performance of *HMS Pinafore* by a school operatic society. The 'at homes' have neat ticks marked in the corners to show that they have been acknowledged. A log fire burns in the grate, and the bellows that encouraged it lie on the brick hearth.

Betjeman captured all this atmosphere of Home Counties well-being before he really knew her. He knew her name and her face and imagined the rest. He met Joan Hunter Dunn during the Blitz in 1940 while he was working at the Ministry of Information. The Ministry had taken over the Senate House of London University where Miss Hunter Dunn was deputy manageress of catering. 'I was taken over with the pots and pans, and together with Mrs. Bruce, the manageress, had the job of providing food for 1,600 people. I was always dashing about in a white coat and I don't see how John Betjeman could have known me terribly well. However, one day he asked me out to lunch and in the taxi on the way to the restaurant he put a copy of *Horizon* magazine into my hand and said, 'I hope you don't mind, but I've written a poem about you.' I must say I was absolutely overwhelmed. It was such a marvellous break from the monotony of the war. It really was remarkable the way he imagined it all. Actually, all that about the subaltern and the engagement is sheer fantasy, but my life was very like the poem.'

Being a Betjeman heroine has not had any adverse effect on her life. 'People who know my maiden name or who find out about it sometimes ask, 'Are you *the* Joan Hunter Dunn?' But I just laugh it off and say that she doesn't exist any more.'

She thought Betjeman was one of the most interesting and amusing of the motley collection of poets, journalists and artists who were press-ganged together at the Ministry. 'He is also a very good character and a very religious man. They say that God has His agents on this planet, and I am sure that John Betjeman is one of them.'

Betjeman can still remember vividly Miss Hunter Dunn's lithe, tigerish energy and coolness in a crisis. 'The raids that went on drew us together in the evenings. I don't say by "us" that I mean Joan and I, but all of us at the Ministry in those days, especially when we had to wait between raids before bicycling home. "Mini" was mostly pale green intellectuals like yours truly. Joan Hunter Dunn was quite different from the rest of us. She had bright cheeks, clear sunburned skin, darting brown eyes, a shock of dark curls and a happy smile. Her figure was a dream of strength and beauty. When the bombs fell she bound up our wounds unperturbed. She was so marvellous at first aid. I used to wish desperately for a small wound from a bomb so that she would minister to me. When I first saw her I said to my friends Osbert Lancaster and Reginald Ross-Williamson, "I bet that girl is a doctor's daughter and comes from Aldershot."

'When I got to know her, I found I was right, and it is my only experience of poetic prescience. I wrote the verses in the character of a subaltern at Aldershot but they were really my own imaginings about her. When I showed her the poem she told me she lived in Farnborough, Hampshire, but I considered that near enough to Aldershot to count. She was one of the most cheerful, sweet and gentle girls I ever knew. Oh, goodness, I wish you had seen her striding about the Ministry. The spirit of Surrey girlhood and a pine-scented paradise.'

Joan Hunter Dunn had an almost classical upper-middle-class girlhood of the Thirties. Her father was a doctor with many Army officers from Aldershot among his patients. He had a Victorian mansion with stables at the back in which he kept his two cars, a Talbot and an Austin. There was a chauffeur called Pickett, who was clever with his hands. 'Whenever anything was broken, Daddy or my brother always used to say, "Pickett will mend it." He was a terribly good chap. You know, typical old retainer type. He came to Father as a boy to clean knives and boots. Then he went off to fight in the First World War, and when he came back he went into livery.'

Pickett's wife did the cooking, and there were also various parlour maids and cleaning women. 'It's really amazing to look back on, when you think that hardly anyone has servants nowadays. It was really gracious living. But you know, we loved them and they loved us. We used to give them lovely presents at Christmas.'

Joan had two sisters, Rosamond and Betty, and a brother, Christopher. They all went to boarding schools, except for Rosamond, who had a French governess called Violet d'Boissiere.

The great treats of Joan's early life were visits to the patients with her father, for whom she had a very deep affection, bicycle rides with Christopher and games of tennis with Rosamond. 'One of my father's patients, Mrs. Willis, had a big house at Frimley with a hard court. She used to let Rosamond and me play on it whenever we liked. We used to cycle there from home and after we'd played tennis she would give us date cakes and lemonade.'

After five years at a convent school at St Leonard's-on-Sea, Joan went to Queen Anne's, Caversham, a girl's public school near Reading. She was not a brilliant scholar, but she was always in the top half of her class. She was very good at games. 'I think I was on most teams it was possible to be on, and I was head girl of my house.' They put her on the defence wing in the lacrosse team because she was such a fast runner. Two of her front teeth were knocked out in a match against Wycombe Abbey.

At eighteen, Joan Hunter Dunn went to Queen Elizabeth College, London University, to study household and social science. On holidays, she occasionally played tennis at Aldershot and went to dances at the officer's club. After taking a diploma in institutional management, she got a job at Guy's Hospital making up diets and lecturing nurses on elementary dietetics. When the war started, she had just settled into a new job at the Senate House of London University. The Ministry of Information moved in, Betjeman admired her from afar and composed his Surrey pinewood fantasy about her, and a civil servant fell in love with her. The first time he took her out he asked her if she knew of a place where he could go on leave with his friend, a naval commander. Holiday accommodation at that time was scarce but Joan knew of somewhere – Amroth Castle, which had been converted into an hotel in Pembrokeshire.

She arranged their booking and when they got there he sent a telegram asking her to join them. His birthday fell in the middle of the leave, so she baked him a cake, sent most of her luggage ahead by post and nursed the cake all the way to Wales. 'I must have been in love with him to do that.' He proposed to her in the hotel at 6.35 on 2 October 1944, after they returned from a mackerel fishing trip. A photograph of the ivy covered castle, and the exact time of the proposal are in Joan's 'Bride's Book'.

This book, like all Joan's mementoes, is well-documented. Apart from the usual lists of guests and gifts it contains her thoughts on her wedding day entitled: Jan 20th 1945. THE LAST HOURS OF 'ME' AS J.H.D. It begins: 'I had slept in the spare bedroom at home ('Red House') and woke to find a beautiful breakfast of boiled egg! What luxury, but this was my wedding day. The sky was grey, and heavy snow soon began to fall, but later the sun came out and the sky was blue and Farnborough looked whiter and brighter to me that ever before. I lay in bed for a bit and thought deeply about this day . . .'

Dr. George Hunter Dunn was determined that it should be a great day for his second daughter. He must have been very proud of her, and in a letter to her on her engagement had said, 'I know all your qualities and capabilities pretty well, and what a grand little homemaker you will be, and I know how lucky any man would be to have you as his wife.'

Despite the shortages, Mrs. Hunter Dunn succeeded in making it quite an impressive wedding. There were 300 people in St Mark's Church, Farnborough, and 130 guests at the reception. The Bride's Book gives details:

'Taxis – four hired. Smith. All day.
Caterers – Bonnets, Aldershot. Very good.

Drink – Claret cup and gin (6 botts.)
Eats – Sandwiches, petit fours, toasted savories, trifles, chocolate biscuits.
Florals – Chrysanthemums white and gold. Carnations. Hired pots and flowers for church. Lilies on altar.
Service – Fully choral.'

Joan's veil was old Honiton lace and had been worn by Granny Dunn at her wedding. Her stockings were made of pure silk, 'Last pair, 4s. 11d. pre-rations from Peter Robinson's,' says the Bride's Book.

The honeymoon was in Devon, but they spent the first night at the Savoy: 'Left Farnborough to catch train from Ashvale. Blinding snow-storm when we arrived. *No* taxis! Took tube to Strand then taxi 100 yards to Savoy!! Beautiful apartment. Dined and danced. Roast plover.' The bill for the apartment, carefully preserved in the Bride's Book, was £2 19s. 8d.

It was a marvellously happy marriage. They moved around the world a lot as her husband worked hard and was steadily promoted and given important jobs in Empire outposts like Kuala Lumpur, Singapore and Salisbury, Southern Rhodesia. He died suddenly two years ago while they were in Rhodesia. Their three sons were at school in England, Andrew at Winchester, Charles and Edward at prep school. The masters broke the news to them. 'I shall always be grateful for the help they gave us.'

Most of the time she is alone from choice. 'But I don't mind the boys being away at school. I think it would be a bad thing if they were tied to their mother's apron strings. I can't teach them manly things and give them the discipline they get from their masters.' Most of her social outings are bound up with their scholastic careers – meeting other mothers at open days, school plays and at cricket matches.

She is now beginning to get adjusted to being a widow and is taking more of an interest in village life. Recently she has been arranging the flowers on the altar of the parish church. She hopes to convert part of her house into a flat and let it to an unmarried mother. 'Because she would be company for me and I would enjoy looking after the baby.'

She asked if I knew why the poem had caught on so much and why it was one of the best-known of Betjeman's works. I said I thought it was because it had showed her as the perfectly desirable synthesis of English girlhood – wholesome, athletic and comfortably off. 'Yes,' she said, 'I suppose you're right.'

Peter Crookston has been the editor of the Observer Magazine *and* World *magazine. He is currently editor of* Heritage Today.

JOHN LENNON: 'WE'RE MORE POPULAR THAN JESUS NOW'

—

Maureen Cleave

Evening Standard
March 4 1966

When this article first appeared in the London Evening Standard, *John Lennon's aside about the Beatles being more famous than Jesus raised few eyebrows. Reprinted in American fan magazines a couple of months later, however, just as the group were beginning a tour of one-night stands across America, there was fury right across the Bible Belt. Beatles records were publicly burnt, death threats were made and Lennon was forced to apologize. He felt humiliated, and the experience probably accelerated the end of the Beatles' touring career. After 1966 they never played together in public again.*

The Beatles are now the most famous people in the English speaking world. They are famous in the way the Queen is famous. When John Lennon's Rolls-Royce, with its black wheels and its black windows, goes past, people say 'It's the Queen' or 'It's the Beatles'. With her they share the security of a stable life at the top. They all tick over in the public esteem – she in Buckingham Palace, they in the Weybridge-Esher area. Only Paul remains in London.

The Weybridge community consists of the three married Beatles; they live there among the wooded hills and the stockbrokers. They have not worked since Christmas and their existence is secluded and curiously timeless. 'What day is it?' John Lennon asks with interest when you ring up with news from outside. The fans are still at the gates but the Beatles see only each other. They are better friends than ever before.

Ringo and his wife, Maureen, may drop in on John and Cyn; John may drop in on Ringo; George and Patti may drop in on John and Cyn and they might all go round to Ringo's – by car, of course. Outdoors is for holidays.

They watch films, they play rowdy games of Buccaneer; they watch television till it goes off, often playing records at the same time. They while away the small hours of the morning making mad tapes. Bedtimes and mealtimes have no meaning as such. 'We've never had time before to do anything but just be Beatles,' John Lennon said.

He is much the same as he was before. He still peers down his nose, arrogant as an eagle, although contact lenses have righted the short sight that originally caused the expression. He looks more like Henry VIII than ever now that his face has filled out

– he is just as imperious, just as unpredictable, indolent, disorganized, childish, vague, charming and quick-witted. He is still easy-going, still tough as hell. 'You never asked after Fred Lennon,' he says, disappointed. (Fred is his father; he emerged after they got famous.) 'He was here a few weeks ago. It was only the second time in my life I'd seen him – I showed him the door.' He went on cheerfully 'I wasn't having *him* in the house.'

His enthusiasm is undiminished and he insists on its being shared. George has put him on to this Indian music. 'You're not listening, are you?' he shouts after twenty minutes of the record. 'It's amazing this – so cool. Don't the Indians appear cool to you? Are you listening? This music is thousands of years old; it makes me laugh, the British going over there and telling them what to do. Quite amazing.' And he switched on the television set.

Experience has sown few seeds of doubt in him; not that his mind is closed, but it's closed round whatever he believes at the time. 'Christianity will go,' he said. 'It will vanish and shrink. I needn't argue about that; I'm right and I will be proved right. We're more popular than Jesus now; I don't know which will go first – rock 'n' roll or Christianity. Jesus was all right but his disciples were thick and ordinary. It's them twisting it that ruins it for me.' He is reading extensively about religion.

He shops in lightning swoops on Asprey's these days and there is some fine wine in his cellar, but he is still quite unselfconscious. He is far too lazy to keep up appearances, even if he had worked out what the appearances should be – which he has not.

He is now twenty-five. He lives in a large, heavily panelled, heavily carpeted mock Tudor house set on a hill with his wife Cynthia and his son Julian. There is a cat called after his aunt Mimi and a purple dining room. Julian is three; he may be sent to the Lycee in London. 'Seems the only place for him in his position,' said his father, surveying him dispassionately. 'I feel sorry for him, though. I couldn't stand ugly people even when I was five. Lots of the ugly ones are foreign, aren't they?'

We did a speedy tour of the house, Julian panting along behind clutching a large porcelain Siamese cat. John swept past the objects in which he had lost interest: 'That's Sidney' (a suit of armour); 'That's a hobby I had for a week' (a room full of model racing cars); 'Cyn won't let me get rid of that' (a fruit machine). In the sitting room are eight little green boxes with winking red lights; he bought them as Christmas presents but never got round to giving them away. They wink for a year; one imagines him sitting there till next Christmas surrounded by the little winking boxes.

He paused over objects he still fancies: a huge altar crucifix of a Roman Catholic nature with IHS on it; a pair of crutches, a present from George; an enormous Bible he bought in Chester; his gorilla suit.

'I thought I might need a gorilla suit,' he said; he seemed sad about it. 'I've only worn it twice. I thought I might pop it on in the summer and drive round in the Ferrari. We were all going to get them and drive round in them but I was the only one who did. I've been thinking about it and if I didn't wear the head it would make an amazing fur coat – with legs, you see. I would like a fur coat but I've never run into any.'

One feels that his possessions – to which he adds daily – have got the upper hand; all the tape recorders, the five television sets, the cars, the telephones of which he knows not a single number. The moment he approaches a switch it fuses; six of the winking boxes, guaranteed to last till next Christmas, have gone funny already. His cars – the Rolls, the Mini-Cooper (black wheels, black windows), the Ferrari (being painted black) – puzzle him. Then there's the swimming pool, the trees sloping away beneath it. 'Nothing like what I ordered,' he said resignedly. He wanted the bottom to be a mirror.

'It's an amazing household,' he said. 'None of my gadgets really work except the gorilla suit – that's the only suit that fits me.'

He is very keen on books, will always ask what is good to read. He buys quantities of books and these are kept tidily in a special room. He has Swift, Tennyson, Huxley, Orwell, costly leather-bound editions of Tolstoy, Oscar Wilde. Then there's *Little Women*, all the William books from his childhood; and some unexpected volumes such as *Forty-One Years In India*, by Field Marshal Lord Roberts, and *Curiosities of Natural History*, by Francis T. Buckland.

This last with its chapter headings – Ear-less Cats, Wooden-Legged People, The Immortal Harvey's Mother – is right up his street.

He approaches reading with a lively interest untempered by too much formal education. 'I've read millions of books,' he said, 'that's why I seem to know things.' He is obsessed by Celts. 'I have decided that I am a Celt,' he said. 'I am on Boadicea's side – all those bloody, blue-eyed blonds chopping people up. I have an awful feeling wishing I was there – not there with scabs and sores but there through *reading* about it. The books don't give you more than a paragraph about how they *lived*; I have to imagine that.'

He can sleep almost indefinitely, is probably the laziest person in England. '*Physically* lazy,' he said. 'I don't mind writing or reading or watching or speaking, but sex is the only physical thing I can be bothered with any more.'

Occasionally he is driven to London in the Rolls by an ex-Welsh guardsman called Anthony; Anthony has a moustache that intrigues him.

The day I visited him he had been invited to lunch in London, about which he was rather excited. 'Do you know how long lunch lasts?' he asked. 'I've never been to lunch before. I went to a Lyons the other day and had egg and chips and a cup of tea. The waiters kept looking and saying: `No, it *isn't* him, it *can't be* him'.'

He settled himself into the car and demonstrated the television, the folding bed, the refrigerator, the writing desk, the telephone. He has spent many fruitless hours on that telephone. 'I only once got through to a person,' he said, 'and they were out.'

Anthony had spent the weekend in Wales. John asked if they'd kept a welcome for him in the hillside and Anthony said they had. They discussed the possibility of an extension for the telephone. We had to call at the doctor's because John had a bit of sea urchin in his toe. 'Don't want to be like Dorothy Dandridge,' he said, 'dying of a splinter fifty years later.' He added reassuringly that he had washed the foot in question.

We bowled in a costly fashion through the countryside. 'Famous and loaded' is how he describes himself now. 'They keep telling me I'm all right for money but then I think I may have spent it all by the time I'm forty so I keep going. That's why I started selling my cars; then I changed my mind and got them all back and a new one, too.

'I want the money just to *be rich*. The only other way of getting it is to be born rich. If you have money, that's power without having to be powerful. I often think that it's all a big conspiracy, that the winners are the Government and people like us who've got the money. That joke about keeping the workers ignorant is still true; that's what they said about the Tories and the landowners and that; then Labour were meant to educate the workers but they don't seem to be doing that any more.'

He has a morbid horror of stupid people: 'Famous and loaded as I am I still have to meet soft people. It often comes into my mind that I'm not really rich. There are *really* rich people but I don't know where they are.'

He finds being famous quite easy, confirming one's suspicion that the Beatles had been leading up to this all their lives. 'Everybody thinks they *would* have been famous if only they'd had the Latin and that. So when it happens it comes naturally.

'You remember your old grannie saying soft things like: "You'll make it with that voice." Not, he added, that he had any old grannies.

He got to the doctor two and three quarter hours early and to lunch on time but in the wrong place. He bought a giant compendium of games from Asprey's but having opened it he could not, of course, shut it again. He wondered what else he should buy. He went to Brian Epstein's office. 'Any presents?' he asked eagerly; he observed that there was nothing like getting things free. He tried on the attractive Miss Hanson's spectacles.

The rumour came through that a Beatle had been sighted walking down Oxford Street. He brightened. 'One of the others must be out,' he said, as though speaking of an escaped bear. 'We only let them out one at a time,' said the attractive Miss Hanson firmly.

He said that to live and have a laugh were the things to do; but was that enough for the restless spirit?

'Weybridge,' he said, 'won't do at all. I'm just stopping at it, like a bus stop. Bankers and stockbrokers live there; they can add figures and Weybridge is what they live in and they think it's the end, they really do. I think of it every day – me in my Hansel and Gretel house. I'll take my time; I'll get my *real* house when I know what I want.

'You see there's something else I'm going to do, something I must do – only I don't know what it is. That's why I go round painting and taping and drawing and writing and that, because it may be one of them.

'All I know is, this isn't *it* for me.'

Anthony got him and the compendium into the car and drove him home with the television flickering in the soothing darkness while the Londoners outside rushed home from work.

THE MEN WHO NEVER WERE

—

Michael Frayn

Observer
6 March 1966

Throughout the mid-Sixties public debate about the legalization of abortion aroused passionate feelings. In July 1967 abortion was made legal.

It's a weirdly fascinating business watching sober and fair-minded human beings trying to work out a formula for the circumstances in which abortion should be permitted. All possible reasons and permutations of reasons are canvassed and debated; excepting only the reason that the woman concerned wants an abortion, which no one mentions as having any relevance to the question at all.

Of course, this way of thinking is very congenial to a bureaucracy-loving socialist like me, who believes that people shouldn't be allowed any freedom to choose for themselves, but should have all their decisions made for them by faceless officials and so-called experts who think they know what's best for everyone. But I'm rather surprised that the tireless defenders of personal liberty whom we usually find ourselves up against in our insidious erosion of citizen rights haven't been exposing controls and snoopers in this sector with quite their usual vigour.

No, I was being gently ironical. I'm aware that those who deny that a pregnant woman has any personal right to choose whether she wants to give birth do so because they are trying to protect the right of the unborn to be born. And there are two arguments often advanced in this direction which I must admit I find rather compelling.

The first is that few people (if any), once having got themselves born and in a position to say, would prefer not to have been born, however reluctant or unsuitable their mother, or however exhausted and inadequate she subsequently became. The second (and logically similar) argument is that if abortion had been freely available in the past, the world might have been deprived of individuals like Leonardo da Vinci and William the Conqueror (who were illegitimate), and Bach (the eighth of eight children).

These arguments are good ones. The only trouble with them is that they're *too* good. Take the case of that astonishing sixteenth-century figure Ivan Kudovbin. He invented a primitive form of gas-mantle; he wrote 123 flute sonatas, before the sonata form had been invented; he experimented with cheap money and deficit budgeting; he raised a citizen army which drove the Galicians right out of Galicia into Silesia, and the Silesians right out of Silesia into Galicia. He was undoubtedly a genius. But, as we know from studying the history of the period, he was one of the unlucky ones who didn't get born. He Kudovbin, but he wasn't. If he *had* been born he would have preferred to have been born, I'm pretty sure. His loss is a tragedy both to himself and to mankind.

Perhaps Kudovbin was aborted or miscarried – I'm not sure. But I think the trouble was quite probably that he never got conceived. I don't know what went wrong exactly. Perhaps he was the twelfth child in the family, and his parents stopped at eleven. Perhaps his mother was a nun, under vows of chastity. Perhaps his father was away on a business trip the night he should have been commenced. But what seems fairly certain mathematically is that the tragedy of his non-birth could have been averted if everyone had really taken the matter seriously.

Think of it. If the available reproductive plant had been fully utilized from the beginning of time, and every woman had been kept bearing a child a year from puberty to menopause, billions upon billions more people would have been born. Nearly all of them, once born, would have preferred to have been born. And among them, presumably, would have been the usual proportion of geniuses. Kudovbin after Kudovbin – composers who wrote greater polyphonic music than Bach; Elizabethan dramatists more universal than Shakespeare; Elizabethan monarchs more Elizabethan than Elizabeth.

The steamboat would have been invented in time to take people to the Crusades; the United Nations in time to reach a negotiated settlement instead. Frozen fish-fingers would have come in about the beginning of the Renaissance.

Just think for a start how many innocent babes – potential great men among them – have been kept out of this world because of legal or moral sanctions against fornication, adultery, rape, and intercourse below the age of consent! Sentimentalists have opposed these creative and life-enhancing activities on various short-sighted grounds, such as the well-being of the woman concerned, and the desirability of stable family and social life. Have they ever stopped to consider the well-being of poor little Vsevolod and Tatiana Kudovbin, who as a result of their interference never even started being, well or ill?

But then, people never stop to think about the rights of the unborn. So-called reformers struggled for years to get slavery abolished, using a variety of spurious moral arguments, but really on the shallow hedonistic grounds that the slaves themselves didn't much care for it. Didn't they, indeed! Nobody stopped to consider that without slavery there would in years to come be no Buddy Bolden, no Jelly Roll Morton, no Blind Lemon Jefferson; hence no syncopated popular music of any sort; hence no Beatles and no Cilla Black. So much for Cilla Black, for all Wilberforce cared.

The simple truth is, that it's an ill wind that blows nobody any silver linings. So carry on persecuting people; they may be Dostoyevsky. And don't hesitate to martyr any likely-looking candidate; remember, he may not get canonized otherwise.

Although now principally a playwright – his most successful plays include Alphabetical Order, Noises Off *and translations of Tolstoy, Anouilh and Chekhov – Michael Frayn has recently returned to journalism with a column for the* Guardian.

THE MOORS MURDERS

—

Maurice Richardson
Observer
8 May 1966

A terrified call by Myra Hindley's brother-in-law, David Smith, first alerted police to what was to become one of the most infamous and saddest murder trials in Britain this century. At least five children are now believed to have been tortured and murdered. Both Hindley and her lover Ian Brady are still in jail.

'If those two were sane they'd have gone mad long ago.' I was rather impressed by this comment – by a local hall porter – on the psychology of Ian Brady and Myra Hindley. Behaviour so atrocious can only be described in terms of Irish or Hegelian logic, the logic of contradictions. How does one begin to explain it?

It is all very well to say that we were all once polymorph-perverse infants, and that Mr. Everyman's unconscious teems with sado-masochistic impulses. True, of course. But there is nothing impulsive about their dreadful calculated performances and the elaborate decoying that must have preceded them. I find it less difficult to empathize with Jack the Ripper than with these two. Odd how one always calls them Brady and Myra.

The other peculiar feature here is the dual element. *Folie à deux* in which two people go mad together is not unknown. An hysteric who falls in love with a psychotic will share the psychotic's delusions so long as they are together. Separate them, and the hysteric recovers while the psychotic remains insane. And according to Freud hysterical women may share the perversions of their lovers.

This looks very much like such a case. Indeed I am convinced it is one. Myra is an 'hysteric', Brady is a psychopathic sadistic pervert: it is conceivable that his perversion may mask a germinating psychosis. His passion for the Nazis (which the prosecution decided to play down so as not to appear to be overloading their case with politics) is no accident: he was looking for some sort of social sanction for his violent impulses. In a Nazi regime he might have flourished, become a Belsen guard, and Myra with him, or perhaps have risen to a higher post. He is a remarkable specimen of lumpen-proletarian intellectual. Strange to think that he was only eight when Hitler died. His enthusiasm for the Nazis started when he was a schoolboy.

Their backgrounds: What would have happened if they had never met? You can't tell about Myra, but I think Brady would have got into bad trouble anyway. He had a hopeless start and probably drew something sinister in the chromosomal lottery. Born 2 January 1938, in the notorious Gorbals in Glasgow. Nobody knows who his real father was. Mother a teashop waitress, who registered his birth in her maiden name, Stewart. He was brought up by a good foster-mother and took her name: Sloan. He was quite bright at school, but a persistent thief, and showed a cruel streak. He was put on probation on condition he went to live with his mother, who had married and moved to Manchester.

He stole again, was sent to Borstal (Hull and Hatfield), then settled down for a bit. His first job was working with his stepfather in the Manchester meat market. He had a spot of bother over pinching some lead, but no further convictions apart from a drunkenness charge. At Millwards, the chemical works, where he started as a stock clerk in February 1959, he had the reputation of being a meticulous worker, unsociable, yet not particularly difficult to get on with, though given to fits of violent temper if crossed or if he had lost at betting.

Myra's people are fairly solid working-class from Manchester and the industrial fringe of Cheshire. We saw her mother in court: she had a long, sad, rather distinguished face and wore a thin, black scarf over her head. Myra was brought up by her Gran; her sister Maureen, who married David Smith, stayed with Mum and Dad; but they all lived within a stone's throw of one another in Gorton, a pretty tough working-class quarter of Manchester.

Myra went to a secondary modern school, stayed on and took a commercial course. At thirteen she saw a boy drown in a canal; this had a profound effect on her. She became religious, thought of becoming a Roman Catholic and received instruction. Later she became a bit flighty and unstable. She was said to be a good baby-sitter. There was an engagement that bust up. She had several secretarial jobs before she fetched up at Millwards in 1960.

Myra fell in love with Brady immediately and set her cap at him. For months he wouldn't take the slightest notice of her. She kept a diary with entries such as, 'He wouldn't look at me . . . I almost got a smile out of him today . . . Ian wore a black shirt and looked smashing . . .He's a crude uncouth pig . . .' Then the tone changes: 'Took Ian home: he was ever so gentle.'

As their association developed, Myra became tougher, 'posher', more flamboyant, going in for multi-coloured hair-dos, also more secretive. Asked why they didn't marry, she said Ian didn't hold with marriage, it was meaningless.

It's difficult to get their relationship straight. We know she was obsessed by him. ('I loved him . . . I still . . . I love him,' she said in the box.) He must have had quite strong affection for her. His attitude now is not unchivalrous.

One is inclined now to picture them as spending all their time in abnormal or criminal activities: taking pornographic photographs (he took many of the pair of them), planning crimes, visiting victims' graves on the moors – that strange Gothic obsession of theirs. In fact, for much of the time they must have led a quite ordinary domestic life. Their family photograph album, the respectable one in a tartan cover, is full of the usual banal snapshots; there is one of Myra in a black evening dress with a cocktail glass in her hand; one of Brady picnicking on the moors, looking jovial, brandishing a bottle; several of them playing with the dogs.

Both were very fond of these dogs. Brady spent hours combing them. He still believes, you could tell from his evidence, that the police destroyed Puppet – who died under an anaesthetic being X-rayed – to punish him. Myra, when told of Puppet's death, said to the policewoman, 'You're a lot of f-----g murderers.'

I wonder what a quiet evening was like at 16 Wardle Brook Avenue – on the Hattersley over-spill estate, an abysmally under-planned housing expedient with its skyscraper flat blocks and rows and rows of little, grey, brick boxes?

Brady would be playing records of Hitler's speeches; or reading aloud from *Mein Kampf*, or one of his favourite paperbacks; a history of torture or a book of Nazi atrocities. Myra might be learning German, which she did with Brady's encouragement, dyeing her hair a still brighter shade of Nordic blonde, or cleaning her revolvers. (We heard in evidence during the committal proceedings how she always hankered for a Luger.)

It's too easy to make them sound like a family out of a horror comic. I'm afraid that doesn't help one to distinguish between the precise shades of criminality and psychopathy.

In the box we heard Brady speak for the first time on Tuesday afternoon, but it was during a legal submission and couldn't be reported because the jury were out. He has a strong Scots accent and a schoolmasterly manner. Pedantry and perversion, photography and pornography join hands in this case. He is fond of words like 'approximately' and 'phraseology'.

He had a little spat with the Attorney-General, who was testing him out like a matador indulging in some preliminary cloak-play, about taking the oath. The Attorney-General suggested, after Brady had said he didn't believe in it, it was just a symbol, that he could have affirmed. 'I suppose there are more theatrical ways of getting round it,' Brady said with heavy sarcasm. You could sense adolescent aggression and scorn coming off him like steam. Having heard him I could now believe that David Smith was really frightened of him.

On the Friday during his examination in chief by his own counsel, his manner was more subdued. At his day-long cross-examination by the Attorney-General on Monday he was a bit more fiery, but for long periods he was merely answering 'No' or 'I wouldn't know' (which he tended to pronounce 'noo').

The cross-examination of the accused in a murder trial is always the obvious highspot, like Act IV in a Shakespearean tragedy. This cross-examination was perfectly successful. It compelled Brady to tell lie after lie. It went a long way towards corroborating Smith's evidence about the murder of Evans. It made hay of Brady's 'explanation' that the tape recording of Lesley Ann Downey was made as a kind of insurance in case anyone else interfered with the child, of his attempts to incriminate Smith and exculpate Myra.

None the less for some of us it was a bit of an anticlimax in that it never managed – how could it? – to get right inside Brady's mind. He knew he was done for and didn't hide it: 'My train of thought now is that I will be convicted anyway.' Yet he went on keeping up some sort of front and using a form of quibbling ingenuity that must be characteristic.

Perhaps one of his most revealing answers came when the Attorney-General asked him about his collection of pornographic books. 'There are better collections than that in Lords' manors all over the country,' said Brady. This made one wonder if he mightn't be seeing himself as a latter-day de Sade. Obviously his head is stuffed with romantic compensatory fantasies.

Myra was in the box for nearly as long as Brady. She spoke in a low, rather husky voice in that flat north midland accent, with an occasional hint of a Scots intonation.

She complained of a sore throat and for a moment I thought she might be going to crack. Then when they asked her to speak up, she snapped at them. You realized she was in control of herself. Very articulate, she had Brady's barrack-room-lawyer's facility for raising sudden quibbles.

Of the two I think she is possibly the more intelligent. Brady is the pseudo-intellectual, a mood-man. She has a down-to-earth quality. If you were to give an IQ test to the two accused and the two principal witnesses, I suspect the order might be first Myra, then David Smith, then Brady, with Maureen Smith (Myra's sister) last.

Her account of her role during the Lesley Ann Downey tape-recording was preposterous. And when she was contrite, admitting to having been cruel, she seemed to go just so far and no further. And, whenever possible, she revived the fiction that Smith had brought the child to the house and taken her away. She, too, showed remarkable stubbornness in maintaining her front; I felt there was something specifically north-country here. She hated being made to read aloud one passage from the tape transcript when she said to the child, 'don't dally.' It seemed to me that the word 'dally' was too unsophisticated for her liking.

The Attorney-General was scrupulously polite, always calling her Miss Hindley: 'Your shame is a counterfeit shame, Miss Hindley . . . oh Miss Hindley . . .' She stayed self-possessed. When the Attorney-General asked her why they had kept one photograph of her standing by the grave of John Kilbride – because it was 'hardly the most attractive picture of you, Miss Hindley?' – she came back instantly, 'There are a lot of unattractive pictures of me.'

I got the impression of a distinctly powerful personality, whatever she may have been like before she took up with Brady.

In the dock: Brady is thin, bony, rather gangling. Lean face with straight nose jutting out under his rather flat forehead. His dark brown hair is neat and tidy, yet looks faintly dusty. His clothes – grey suit, pale blue shirt, ultramarine, mildly artistic tie – are dateless, not like those of David Smith, who goes in for the gear. One of the first things you notice about him is his bad colour: pale mud. He really does look terribly sick.

Myra by contrast is blooming. Her hair, naturally brown, has been changing colour from week to week. First silver-lilac, then bright canary blonde. She is a big girl with a striking face: fine straight nose, thinnish curved lips, rather hefty chin, blue eyes. Full face she is almost a beauty. The Victorians would have admired her.

She wears a black-and-white speckled coat and skirt and a pale blue shirt open at the neck: it matches Brady's. I suspect she imitates everything he does, even to always keeping her handkerchief neatly folded. At a glance she looks as smartly turned out as a duchess, but when you look closer you see at once that this is mass-produced supermarket chic: there is an ambience of bubblegum and candyfloss.

Both take copious notes and lean over the front of the dock to prod their solicitor, the eupeptic Mr. Fitzpatrick, with a pencil. Occasionally they offer each other a packet of mints. Once during David Smith's evidence Myra flashes Brady a quick bright smile. When he goes into the witness box she gazes at him. When it is her turn, he draws faces on his scribbling pad.

Tea – yes – with some of the hosts of detectives working on this case. We talked about modern youth, violence, censorship, permissiveness and all that. One of them, who is a bit of a sociologist and has a highly specialized knowledge of swinging

Manchester, thought there was a dangerous current of perversion in the air. Kinky had become a household word. He'd seen a shop advertising: NEW LINE IN KINKY RAINCOATS. Why, he said, don't they label them raincoats for sexual perverts and be done with it? He said it twice over. This may be an unduly puritan reaction: it is quite a common one. We shall encounter it more often as a result of this case.

Fantasies: crime reporters are friendly fellows. They go in a good deal for professional cynicism and make use of the whimsicalization of horror as a defence. The Charles Addams drawings and the TV Munster series are much to their liking. I asked one of them if he ever dreamed about his case. He said no, but he'd one rather nightmarish experience when his routine method of sending himself to sleep had failed him. This, which he adapted from Hemingway, consisted in playing an imaginary round of golf on his favourite suburban course, which he knew backwards. Ordinarily, he would drop off after a few holes.

This time it was no use. As soon as he drove into a bunker his ball turned into a child's hand.

I haven't myself dreamed about the case at all, but occasionally in court towards the end of an afternoon I've caught myself lapsing into fantasies. These have taken the form of carrying out vengeance on the accused, which shows how careful you have to be. Once, I said to myself: If I were to put on Batman's gear, swoop down on the dock, which I could easily do from my seat in the gallery, what would the *News of the World* pay for my life story?

I lie awake at 2 a.m. because some race-going son of Belial – there are nightclubs now even in Chester – has jammed the horn of his car. I try to find a suitable text in Sartre's *Saint Genet*, which a kind local friend has lent me; he thinks that Brady might conceivably turn into his opposite. I'm afraid he has a long way to go, and he lacks Genet's talent. How about this?

Thus the evil doer is the Other. Evil – fleeting, artful, marginal evil – can be seen only out of the corner of one's eye and in others . . . The Enemy is our twin brother, our image in the mirror . . . For peace-time, Society has, in its wisdom, created what might be called professional evil doers.

These evil men are as necessary to good men as whores are to decent women. They are fixation abscesses. For a single sadist there is any number of appeased, clarified, relaxed consciousnesses. They are therefore very carefully recruited. They must be bad by birth and without hope of change.

H'm. I think I know what Mr. Justice Fenton Atkinson would say to that. And I rather think I agree with him. We've had rather a surfeit of evil up here. Evil is horrible; it is also banal. I incline at this moment to agree with my favourite crime reporter, who likes to pretend that all murders are fish-and-chip cases – something to wrap the supper in.

And if this sounds unduly philistine let me put it another way. I quote from the schoolmaster Wagner, a celebrated German mass murderer, a paranoiac who went mad in 1913, killed his wife and four children, burned down some houses and a school, and shot nine men. Recovering some sanity, he declared:

The feeling of impotence brings forth the strong words. The bold calls to battle are emitted by the trumpet called persecution-insanity. The signs of the truly strong, however, are repose and good will.

A big murder trial when capital punishment has been abolished is like a Portuguese bullfight. I'm an abolitionist myself, but naturally I can't help wondering how differently those two would behave if they were facing the death penalty. I also wonder if there may not be something in the idea that we, the public, feel that an execution acts like a symbolic scapegoat ceremony.

Waiting for the verdict you feel like a privileged spectator at the Apocalypse. The time factor, however, raises acute mundane problems. Back in court the sense of dramatic symbolism becomes very strong. The prisoners are brought up from the pit to which they will return. The body of the court is the world. The judge re-enters at his own detached prophetic level.

But now, perhaps for the first time, you realize that the jury, as they troop down into their box, have become invested with superior power. Their foreman, who looks like, and, I think, is, an intelligent grocer, has acquired *charisma*.

Mr. Justice Fenton Atkinson has made a great impression here. Always utterly in control, he has been exquisitely civil to everybody. His personality, unlike that of some judges, has a therapeutic quality: it had done a lot to desensationalize the atmosphere. He pronounces sentence in the same quiet tone he has used throughout and refrains from any additional execration. He has already said all he needs to say in two words of his brilliant summing-up: 'utmost depravity'.

As far as I could see, and I was standing quite near, neither Myra nor Brady showed any emotion. They were whisked away, one after the other, in a trice. Brady made a wonderfully characteristic last public utterance when asked – between verdict and sentence – if he had anything to say: 'Only that the revolver was bought in July, '64.' (This referred to a question which the jury had returned, briefly, to ask.) Myra said nothing. She may have swayed slightly.

Raining hard. The crowd outside, which includes a few small children, forms a lane by the door out of which they think They will emerge – though this looks to me like a police diversion. An old white-haired woman, with her leg in an iron brace, is brandishing an enormously thick stick. A Welshman is muttering, 'Ghouls, all bloody ghouls the lot of you! Who's taken my car keys?'

Maurice Richardson's book of collected articles, Fits and Starts, was published in 1979, a year after his death.

LIGHT AND HARD AND READY TO RUMBLE

—

Hugh McIlvanney

Observer
21 May 1966

There never was a world heavyweight like Muhammad Ali. Good looking and witty, he amused press and public with his repartee, and battered opponents with the swiftness of his fists.

Stripped of his title in 1967 for refusing to be drafted – 'I ain't got no quarrel with them Viet Congs' – Muhammad Ali later regained it and fought on until retiring in 1979. Sadly, he now suffers from a form of Parkinsonism, almost certainly the a result of taking too many blows to the head during his boxing career.

Whatever the ultimate results of the mounting pressure now being applied in America to the heavyweight champion of the world, one man who is not likely to benefit is Henry Cooper. When Muhammad Ali leaves Miami for London soon after lunch tomorrow he will weigh less in his street clothes than he did stripped for action against the Canadian George Chuvalo in March. He is, in his own words, 'light and hard and ready to rumble' a full fortnight before he is due to defend his title against Cooper at Highbury Stadium.

'I've never seen you looking so skinny this long before a fight,' said one incredulous local reporter as the champion drummed the speed-ball in the Fifth Street gym. 'If you get any lighter you will be white,' he added and laughed loudly at his own wit. Muhammad Ali did not acknowledge the pun (he rarely sees jokes other than his own). 'Usually I'm 215lb or more at this stage,' he admitted. 'Today I'm 207. I'm like I was when I fought Liston the first time. When I'm like this I got moves you can't even see, and I punch harder, too. That's how it's going to be from here on. I'm giving nothing away. There's so much pressure. They're trying everything to get my title away from me. In Toronto the referee let the man hit me low a hundred times. I'm telling you man, it's a little war. I don't have no return clauses. I got to be well ready.'

For a man seeking that kind of readiness few places have more to offer than the gym that brings a little seedy glamour to the nondescript shops, offices and cheap hotels which make up Fifth Street. One stair up, above a drug store and a shoe repair shop, it is big (thirty yards long and almost as wide), bare and busily peopled on most days with successful professionals (Florentino Fernandez, Gomeo Brennan, Luis

Rodriguez). A few feet from the ring a machine peddles iced Coca Cola but the gym's most bizarre feature is a small room with a 'Ladies' sign reinforced by the warning: 'For women only – fighters keep out.' Angelo Dundee, the small energetic Italian who trains and manages the world champion for the group of Louisville businessmen who hold his contract, dismissed the sign as a sexual fantasy. 'We use that place to store equipment. We never have women here.'

They have had one woman this week, however, Oriana Fallaci, the Italian novelist and journalist, a slight, aggressively curious interloper among the snorting, preoccupied fighters. 'Have you seen the de Sade play?' she said. 'This is it. They're all man.' When Muhammad Ali shook her hand with his eyes averted she asked one of the sparring partners, Chip Johnson, a big, outrageously good-natured negro who was himself flattened by Cooper in one round, to prove his friendship for her by knocking his employer down. Johnson widened his eyes and showed his gold teeth. 'Better lose a friend than lose my head, ma'am. This man is superman.'

Unfortunately, Superman has soft hands. Before sparring with Chip Johnson, the less experienced Willie Johnson and, most impressively, with Jimmy Ellis, a boxer of undoubted class who, at twenty-six, is two years older than the champion but only now growing up to heavyweight, he had pads of foam rubber taped across his knuckles. It was about 2 p.m. Outside the temperature was in the high seventies, and soon he looked as if he had just stepped out of the showers. He boxed six sharp rounds, bringing his total sparring so far to about forty rounds. Ellis's impersonation of Cooper's left hook was close enough to raise a bruise under his left eye. 'I got tagged,' he said later.

To reach the dressing-rooms he had to pass under a large, wrinkled Stars and Stripes, a ponderous cue for questions about his pronouncements on Vietnam that infuriated the majority of Americans. He volunteered no retraction. 'You turn on the radio and you hear: "Twenty-seven Americans was killed in Vietnam today. Two hundred Vietmanese [sic] was killed." Man, it's terrible. I don't like to hear about people being killed. Not anybody.' Then, forced to be more specific about his own attitude: 'America's a white man's country. They got more to fight for than I have.' At that point the conversation gave way to a lecture by Sam Saxon (Cap'n Sam, head of the Black Muslim Mosque in Miami), who has a shoeshine concession at Hialeah and Tropical Park racecourses but makes a more congenial living as bodyguard-companion to the champion. Homilies are Saxon's speciality and he has the kind of physique that encourages people to listen. 'There are 257,255,000 square miles of land in the world,' he announced, throwing in precise figures for the Atlantic and Pacific oceans to show that he knew where the rest of the globe had gone. 'There's room for everybody if they stay where God intended.'

It was agreed that someone who had 'come all the way from London, England', should spend an afternoon with the champion. When he was dressed to go home, in a blue and yellow check shirt and jeans, we walked a hundred yards to a garage where Saxon had parked a white Cadillac. Muhammad Ali was whistling 'A Hard Day's Night', as we drove north-west towards the negro quarter. He stopped, took two metal weights in his hands and began shadow-boxing in the back seat. 'Go round by Sonny's,' he instructed, 'I need a haircut.' The car swung along Second Avenue past open snack counters and cocktail lounges dark as sepulchres to drop us outside 'Nat and Sonny's Downtown Barber Shop and Processing Capitol'. It was closed but a man who unlocked the door said Sonny was expected back momentarily. 'I'll lay around here awhile,' said Muhammad Ali. His idea of laying around seemed to be to move along the pavements at a pace that would have worried an Olympic walker, swooping into soda fountains or disappearing in the gloom of the lounges to kid briefly with the black men who greeted him, and move on as impulsively as he had come. All the time he was enjoying his favourite pastime, talking and playing with children. He cannot let one pass without trying to establish a personal relationship. 'You been good? You gonna give me a hug?' He lifts them high and snuggles them against the smooth, handsome face. Generally they are reserved at first, then recognition shines in their faces as if someone had switched on a light behind their eyes. 'Hey, you're Cassius Clay,' they yell and mob him with questions and demands for autographs. 'Kiss me right here,' one teenage schoolgirl told him, pointing to a discreet spot on her cheek. 'I'm shy,' he said.

After two more checks at Sonny's he signalled a cab, but when we had gone a few yards he told the driver to turn back round the block. We got out and he began to pursue two pretty, brightly dressed young black girls who were crossing the street towards the lounge of the King's Hotel. 'Hey, woman,' he shouted. There was a whispered conversation, then the girls, who had laughed a lot, turned away from the hotel and waved. 'See you,' they called. He turned to me: 'Them girls is prostitutes and I'm trying to convert them.' But he claimed only the most partial success. 'They stopped smokin' but they're still drinking and prostitutin'.'

Finally we took another taxi and drove farther out to the north-west of Miami, to a residential area occupied by lower-middle-class blacks where he has a small, rather boxlike house. Built of cement blocks, it cost around $11,000, appreciably less than the price of most semis in Finchley. In the cramped living-room the only pictures are of Elijah Muhammad and, less conspicuously, the champion. A copy of the Muslim newspaper *Muhammad Speaks* is pinned prominently above the sideboard. At one end of the room is a screen for home movies. He likes 'scary horror movies, westerns and science fiction'. Apart from films and TV he contents himself with going for drives or making strange pilgrimages to Miami Airport. Once he was deeply afraid of flying but now he is fascinated by planes. 'It's nice out there, nobody bothers you.'

Three 'sisters' in white smocks (part of the large entourage that helps to keep him comfortable but broke) had cooked a kosher meal in the kitchen that opens off the living-room. After prayers, said with the hands outstretched, palms upwards, Muhammad Ali had salad and cooked vegetables and then disposed of half-a-dozen lamb chops as if they were digestive biscuits.

Later the two of us went for a walk and he played the Pied Piper again. I suggested that even after one failed marriage he must want children of his own. 'I think I will be married before the year is over,' he said seriously. No, he wasn't going steady, but it would not be hard to find the girl. When we were back at the patch of unfenced lawn in front of his home, he flopped down on a sun chair and prepared to hold court among more children. Leaving him, I had the wild thought that if Henry Cooper stayed at home on 21 May and sent along his young son, Henry Marco, Muhammad Ali might give him the title as a present.

Now writing for the Sunday Times, *Hugh McIlvanney remains the outstanding sports journalist of the past thirty years.*

MEMOIRS OF A TELEVIEWER

———

Keith Waterhouse

Punch
20 July 1966

When it comes to the relationship between the viewer and his television some things, it seems, never change.

Considering what a slice it's taken out of all our lives it's surprising – or come to think of it, perhaps it's not really surprising – how difficult it is to look back on twenty years of television with anything like affection. I'm the first one to go overboard for the golden age of radio and I can match anyone catchphrase for catchphrase on *ITMA* or *Band Waggon* or *Monday Night at Eight*; but even with Leslie Bailey's Scrapbook to drum up the enthusiasm I couldn't see myself getting nostalgic about *The Grove Family* or *What's My Line?*

The other surprising thing, or the other non-surprising thing if you like, is how little television has changed in all these years. I suppose nowadays it's rather more possible to switch on a set without seeing Pat Smythe taking the water-jump, and of course we've got BBC2 and the commercial; but if you were to draw the curtains and give a TV dinner on a plastic tray I could watch *Mrs. Thursday* in the firm belief that it was 1946. And next day in the pub – 'Did you see the play last night?' – the belief would be even stronger. For here we come to the real surprise, and that's how much people still *talk* about television. The novelty value, for something so patently un-novel, is amazing. Are schoolmasters' conferences *still* complaining about the undesirable effects of television? Yes, they are. Are doctors *still* inventing boring new complaints: TV neck and TV shoulder and all the rest of it? Yes, by the casebook. If television hadn't killed vaudeville stone dead there'd be music hall songs about it: 'I saw you on the Telly, Nelly' or 'All the nice girls love a Dalek.' Instead we sing TV jingles. And we talk.

We talk about television as if it were the latest electric brougham, come to scare the horses off the roads. Still, twenty years on, we're wondering if TV should have a red flag in front of it. It's practically impossible for anyone to mount a programme about anything without a nationwide protest from nationwide protestants. It's impossible to raise ever so diffidently the question of another channel without someone calling for a university of the air or something equally depressing, as if we had just been marking time with *Coronation Street*, for the return of the fabulous era of the nightschool and the mechanics' institute lantern lecture. It's impossible, indeed, to mention TV at all in what are laughingly called responsible circles without having one's ear bent on the need for more balance, less political bias and longer, possibly continuous, programmes about emergent Africa.

Of course, all this is a minority view. (Definition: that which gets catered for after 11.15 p.m. on ITV.) To go along with this view one must accept that TV is only illustrated radio after all and that it has a power for good or evil roughly equivalent to the hula-hoop. I grant that there are probably a dozen or twenty documentaries a year that come up to the standard of a feature in one of the colour supplements, but beyond that, and apart from wrestling matches and the occasional assassination, I don't find TV the exciting visual medium it's cracked up to be. (The fact that a man employed, say, to deliver a news broadcast about aviation chooses to do so from the roof of London Airport, where he has to bawl his head off to make himself heard, doesn't make it any more visual, either.) If one accepts this view then this whole talk-talk-talk situation seems as ludicrous as if the whole nation were to gather in bars and restaurants every day to discuss the contents of the *Daily Sketch*.

Perhaps we're not quite as dotty about TV and its effects as we once were. One thing I do remember with affection is that marvellous House of Lords debate on commercial television, when half their lordships referred to it as 'the wireless', when Lord Hailsham as he then was – before he became one of Eamonn Andrews' Sunday night people – asked: 'What guarantee have we that this scheme will be commercially successful?' and when one noble lord after another cheerfully admitted not having a set and in some cases not having ever seen a television programme. Things aren't as bad as that now. It's a long time since the *Evening Standard* was able to run a series of paragraphs called 'People Without TV' which I remember seemed to include practically everyone in the Government; and the ghastly word 'telly', which once conjured up a whitish flickering vision of awful drab families in Dagenham munching Mars bars and neglecting bingo, has entered the mock-cockney vocabulary of Kensington mums who no longer pretend that they have got it for the au pair girl. But even now the boring debate rages on, and the general theme of it is that if we have got to have television it ought to be good for us, like brimstone and treacle. Inside every viewer, it seems, is a little Lord Reith trying to get out.

When the Education Act of 1870 was passed, thus giving a large section of the public the opportunity of reading *Tit-Bits*, there was a strong outbreak of Matthew Arnoldism to the effect that if the public was going to read at all it might as well be reading *The Times*. To which, according to Reginald Pound's book *The Strand Magazine*, Newnes responded: 'At least its contents are wholesome and many of those readers may be led to take an interest in higher forms of literature.' From *Tit-Bits* to Tolstoy – or, as things more mundanely turned out, from *Tit-bits* to the telly.

'I believe I'm going to be rich,' said Newnes. 'It's a licence to print money,' said Roy Thomson, and that's not the only parallel. The Television Act produced the same response as the Education Act on the part of the let-them-eat-Matthew-Arnold faction, and the same defensive reaction on the part of those responsible for television. The ITV companies, which as everyone knows are dedicated to the manufacture and dissemination of hogwash, still spend pages of their annual reports every year in solemn defence of their 'serious' outlook and in listing the obscure, 'serious' fifteen-minute programmes about religion, art and politics which they shuffle on to the air when everyone has gone to bed. The BBC, in order to get its lists on the third channel which is now BBC2, ran for years a priggish campaign in which it boasted of its own 'taste, cultural aims and general sense of responsibility' and warned of the calamitous Gresham's Law effect of commercial television. It's with apparent reluctance that either side admits to being in the entertainment business, possibly because it is unacceptable or incomprehensible to the English mind that anything should publicly admit to be entertainment without being immediately closed down by the police. (I still half expect *Sunday Night at the Palladium* to be raided one of these days.)

The reluctance to concede that television might be a pleasant time-waster like patience or clock golf is one deeply ingrained in the English character. It seems to me more than coincidence that twenty years after the resumption of TV and a dozen years after the commencement of ITV, viewing hours should be roughly equivalent to the permitted hours for consuming alcohol on licensed premises. Why can't I watch TV at breakfast-time? Even if I wanted to watch something wholesome like *Panorama* (which I don't – I've always thought Yogi Bear would go well with a lightly boiled egg) the most hardened and compulsive viewer would shudder at the idea and shrink back, as if I had suggested absinthe at the Methodist picnic. Perhaps it is, after all, more than native English Puritanism. My belief is that the Reith Sunday (*5.30 pm Recital: 6.0 pm Religious poetry of the 17th century; 9.05 pm Hastings Municipal Orchestra*) got deep into the national unconscious in the u-days of broadcasting. Now TV entertainment parallels bed-wetting in its inducement of a guilt trauma.

I'm not being cynical about all this, or at least not much. It really does seem a pity that in searching for Our Very Own Golden TV Centre we refuse to allow television to slip into the natural order of things and continue to saddle it with a significance which it simply doesn't have. From time to time I go to the United States, where of course there's multi-channel TV operating more or less round the clock. The thing that impresses me is that in spite of something like 120 viewing hours a day – well over four times the English ration – *nobody talks about it*. It's accepted as one of the amenities of life, like company water. A large part of its output is of course junk of an almost inspired order, and another large part of its output is the slick, packaged show (which, come to think of it, is rather better than the show done up like a parcel of secondhand clothes which is what we usually get here in between 'serious' programmes). But at its best – for example, in the *one-hour* news reports which New Yorkers can see every night of the week – American television has a vitality and urgency which completely escapes our own guilt-ridden, Charter-watching, Gresham's Law-obsessed product. I think the Americans have come to terms with television – they no longer imagine that it's Joanna Southcott's box. The relaxed attitude of both viewed and viewer often, paradoxically, produces a spontaneous excitement. I wonder if that will ever happen here? It would certainly be something to talk about in the pub next morning.

Keith Waterhouse remains one of the most prolific, versatile and readable writers in Britain. In addition to writing a column in the Daily Mail, *he is a novelist and playwright.*

THE WORLD CUP FINAL

—

Hugh McIlvanney

This article is an extended version of the report which appeared in the Observer *on 31 July 1966.*

Wembley does not always stir the spirit. As a football stadium it is overrated. The slow, sweaty crush out of the tube station and the long trudge along Stadium Way, where ticket touts and vendors of smelly hot-dogs wait in ambush, are not immediately rewarded. The closer you come to the place the shabbier it looks, twin towers notwithstanding. Under the stands there is the grey, cavernous gloom of most English grounds.

But Wembley is lucky enough to have occasions that work a metamorphosis, that can make grown men persuade themselves that the hideously inconvenient journey from London is an adventure and can transmute the undistinguished concrete bowl into what the more imaginative chroniclers of our time would call 'a seething cauldron'. FA Cup finals can do that, especially when one of the clubs comes from the North of England and brings its raucous trainloads of supporters to drink at dawn in Covent Garden and spill their beery optimism over the terraces. One wondered if the World Cup could do as much for Wembley. In the event, it did far more. It was impossible to define the atmosphere precisely but it was palpable, and it was unique. It was like walking into an ordinary, familiar room and knowing instinctively that something vital and unbearably dramatic was happening, perhaps a matter of life and death. The people hurrying and jostling and laughing nervously inside had a flushed, supercharged look, but if they were high it was with excitement. 'It's bloody electric,' said one of the doormen. He had found the word.

Down on the field the combined bands of the Portsmouth Command and the Portsmouth Group, Royal Marines, had found the music, a tune for each of the sixteen competing nations. The North Koreans, whose own community singing is probably a little hard to follow, had to settle for a thing called Oriental Patrol. It did not matter much, for the roaring and chanting from the terraces, where the red, black and yellow flags of Germany were in no danger of being submerged among the Union Jacks and English banners, was loud enough to make everything sound alike. It might have been Liverpool's Anfield (England did wear red), and there can be no finer tribute. The weather was to fluctuate unpredictably between bright sunshine and squalls of driving rain, the fortunes of both teams to swing wildly between elation and frustration, but the crowd would remain constantly exhilarated, buoyed by an incredible flood of incident. When the bands played the National Anthem the

English supporters came together in a great chauvinistic choir. *Deutschland uber Alles* boomed out in its wake and the battle was on.

The Germans began rather nervously, standing off from the tackle and letting the England forwards move without conspicuous hindrance up to the edge of the penalty area. Bobby Charlton and Peters were able to work the ball along the left at their leisure and there was anxiety in the German defence before the cross was cleared. But that was a tranquil interlude compared with what happened after eight minutes. An intelligent crossfield pass from Hurst set Stiles free on the right and his high centre beat Tilkowski before Hottges headed it away. The ball was returned smartly by Bobby Charlton and Tilkowski had so much trouble punching it off Hurst's head that he knocked himself out. The goalkeeper was prostrate, the whistle had gone and the defenders had stopped challenging before Moore put the ball in the net. The crowd cheered anyway, in the hope that next time it would be the real thing. They had reason to be optimistic, for England were dominating these early moments, running and passing with fine confidence on the wet surface. Without Schulz, patrolling tirelessly behind the main line of four backs, calmly averting crises, Germany would have come under severe strain. Many of their problems came from Bobby Charlton, wandering purposefully all over the field, bringing composure and smoothness wherever he appeared, again making comparisons with Di Stefano seem relevant. Beckenbauer, asked to rein in his own aggressive impulses to concentrate on subduing the Manchester United player, was in for a thankless first half.

Yet it was Jack Charlton, carrying the ball forward on his forehead with a skill that would have done credit to his brother, who initiated England's next important attack. He strode swiftly out of defence and his perfectly judged diagonal pass let Peters hit a quick, powerful shot from well outside the area. Tilkowski, already revealing an uncertainty that sharpened the appetite of the England forwards, dived desperately to his left and punched the ball round the post. Hurst met Ball's corner but sent the volley too high. At that point Weber chose to give the sort of agonised performance that had been one of the less admirable characteristics of the German players in the competition. But Gottfried Dienst quickly made it plain that nobody was being fooled and suggested it was time to get on with the game. Peters certainly did, surging in from the right wing to shoot only two feet wide from twenty-five yards.

Then, stunningly, in the thirteenth minute England found themselves a goal behind. And it was a goal that anyone who had seen their magnificent defensive play earlier in the tournament could hardly believe. Held glided a high cross from the left wing and Wilson, jumping for the ball in comfortable isolation, amazingly headed it straight to the feet of Haller, standing in an orthodox inside-right position a dozen yards out from Banks. The blond forward had time to steady, pivot and aim his right-foot shot along the ground into the far corner.

There were fears that the Germans would try to make that goal win the cup, that an open, invigorating match would be reduced to an exasperating siege. It took England only six minutes to reassure us. Overath had been warned for a bad foul on Ball and now he committed another one on Moore, tripping the England captain as he turned away with the ball. Moore himself took the free kick and from forty yards out near the left touchline he flighted it beautifully towards the far post. Hurst, timing his run superbly to slip through the defence much as he had done against Argentina, struck a flawless header low inside Tilkowski's right-hand post. Moore held one arm aloft in a gladiator's salute while Hurst was smothered in congratulations. It was another reminder of the huge contribution West Ham were making to England's success in the World Cup.

There were many free kicks but a high percentage of them could be traced to the officiousness of the referee. When Dienst took Peter's name for shirt-pulling, Schnellinger placed the kick carefully for Seeler to outjump the English defence and force in a header. But the ball curved tamely into Banks's hands. Seeler was generally more damaging, both in the air and on the ground, and one through pass in front of Haller demanded an alert intervention from Banks.

At that stage, however, the more sustained aggression was still coming from England. Moore was showing wonderful control and assurance, driving up among his forwards, joining readily in the moves begun by Bobby Charlton. It was unfortunate that Charlton could not be in two places at once. Several of the attacks he conceived in deep positions cried out to be climaxed with his striking power. Peters, who was his partner in much of the midfield work, was also the one who went nearest to his cleanness of shot, but so far most of the West Ham man's attempts had been from a range that favoured the goalkeeper, even a goalkeeper like Tilkowski. Thus it was Hurst, with his instinct for being in the right place at the right time and his marvellous ability in the air, who was the most direct threat to the Germans. He proved it again when Cohen crossed the ball long from the right and he rose to deflect in another header which Tilkowski could only scramble outside his right-hand post. Ball turned the ball back into the goalmouth and the desperation was unmistakeable as Overath came hurtling in to scythe it away for a corner.

With about ten minutes left of the first half the Germans, quite suddenly, put strenuous pressure on the English defence. They were using the gifted, resourceful Overath to create in midfield, with Haller between him and the three striking forwards, Seeler, Held and Emmerich. Beckenbauer joined the link-men when he could afford to leave Bobby Charlton, but that was a luxury he rarely enjoyed until the Englishman's selfless running began to slow him down in the second half. Held was the most persistently dangerous of his team's forwards throughout the two hours of the match and it was his determination that began this period of German ascendancy before the interval. Ball and Cohen made the mistake of toying with him near the byline and Jack Charlton, who was maintaining the remarkable standard of his World Cup performances, had to come in with a prodigious sweeping tackle to rescue them. It cost Charlton a corner and the corner almost cost England a goal. The ball went to Overath and from twenty yards he drove it in fiercely at chest height. Banks beat it out and when Emmerich hammered it back from an acute angle the goalkeeper caught it surely.

After forty-two minutes Hunt had the kind of miss that was bound to revive comparisons with Greaves. Wilson headed into goal and Hurst again soared above everybody to steer the ball down to Hunt. But the Liverpool man came round behind it rather ponderously and by the time he forced in his left foot volley Tilkowski was in the way.

One of the features of the play was that defensive errors were occurring far more frequently than they had done in most previous games in the series. After Wilson's disaster, the Germans had been slightly the shakier but they could be excused their bewilderment as Bobby Charlton stroked a subtle pass into their midst. Peters could not quite reach it. Then, to stress the hectic, fluctuating pattern of the first half that was just ending, Overath had a bludgeoning twenty-yard shot turned brilliantly over the cross bar by Banks.

The rain came again at the beginning of the second half, falling like sequins in the sunshine. Charlton fell, too, rather more heavily, after being tacked by Schulz, but the claims for a penalty were understandably half-hearted. The first to assert himself was Ball, and it was no brief flourish. From then until the Cup was won he was the most impressive player on the field. In the first half he had worked with his usual inexhaustible energy but had never quite shaken off Schnellinger, who set out to track him everywhere. A redhead and a blond, they were invariably close enough to be advertising the same shampoo. But after the interval Schnellinger, who has held some of the most menacing forwards in the game, found Ball too much. The little man simply went on and on, becoming more impertinently skilful, more astonishingly mobile by the minute. However, in the long period of deadlock following the interval, when both sides were steadying their heartbeats after the tumult of that first three-quarters of an hour, even Ball's dynamism was not enough. Charlton was suffering for the way he had punished himself to mould England's pattern in the first half and, if Hurst was still outleaping the German defenders, Hunt lacked the pace or inventiveness to outwit them on the ground. Both defences were in command, England's closing on the opposition with consuming vigour, Germany's blocking the path to goal like a white wall in which the cement was hardening.

Fortunately for England, the wall was not as formidable as it looked. With thirteen minutes to go Ball won a corner, took it himself and saw the ball diverted to Hurst. His shot from the left was deflected across goal by a defender and Peters, strangely neglected by the Germans, came in to take the ball on the half-volley and sweep it in from four or five yards. It was another West Ham goal, and there were more to come.

With only four minutes remaining, England had a chance to crush their opponents. An inspired pass from Ball sent Hunt clear on the left. Bobby Charlton and Hurst were on his right and only Schulz stood between them and the goal. It was a three to one situation, something that should bring a goal at any level of football. But Hunt's pass was ill-timed, slackly delivered and too square. Bobby Charlton was committed to a hasty swipe and the result was a mess.

In the very last minute England were made to pay a cruel price for that carelessness. Jack Charlton was doubtfully penalized after jumping to a header and from the free kick Emmerich drove the ball through the line of English defenders. As it cannoned across the face of the goal Schnellinger appeared to play it with a hand, but the referee saw nothing illegal and Weber at the far post was able to score powerfully. The fact that these German defenders were crowding in on Banks indicates what a despairing effort this attack was. Such an injustice, coming just fifteen seconds from the end of the ninety minutes, would have broken most teams. But England, after a momentary show of disgust, galloped into extra time as if the previous hour-and-a-half had never happened. Appropriately, it was Ball who showed the way with a wonderful run and a twenty-yard shot which Tilkowski edged over the bar. Bobby Charlton followed with a low one that the goalkeeper pushed against his left-hand post.

The Germans looked weary but their swift breaks out of defence were still dangerous. A pass from Emmerich gave Held an opening and only unaccustomed slowness in controlling the ball enabled Stiles to clear. Held compensated for this by sprinting away from all challengers and turning the ball back invitingly across goal. But there was no one following up.

Having lost their lead through one controversial goal, England now regained it with another in the tenth minute of extra time. Ball made space for himself on the right and when the ball went across, Hurst resolutely worked for a clear view of goal. His rising right-foot shot on the turn from ten yards was pushed against the underside of the crossbar by Tilkowski and when it bounced the England players appealed as one man for a goal. The referee spoke to the Russian linesman on the side away from the main stand and, after an agony of waiting, awarded a goal. The delayed action cheers shook the stadium.

But this match had not yet taken its full toll of our nerves. The hammer blow England had received at the end of the hour and a half was almost repeated in the final minute of extra time when Seeler lunged in and narrowly failed to make decisive contact with a headed pass by Held. And that was only the prelude to the climax. Nonchalantly breasting the ball down in front of Banks, Bobby Moore relieved a perilous situation and then moved easily away, beating challengers and exchanging passes with Ball. Glancing up, he saw Hurst ten yards inside the German half and lifted the pass accurately to him. The referee was already looking at his watch and three England supporters had prematurely invaded the pitch as Hurst collected the ball on his chest. At first he seemed inclined to dawdle-out time. Then abruptly he went pounding through in the inside-left position, unimpeded by the totally spent German defenders, his only obstacle his own impending exhaustion. As Tilkowski prepared to move out, Hurst summoned the remnants of his strength, swung his left foot and smashed the ball breathtakingly into the top of the net.

The scene that followed was unforgettable. Stiles and Cohen collapsed in a tearful embrace on the ground, young Ball turned wild cartwheels and Bobby Charlton dropped to his knees, felled by emotion. Within seconds the game was over and the players, ignoring the crippling weariness of a few minutes before, were hugging and laughing and crying with their manager, Alf Ramsey, and the reserves who must go through the rest of their lives with bitter-sweet memories of how it looked from the touchline. 'Ramsey, Ramsey,' the crowd roared and in his moment of vindication it was a tribute that no one could begrudge him.

Eventually Moore led his men up to the Royal Box to receive the Jules Rimet trophy from the Queen and the slow, ecstatic lap of honour began. 'Ee-aye-addio, we've won the Cup,' sang the crowd, as Moore threw it in a golden arc above his head and caught it again. England had, indeed, won the Cup, won it on their merits, producing more determined aggression and flair than they had shown at any earlier stage of the competition. As hosts, they had closed their World Cup with a glorious bang that obliterated memories of its grey, negative beginnings. In such a triumph there could be no failures (the very essence of Ramsey's England was their team play), but if one had to name outstanding heroes they were Ball, Moore, Hurst and the brothers Charlton, the one exhibiting the greatness we always knew he had, the other attaining heights we never thought he could reach.

The Germans had been magnificent opponents and they deserved their own lap of honour at Wembley and the acclaim that awaited them at home. If they were in the West End of London that Saturday night they must have seen some interesting sights.

The area was taken over for one great informal party. Some people said it was another VE night, but perhaps that was not the most tactful analogy. At the Royal Garden Hotel, where the English team were spending the night to unwind, there were visits from Harold Wilson and George Brown, who joined in the singing with the crowds outside. Hundreds of people were still dancing a conga around Charing Cross Station at midnight and nearby, in Trafalgar Square, there was the ritual of leaping into the fountains. For most of the nation, however, it was enough to be bathed in euphoria.

England 4, West Germany 2.

FROM THE EDINBURGH FESTIVAL

—

Ronald Bryden
Observer
28 August 1966

Rosencrantz and Guildenstern Are Dead *was the play which launched the career of Tom Stoppard. Within a year it was playing at the National Theatre in London.*

The best thing at Edinburgh so far is the new play by Tom Stoppard staged in Cranston Street Hall by the Oxford Theatre Group, *Rosencrantz and Guildenstern Are Dead*. Mr. Stoppard has taken up the vestigial lives of Hamlet's two Wittenberg cronies, and made out of them an existentialist fable unabashedly indebted to *Waiting for Godot*, but as witty and vaulting as Beckett's original is despairing.

The play does not pretend to know more of the pair's lives than Shakespeare: it's point is, neither do they. While the violent drama at Elsinore unrolls off-stage, occasionally sucking them into its fury, they spin coins endlessly in ante-rooms, wondering what is going on, what will happen next, what will become of them? They sense that they should escape, but what to? The tragedy of Denmark offers them the only significance, the only identities life has held out to them – it offers them roles.

Behind the fantastic comedy, you feel allegoric purposes move: is this our relation to our century, to the idea of death, to war? But while the tragedy unfurls in this comic looking-glass, you're too busy with its stream of ironic invention, metaphysical jokes and linguistic acrobatics to pursue them. Like *Love's Labour's Lost*, this erudite comedy, punning, far-fetched, leaping from depth to dizziness, is the most brilliant debut by a young playwright since John Arden's.

After several years as chief drama critic of the Observer, *Ronald Bryden joined the Royal Shakespeare Company in 1972 as a play adviser. He is now a professor of drama at Massey College, Toronto.*

PAUL McCARTNEY

—

Hunter Davies
Sunday Times
18 September 1966

At this point the Beatles had finished touring. Their future was uncertain. But Lennon and McCartney were without equal as writers of popular songs. The release of the album Revolver *showed the path they were to follow.*

Paul McCartney was in his new mansion in St John's Wood. He lives alone. A Mr. and Mrs. Kelly look after him. Nothing so formal as housekeeper and butler. Their job, he says, is just to fit in.

The house has a huge wall and an electrically operated black door to keep out non-Beatle life. Inside there is some carefully chosen elderly furniture. Nothing flash, affected or even expensive-looking. The dining-room table was covered with a white lace tablecloth. Very working-class posh.

Mr. McCartney, along with Mr. Lennon, is the author of a song called 'Eleanor Rigby'. No pop song of the moment has better words or music.

'I was sitting at the piano when I thought of it. Just like Jimmy Durante. The first few bars just came to me. And I got this name in my head – Daisy Hawkins, picks up the rice in the church where a wedding has been. I don't know why. I can hear a whole song in one chord. In fact, I think you can hear a whole song in one note, if you listen hard enough. But nobody ever listens hard enough.

'Okay, so that's the Joan of Arc bit. I couldn't think of much more, so I put it away for a day. Then the name Father McCartney came to me – and all those lonely people. But I thought people would think it was supposed to be my Dad, sitting knitting his socks. Dad's a happy lad. So I went through the telephone book and I got the name McKenzie.

'I was in Bristol when I decided Daisy Hawkins wasn't a good name. I walked round looking at the shops and I saw the name Rigby. You got that? Quick pan to Bristol. I can just see this as a Hollywood musical . . .

'Then I took it down to John's house in Weybridge. We sat around, laughing, got stoned and finished it off. I thought of the backing, but it was George Martin who finished it off. I just go bash, bash on the piano. He knows what I mean.

'All our songs come out of our imagination. There never was an Eleanor Rigby.

'One of us might think of a song completely, and the other just add a bit. Or we might write alternate lines. We never argue. If one of us says he doesn't like a bit, the other agrees. It just doesn't matter that much. I care about being a songwriter. But I don't care passionately about each song.

'"Eleanor" is a big development as a composition. But that doesn't mean "Yellow Submarine" is bad. It was written as a commercial song, a kid's song. People have said, "Yellow submarine? What's the significance? What's behind it?" Kids get it straight away. I was playing with my little step-sister the other day, looking through a book about Salvador Dali. She said, "Oh look, a soft watch." She accepted it. She wasn't frightened or worried. Kids have got it. It's only later they get messed up.

'I tried once to write a song under another name, just to see if it was the Lennon-McCartney bit that sold our songs. I called myself Bernard Webb – I was a student in Paris and very unavailable for interviews. The song was "Woman", for Peter and Gordon. They made it a big hit. Then it came out it was me. I realized that when I saw a banner at a concert saying "Long Live Bernard Webb".'

'We'd need a properly controlled experiment to find out how much our names really mean, now, but I can't be bothered. I can't play the piano, or read or write music. I've tried three times in my life to learn, but never kept it up for more than three weeks. The last bloke I went to was great. I'm sure he could teach me a lot. I might go back to him. It's just the notation – the way you write down notes, it doesn't *look* like music to me.

'John's now trying acting again, and George has got his passion for the sitar and all the Indian stuff. He's lucky. Like somebody's lucky who's got religion. I'm just looking for something I enjoy doing. There's no hurry. I have the time and the money.

'People think we're not conceited, but we are. If you ask me if I wrote good or bad songs, I'd be thick to say bad, wouldn't I? It's true we're lucky, but we got where we are because of what we *did*.

'The girls waiting outside. I don't despise them. I don't think fans are humiliating themselves. I queued up at the Liverpool Empire for Wee Willie Harris's autograph. I wanted to do it. I don't think I was being stupid.

'I can go out and around more than people think, without being recognized. People never really believe it's you. They don't expect to see you in the street, so you can get away with it.

'I think we can go on as the Beatles for as long as we want to, writing songs, making records. We're still developing. I've no ambitions, just to enjoy myself. We've had all the ego bit, all about wanting to be remembered. We couldn't do any better than we've done already, could we?'

Hunter Davies is one of the great newspaper interviewers, while his biography, The Beatles, *remains the best account of the group. The author of many other books, he recently published an anthology of interviews.*

NOW THERE IS ONLY ONE

—

Cassandra
Daily Mirror
30 September 1966

Nowhere was the Cold War more bleakly unyielding than in Spandau Prison, Berlin.

One overcast morning in Berlin more than seventeen years ago – it was 16 March 1949 – a small Volkswagen motor-car drew up outside the main gate of Spandau Prison in West Berlin.

The cheerful occupant (the smile was about to fade from his ruddy countenance) popped a Contax camera out and took a picture of the sombre, red-bricked gaol with its twin entrance turrets and its massively heavily-barred gates.

In a trice bedlam – organized bedlam – broke loose. Whistles blew. Voices Bellowed: *'Halte!'* And white-helmeted guards raced out, shouting.

They hurled open the door of the car, grabbed the photographer, seized his camera and, in a matter of seconds, rushed him into the main guardroom – which is first on the left up some stone steps when you've been slung through the main gate.

Those detained against their will that day in the Allied Prison Berlin Spandau, Wilhelm Strasse, 23, suddenly increased.

There were on that grey morning long ago: Grand Admiral Doenitz, Deputy Fuehrer Rudolf Hess, Hitler Youth Leader Baldour von Schirach, Reichsbank Minister Walther Funk, Grand Admiral Erich Raeder, Minister of War Production Albert Speer, Foreign Minister and Protector of Bohemia and Moravia Baron Konstantin von Neurath.

AND ME.

It was a daft thing to do.

There are notices forbidding entrance and the taking of photographs. The guards on the watchtowers have orders to shoot and the whole hideous circular structure is surrounded by a high-voltage electric fence.

The Americans – who fortunately at the time were doing their monthly rota of duty and not the Russians – were suitably rude, and after weak-kneed protests from me ending in my passport being taken away, the British Colonel was informed.

In those days our military divided everything in life and our behaviour towards it into two classes: 'Good Show and Tickety-boo!' and 'Not Good Show and Not Tickety-boo.'

The Colonel told me that things were a damn bad show and distinctly non-tickety-boo. But he got my release and my camera back – minus the film, of course – and inside three hours I was free.

Today I stood outside Spandau again. Neurath, Raeder and Funk are dead. Doenitz is alive and remarkably chirpy, living near Hamburg, after having served his ten years.

And now within a few hours Baldur von Schirach and Albert Speer, having been entombed for some 2,000 days and nights, are about to be released.

Only Deputy Fuehrer Rudolf Hess, the crazed husk of a man now in his seventy-third year, will be left to die alone in Spandau. There is no release for him.

He has now been under lock and key since the night of 10 May 1941, twenty-five endless years ago, when he climbed into his Messerschmitt and flew to Scotland on his hare-brained romantic scheme to see the Duke of Hamilton and impose peace on Great Britain.

Schirach and Speer, by the time you read these words, will have spent their last night in Spandau. They will emerge to a baffling new world they have never seen.

Their names are forgotten, and most of the younger people in Germany have never heard of them.

There will be at least one hundred cameramen outside the Spandau gates, and it is highly unlikely that any of them will be arrested for non-tickety-boo behaviour.

The telly will be there (neither Speer nor Schirach has ever seen it) and nobody will give the Hitler salute.

At the stroke of midnight Speer and Schirach, met by their relatives in two cars, will emerge from the inner courtyard. It will be twenty years to the day, almost to the hour, since they were sentenced at Nuremberg.

Speer, the least repulsive and easily the most intelligent of the seven convicts of Spandau, will drive about a mile to the nearby Gerbus Hotel in the fashionable Grunewald district.

For one-third of his life he has been unable to move more than forty yards from his cell, measuring only eight feet long by five feet wide. It is furnished with an army cot-type bed, a rough wooden chair, a tiny table and a lavatory basin.

For two decades that has been the entire world of Number Five Spandau, for Speer, in common with the others, is not even granted the identity of his own name. At one minute past midnight tonight one-time brilliant Minister of War Production will be on his way to a suite in a luxury hotel with the complete freedom of Western Germany and a welcome in such other countries as may care to admit him.

Both he and Schirach may be rich men, for the figure of half a million marks in fees from a German magazine has been mentioned. Speer will join his brave and affectionate wife and their six children in a more than comfortable home in Heidelberg.

Few men in the history of the world have faced such a sudden transition and will undergo such an emotional storm as Speer. He has been plunged from the flaunting, ruthless heights of Nazi comfort into a completely new world that he has never seen.

As with Speer so with Schirach. True his wife has deserted him, and his health, and especially his eyesight, has been bad. But his son Klaus, now aged thirty-one, a successful lawyer, is expected to meet him, and there are said to be ample family funds available.

Rudolf Hess, silent, solitary and half mad, alone remains. What is he thinking of today when his lucky companions Speer and Schirach will vanish from his life for ever?

He is finally and completely on his own.

The Russians, it is said, will never free him and even if they were inclined to do so they are highly unwilling to surrender this pitiable symbol of four-Power authority in Berlin.

So far it has cost Great Britain £147,000 to keep the original seven men in Spandau. The United States, Russia, France and West Germany have also paid their share.

Now it is estimated that Hess will cost the best part of £100,000 a year to keep in solitary confinement which, it should be noted, was not described in his sentence in Nuremberg.

Allied justice could easily be going astray here.

If things go on as they are Hess will be attended by a military governor, twenty-eight soldiers, five warders, a varying number of doctors and several cooks.

Different Government departments in London, Washington, Moscow, Paris and Bonn will administer his endless misery.

Never has one ageing demented criminal, chained by life to exist in melancholy torment, had such a retinue in a jail built to hold 500 prisoners.

Commonsense, let alone charity and a feeling for economic house-keeping, cries out that what remains of the man should be left to die outside of the bars.

The price of his evil can never be repaid, for he now has nothing left in expiation.

Britain, the US and France are known to be willing to be rid of their wretched captive.

Can it be that the thirst of Soviet vengeance is not slaked?

*

Details have come through of the final poignant moments when Prisoner Number Seven, as he is known, said goodbye to Schirach and Speer on the day they left and the aged battered creature was left to die in solitary confinement.

He walked in the prison yard on that last afternoon with Schirach, who tried to cheer him up. Speer took a long look at his flowers in the prison garden. Hess listened quietly to it all but said nothing and gave no indication that he had heard the kindly but futile words of encouragement for the empty future and the desolation that lie ahead.

At five o'clock he had a meal, and as was the rule for all three prisoners he put his tray with his plates and his cup in the corridor outside his door.

Then he asked for the chief warder and requested that as a favour the light in the little cell that had been his living tomb for twenty years might be switched off at 5.45 instead of 6.45 p.m. He shuffled in.

They switched it off and the old man was left alone in the dark. There is still a tiny place for pity.

Rudolph Hess remained in Spandau Prison until he managed to commit suicide with an electric flex in August 1987.

As Cassandra, William Connor proved in over thirty campaigning years of service to the Daily Mirror *that a columnist in a tabloid newspaper does not have to pander to the lowest prejudices of his readers. His was a massive influence for tolerance and compassion. He died in 1967.*

ABERFAN: A WHISTLE AND A SHOUT, 'QUIET!' THEN ALL STOPS

—

Tony Geraghty

Guardian
22 October 1966

One hundred and sixteen children and twenty-eight adults died in the South Wales village of Aberfan when a coal slag heap slipped down a mountain, burying them alive.

In the semi-darkness, the front of the school looks in not too bad a shape; it is when you pass through the school gates into the mud and clinker that covers what once was the playground that the full magnitude and near hopelessness of what has happened hits you.

The back of the school, which once faced uphill, has been smashed and laid bare as if the foot of some careless giant had crushed it. The gable ends of the adjoining wings of the building are all that is above ground level.

Below them the classrooms, or some of them, have been cleared of rubble and light shines into them. From the mound behind the school, these rooms, full of old and young men digging furiously, a priest standing among them, have the air of a fairy cavern.

But in spite of appearances, there are other signs that there is nothing hallucinatory about what has happened in Merthyr. The air is thick with dust for a mile around and blindingly light.

The night buzzes with the roar of half a dozen mechanical excavators, some of which dig individual holes at sensitive spots, foraging mechanical arms into the ground in search of life. So many tracked vehicles have moved in here that the ground shifts and changes by the minute and rescue workers, streaming sweat, stumble like moles into the daylight, bumping into one another.

All the noise and activity gradually dies in response to a police whistle. 'Quiet, please!' roars a police sergeant in a voice that must dominate his choir. 'Stop the machines. Stop walking about now, will you?' No explanation is needed. We are all listening for signs of survival somewhere under that beastly oily black mound. After perhaps a minute's pause the whistle blows once more. It is the signal to continue digging.

Just at the back of the school one of the foraging, roaring excavators is picking at a hole about twelve feet deep under the arc lights. In this pit students from Swansea work alongside Civil Defence workers and professional miners. It contains a few grubby pieces of stone and wood. There, the police sergeant explains as he hands an extra light to one of the workers prodding at something, are the remnants of a farmhouse. But the farmhouse, he adds, as if he himself doesn't quite believe it, stood up there, 200 yards away or more up the hill. Now, they believe that this wreckage, mixed with the remains of the school playground, may contain other bodies.

Like others on the site he is utterly calm, chatting even. No matter how fast they work, the rescuers know that for some this can never be fast enough, and that in any case everyone here is in for a long haul.

Barely past the school the main force of the landslip has hammered across Moy Road and thudded into houses on the other side of the street. It is at this point that the street totally ceases to exist. A barrier of oozing clinker is banked completely across the street to a depth varying between twelve and perhaps forty or fifty feet. It is here that thirteen houses stood until this morning.

On the mud fifty or more men dig, and dig, and dig. 'Let's have the pump!' comes the shout. From nowhere it seems, twelve sweating, swearing men stagger like gunners under a limber up the slime under the crushing weight of a heavy water pump. God knows how they will descend safely into the hole where the pump is needed, but just now they don't seem too worried about that.

The mud extends like a glacier for perhaps 400 yards, before more houses spring up from the mess. Somewhere around the bottom of this glacier there is more digging, more light, and a fire is burning. No one knows why.

Aberfan scarred Tony Geraghty emotionally. He says now: 'No other experience – a childhood in the London blitz or military service as a Para followed by work as a war correspondent – touched me like this. I still weep about it sometimes.' Now an author of military histories, inlcuding **Who Dares Wins**, *the story of the SAS, he is currently researching a secret history of the Cold War.*

MAO'S BOLD STROKE

—

Victor Zorza

Guardian
1966

While wrecking China with his Cultural Revolution, Chairman Mao still had time for personal propaganda. Not all journalists reported this momentous event with the same drily detached view as Victor Zorza.

It was a great day for the Chinese, all 700,000,000 of them, when Chairman Mao swam the Yangtse. He was 'relaxed and easy', the official New China News Agency informed the nation yesterday, when he stepped into the water at Wuhan on the Sunday before last, 'braving the winds and the waves'.

Why it was a great day not only for the Chinese but for the people of the whole world is explained by the official news agency: 'The happy news about Chairman Mao's latest swim in the Yangtse soon spread through Wuhan. The whole of this triple city was overjoyed as the news passed from one person to another. Everybody was saying: "Our respected and beloved leader Chairman Mao is in such wonderful health. This is the greatest happiness for the entire Chinese people and for the revolutionary people throughout the world!"'

Chairman Mao is seventy-two, and the corrupt scribblers of the capitalist press have been saying that his prolonged absences from the public scene suggest that all might not be well with his health. That, presumably, is why everybody in Wuhan was remarking so spontaneously on Comrade Mao's fitness.

He stood on deck, says the agency meaningfully, 'with glowing ruddy cheeks and in buoyant spirits,' and when the time came, he 'trod firmly' down the gangway. Then it happened: 'After dipping his body into the water, he stretched out his arms and swam with steady strokes.'

Let no one think that any other man of seventy-two could have done the same: 'The Yangtse was in spate. Its currents were swift. On the broad expanse of water, Chairman Mao at times swam sidestroke, advancing as he cleaved through the waves, and at times he floated and had a view of the azure sky above.' But all those millions in China and elsewhere who think that their beloved leader should not take risks with his life may rest assured.

In the water with him were the first secretary of the provincial party committee, and 'a group of husky young men and women who swam closely beside him' – not to mention the 5,000 other contestants taking part in the cross-Yangtse swim. Nor should anyone imagine that he was out of breath with his exertions. 'As Chairman

Mao advanced through the waves, he chatted with those around him . . . when he discovered that one of the young women knew only one swimming stroke.'

Chairman Mao taught her the backstroke. 'He said: "The Yangtse is deep and its currents are swift, so one can build up one's body and will."'

It seems that there was a moment of panic when 'a ten-metre-per-second wind swept over the broad expanse of the river, throwing up big waves.' A boat moved towards Chairman Mao to take him on board. Repeatedly, the first secretary begged him to have a rest. 'In the best of spirits, Chairman Mao said, "it has not even been an hour yet" – and went on swimming.'

Moreover, the party official insisted, and exactly one hour and five minutes after the beginning of the adventure, Chairman Mao, still evidently in the best of spirits, said playfully to him: 'You are the first secretary of the provincial party committee here, so I obey your order.' The great exploit was over. He had swam thirty li, or just under ten miles – downstream, of course. And at the end of it all, said the news agency, he was still 'vigorous and showed no sign of fatigue'.

Mao always seems to take to the water when the rumours about his health become too persistent. The news agency recalled yesterday that after Mao swam across the river ten years ago he 'wrote a poem full of brilliance and boldness'.

Mao, evidently, likes to live dangerously. The present swimming contest was clearly not without political significance. The swimmers carried placards which proclaimed that 'the imperialists are pushing China around in such a way that China must deal with them seriously'. And the speaker who had opened the proceedings reminded them of the 'great proletarian cultural revolution', which is Chinese for the purge now in progress against those party officials who had dared to challenge Mao's leadership.

China's 'masses of workers, peasants, and soldiers', he said, were 'sweeping away all monsters and demons with the force of an avalanche'. In case any of the monsters think Mao is on his last legs, he isn't – or so they say.

Victor Zorza began writing for the Guardian *in 1950 when he was twenty-five and by the Sixties his reputation as a Kremlinologist extended to more than twenty of the world's leading newspapers, including the* Washington Post *and Le Figaro. In 1969 he won the first Journalist of the Year award for his accuracy in predicting the Soviet invasion of Czechoslovakia. In the early Eighties, after the death of his daughter in a hospice, he gave up political journalism to settle in a remote Himalayan village from where he wrote a weekly column about the life of the poor in the Third World. In recent years he has been involved in launching Russia's hospice movement in Moscow and St Petersburg.*

THE GENERAL GOES ZAPPING CHARLIE CONG

———

Nicholas Tomalin

Sunday Times
1966

The war in Vietnam was the most divisive for America since the Civil War, perhaps not least because it was the first conflict to be televised. Simultaneous with the new communications technology came a new willingness on the part of the US military to accommodate writers on manoeuvres.

After a light lunch last Wednesday, General James F. Hollingsworth, of Big Red One, took off in his personal helicopter and killed more Vietnamese than all the troops he commanded.

The story of the General's feat begins in the divisional office, at Ki-Na, twenty miles north of Saigon, where a Medical Corps colonel is telling me that when they collect enemy casualties they find themselves with more than four injured civilians for every wounded Viet Cong – unavoidable in this kind of war.

The General strides in and pins two medals for outstanding gallantry to the chest of one of the colonel's combat doctors. Then he strides off again to his helicopter, and spreads out a polythene-covered map to explain our afternoon's trip.

The General has a big, real American face, reminiscent of every movie general you have seen. He comes from Texas, and is forty-eight. His present rank is Brigadier General, Assistant Division Commander, 1st Infantry Division, United States Army (which is what the big red figure one on his shoulder flash means).

'Our mission today,' says the General, 'is to push those goddam VCs right off Routes Thirteen and Sixteen. Now you see Routes Thirteen and Sixteen running north from Saigon toward the town of Phuoc Vinh, where we keep our artillery. When we got here first we prettied up those roads, and cleared Charlie Cong right out so we could run supplies up.

'I guess we've been hither and thither with all our operations since, an' the ol' VC he's reckoned he could creep back. He's been puttin' out propaganda he's goin' to interdict our right of passage along those routes. So this day we aim to zapp him, and zapp him, and zapp him again till we've zapped him right back where he came from. Yes, sir. Let's go.'

The General's UH 18 helicopter carries two pilots, two 60-calibre machine-gunners, and his aide, Dennis Gillman, an apple-cheeked subaltern from California.

It also carries the General's own M-16 carbine (hanging on a strut), two dozen smoke-bombs, and a couple of CS anti-personnel gas-bombs, each as big as a small dustbin. Just beside the General is a radio console where he can tune in on orders issued by battalion commanders flying helicopters just beneath him, and company commanders in helicopters just below them.

Under this interlacing of helicopters lies the apparently peaceful landscape beside Routes Thirteen and Sixteen, filled with farmhouses and peasants hoeing rice and paddy fields.

So far today things haven't gone too well. Companies Alpha, Bravo and Charlie have assaulted a suspected Viet Cong HQ, found a few tunnels but no enemy.

The General sits at the helicopter's open door, knees apart, his shiny black toecaps jutting out into space, rolls a filtertip cigarette to-and-fro in his teeth, and thinks.

'Put me down at Battalion HQ,' he calls to the pilot.

'There's sniper fire reported on choppers in that area, General.'

'Goddam the snipers, just put me down.'

Battalion HQ at the moment is a defoliated area of four acres packed with tents, personnel carriers, helicopters and milling GIs. We settle into the smell of crushed grass. The General leaps out and strides through his troops.

'Why General, excuse us, we didn't expect you here,' says a sweating major.

'You killed any 'Cong yet?'

'Well no, General, I guess he's just too scared of us today. Down the road a piece we've hit trouble, a bulldozer's fallen through a bridge, and trucks coming through a village knocked the canopy off a Buddhist pagoda. Saigon radioed us to repair that temple before proceeding – in the way of civic action, General. That put us back an hour . . .'

'Yeah. Well, Major, you spread out your perimeter here a bit, then get to killin' VCs, will you?'

Back through the crushed grass to the helicopter.

'I don't know how you think about war. The way I see it, I'm just like any other company boss, gingering up the boys all the time, except I don't make money. I just kill people, and save lives.'

In the air the General chews two more filtertips and looks increasingly forlorn. No action on Route Sixteen, and another Big Red One general has got his helicopter in to inspect the collapsed bridge before ours.

'Swing us back along again,' says the General.

'Reports of fire on choppers ahead, sir. Smoke flare near spot. Strike coming in.'

'Go find that smoke.'

A plume of white rises in the midst of dense tropical forest, with a Bird Dog spotter plane in attendance. Route Sixteen is to the right, beyond it a large settlement of red-tiled houses.

'Strike coming in, sir.'

Two F-105 jets appear over the horizon in formation, split, then one passes over the smoke, dropping a trail of silver, fish-shaped canisters. After four seconds' silence, light orange fire explodes in patches along an area fifty yards wide by three-quarters of a mile long. Napalm.

The trees and bushes burn, pouring dark oily smoke into the sky. The second plane dives and fire covers the entire strip of dense forest.

'Aaaaah,' cries the General. 'Nice. Nice. Very neat. Come on low, let's see who's left down there.'

'How do you know for sure the Viet Cong snipers were in that strip you burned?'

'We don't. The smoke position was a guess. That's why we zapp the whole forest.'

'But what if there was someone, a civilian, walking through there?'

'Aw come on, you think there's folks just sniffing flowers in tropical vegetation like that? With a big operation on hereabouts? Anyone left down there, he's Charlie Cong all right.'

I point at a paddy field full of peasants less than half a mile away.

'That's different son. We know they're genuine.'

The pilot shouts, 'General, half right, two running for that bush.'

'I see them. Down, down, goddam you.'

In one movement he yanks his M-16 off the hanger, slams in a clip of cartridges and leans right out of the door, hanging on his seatbelt to fire one long burst in the general direction of the bush.

'General, there's a hole, maybe a bunker, down there.'

'Smoke-bomb, circle, shift it.'

'But General, how do you know those aren't just frightened peasants?'

'Running? Like that? Don't give me a pain. The clips, the clips, where in hell are the cartridges in this ship?'

The aide drops a smoke canister, the General finds his ammunition and the starboard machine-gunner fires rapid bursts into the bush, his tracers bouncing up off the ground round it.

We turn clockwise in ever tighter, lower circles, everyone firing. A shower of spent cartridge cases leaps from the General's carbine to drop, lukewarm, on my arm.

'I . . . WANT . . . YOU . . . TO . . . SHOOT . . . RIGHT . . . UP . . . THE . . . ASS . . . OF . . . THAT . . . HOLE . . . GUNNER.'

Fourth time round the tracers flow right inside the tiny sandbagged opening, tearing the bags, filling it with sand and smoke.

The General falls back off his seatbelt into his chair, suddenly relaxed, and lets out an oddly feminine, gentle laugh. 'That's it,' he says, and turns to me, squeezing his thumb and finger into the sign of a French chef's ecstasy.

We circle now above a single-storey building made of dried reeds. The first burst of fire tears the roof open, shatters one wall into fragments of scattered straw, and blasts the farmyard full of chickens into dismembered feathers.

'Zapp, zapp, zapp,' cries the General. He is now using semi-automatic fire, the carbine bucking in his hands.

Pow, pow, pow, sounds the gun. All the noises of this war have an unaccountably Texan ring.

'Gas bomb.'

Lieutenant Gillman leans his canister out of the door. As the pilot calls, he drops it. An explosion of white vapour spreads across the wood a full hundred yards downwind.

'Jesus wept, lootenant, that's no good.'

Lieutenant Gillman immediately clambers across me to get the second gas bomb, pushing me sideways into his own port-side seat. In considerable panic I fumble with an unfamiliar seatbelt as the helicopter banks round at an angle of fifty degrees. The second gas bomb explodes perfectly, beside the house, covering it with vapour.

'There's nothing alive in there,' says the General. 'Or they'd be skedaddling. Yes there is, by golly.'

For the first time I see the running figure, bobbing and sprinting across the farmyards towards a clump of trees dressed in black pyjamas. No hat. No shoes.

'Now hit the tree.'

We circle five times. Branches drop off the tree, leaves fly, its trunk is enveloped with dust and tracer flares. Gillman and the General are now firing carbines side by side in the doorway. Gillman offers me his gun: No thanks.

Then a man runs from the tree, in each hand a bright red flag which he waves desperately above his head.

'Stop, stop, he's quit,' shouts the General, knocking the machine-gun so tracers erupt into the sky.

'I'm going to take him. Now watch it everyone, keep firing round-about, this may be an ambush.'

We sink swiftly into the field beside the tree, each gunner firing cautionary bursts into the bushes. The figure walks towards us.

'That's a Cong for sure,' cries the General in triumph and with one deft movement grabs the man's short black hair and yanks him off his feet, inboard. The prisoner falls across Lieutenant Gillman and into the seat beside me.

The red flags I spotted from the air are his hands, bathed solidly in blood. Further blood is pouring from under his shirt, over his trousers.

Now we are safely in the air again. Our captive cannot be more than sixteen years old, his head comes just about up to the white name patch – Hollingsworth – on the General's chest. He is dazed, in shock. His eyes calmly look first at the General, then at the Lieutenant, then at me. He resembles a tiny, fine-boned wild animal. I have to keep my hand firmly pressed against his shoulder to hold him upright. He is quivering. Sometimes his left foot, from some nervous impulse, bangs hard against the helicopter wall. The Lieutenant applies a tourniquet to his right arm.

'Radio base for an ambulance. Get the information officer with a camera. I want this Commie bastard alive till we get back . . . just stay with us till we talk to you, baby.'

The General pokes with his carbine first at the prisoner's cheek to keep his head upright, then at the base of his shirt.

'Look at that now,' he says, turning to me. 'You still thinking about innocent peasants? Look at the weaponry.'

Around the prisoner's waist is a webbing belt, with four clips of ammunition, a water bottle (without stopper), a tiny roll of bandages, and a propaganda leaflet which later turns out to be a set of Viet Cong songs, with a twenty piastre note (about one shilling and six pence) folded in it.

Lieutenant Gillman looks concerned. 'It's OK, you're OK,' he mouths at the prisoner, who at that moment turns to me and with a surprisingly vigorous gesture waves his arm at my seat. He wants to lie down.

By the time I have fastened myself into yet another seat we are back at the landing pad. Ambulance orderlies come board, administer morphine, and rip open his shirt. Obviously a burst of fire has shattered his right arm up at the shoulder. The cut shirt now allows a large bulge of blue-red tissue to fall forward, its surface streaked with white nerve fibres and chips of bone (how did he ever manage to wave that arm in surrender?).

When the ambulance has driven off the General gets us all posed round the nose of the chopper for a group photograph like a gang of successful fishermen, then clambers up into the cabin again, at my request, for a picture to show just how he zapped those VCs. He is euphoric.

'Jeez I'm so glad you was along, that worked out just dandy. I've been written up time and time again back in the States for shootin' up VCs, but no one's been along with me like you before.'

We even find a bullet hole in one of the helicopter rotor blades. 'That's proof positive they was firin' at us all the time. An' firin' on us first, boy. So much for your fellers smellin' flowers.'

He gives me the Viet Cong's water bottle as souvenir and proof. 'That's a Chicom bottle, that one. All the way from Peking.'

Later that evening the General calls me to his office to tell me the prisoner had to have his arm amputated, and is now in the hands of the Vietnamese authorities, as regulations dictate. Before he went under, he told the General's interpreters that he was part of a hardcore regular VC company whose mission was to mine Route Sixteen, cut it up, and fire at helicopters.

The General is magnanimous in his victory over my squeamish civilian worries.

'You see son, I saw rifles on that first pair of running men. Didn't tell you at the time. And, by the way you mustn't imagine there could have been ordinary farm folk in that house, when you're as old a veteran as I am you get to know about those things by instinct. I agree there was chickens for food with them, strung up on a pole. You didn't see anything bigger, like a pig or a cow, did yuh? Well then.'

The General wasn't certain whether further troops would go to the farmhouse that night to check who died, although patrols would be near there.

It wasn't safe moving along Route Sixteen at night, there was another big operation elsewhere the next day. Big Red One is always on the move.

'But when them VC come back harassin' that Route Sixteen why, we'll zapp them again. And when they come back after that we'll zapp them again.'

'Wouldn't it be easier just to stay there all the time?'

'Why, son, we haven't enough troops as it is.'

'The Koreans manage it.'

'Yeah, but they've got a smaller area to protect. Why, Big Red One ranges right over – I mean up to the Cambodian Border. There ain't no place on that map we ain't been.

'I'll say perhaps your English generals wouldn't think my way of war is all that conventional, would they? Well, this is a new kind of war, flexible, quick moving. Us generals must be on the spot to direct our troops. The helicopter adds a new dimension to battle.

'There's no better way to fight than goin' out to shoot VCs. An' there's nothing I love better than killin' 'Cong. No, sir.'

Voted **What The Papers Say** *reporter of the year in 1966 for his coverage of the Vietnam War, Nicholas Tomalin was killed on the Golan Heights in 1973 while covering the Yom Kippur war for the* **Sunday Times.** *He was forty-two.*

NELL DUNN

—

Hunter Davies
Sunday Times
8 January 1967

No television play has ever caused as much public concern as Jeremy Sandford's Cathy
Come Home, *which like* Up the Junction *and* Poor Cow, *was directed with startling
realism by Ken Loach.*

With the success of his BBC play about homeless families, *Cathy Come Home*,
Jeremy Sandford has done a Nell Dunn. Her *Up the Junction* was also a slice of
working-class realism and was produced by the same television team.

It's hard luck in a way for all the working-class lads when Miss Dunn and Mr.
Sandford, who are terribly upper, have got in first and have done it so well. Miss
Dunn is the daughter of Sir Philip Dunn. One grandfather left £23 million. The other,
the Earl of Rosslyn, was the man who broke the bank at Monte Carlo. Mr. Sandford
is an old Etonian. His parents have a stately home in Herefordshire.

They are married – to each other – and live in a terrace house in Putney, very
working class, in a romantic sort of way. The place is crammed with beat-up furniture
and kids from the street run in and out all the time. Reuben, their younger boy, was
tearing around half naked. When he stopped, his mother filled his baby-bottle with
warm, sweet tea.

Miss Dunn is the one who's fascinated by class, but not in a condescending way.
Her husband is classless. After Eton and before Oxford he decided he wouldn't go
into the Guards for his National Service, like all his friends, or even be an officer.
Instead he became a bandsman in the RAF.

Their parents gave them a house in Cheyne Walk, but when their first boy, Roc,
now nine, was born, she found people objected to washing hanging out and there
was nobody to talk to on walks with the pram. So she started going over the river to
Battersea, and discovered *Up the Junction* land.

'It was so different, it was like arriving in Mexico. I felt happy and relaxed straight
away. I still do. I prefer working-class people. You can get to the bottom of things,
people tell the truth. When you move into a new street you're important, everybody
gapes, wants to know who you are, says hello, looks at your babies. In a place like
Chelsea, you're just ignored.

'I know it's all very well for me to talk like this. I have the security of money behind
me if I ever needed it, so I could move out whenever I want. But I don't want. I'm
very serious about living here.

'What success I've had is ridiculous. Two little books in seven years. *Up the Junction* was just a freak.' She's now working on a film and only hopes the critics won't turn round and lash her next book, *Poor Cow*, due out in April. The paperback rights have already gone for £10,000.

'Some people, like Nell, have success handed to them on a plate,' Jeremy says. 'Others, like me, have to work very hard.' Now he's making money he intends to breed ponies in Wales and open a strip club. 'Most strip clubs are lousy, but one or two are very artistic. It's basic theatre, after all.'

He thinks his wife does have romantic yearnings. 'Upper-class ritual gatherings are so contrived, like the Fourth of June. So it's easy to fall for the *Coronation Street*, womb-like sense of belonging which the so-called working classes have.

'I fell for the rich girl because I think money in girls is sexy and glamorous. They can do what they want. They're not scheming. Middle-class girls are just whores, selling themselves for security.'

His wife says she's not worried about security, or even writing. The thing she cares most about is her children. 'After I was interviewed on television once, Roc said to me, "Don't go on again, because they'll all want you to be their Mum." '

REPORT FROM THE SIX DAY WAR

James Cameron

Evening Standard
11 June 1967

After weeks of growing tension Israel pre-empted an Arab attack by simultaneously striking at her three neighbours – Egypt, Jordan and Syria – on 5 June 1967. So sudden was the attack that much of the Arab air-forces' planes were destroyed on the ground. Within a week a ceasefire had been declared, with Israeli soldiers in control of the entire West Bank of the River Jordan, the Gaza Strip and much of the Sinai peninsula. The repercussions are still to be resolved.

The war has etched its picture over the face of the desert like a surrealist drawing. From the air over Sinai the whole conduct of campaign is physically imprinted on the sand by the tank-tracks – a fantastically elaborate pattern of whorls and loops and intensely meaningful straight lines and sudden stops. It is the most extraordinarily effective record of an engagement I have ever seen, perhaps anyone has ever seen.

Yesterday I went on the first survey of the whole peninsula, perhaps one of the biggest single battlefields ever known, the place where the Egyptian Army died. In a lifetime not too unfamiliar with such things I have never seen anything like this. I believe that only now we and the Israeli people are beginning to realize just how immense this action was, and how complete the conquest. Figures do not really mean very much, even if there were any accurate figures, which naturally there aren't.

An Egyptian force of five infantry and two armoured divisions abruptly eliminated; an army of some 90,000 or more men disintegrated, with some tens of thousands killed or captured, or left, ignored, to wander and struggle somehow or other in the general direction of anywhere. Several million pounds' worth of extremely expensive and sophisticated military ironmongery now reduced to booty or to crushed and blackened scrap. The tanks and vehicles litter the desert like the nursery floor of an angry child. Nothing I have ever experienced so illustrates the extravagance, the mercilessness, the wastefulness of war.

It is somehow imperative to see it physically. From the air one sees the hundreds and hundreds of tanks strewn across the miles of wilderness like broken toys. Some are hideously burned and mangled lumps of complicated metal, some are totally untouched. The Israelis found concentrations of up to forty tanks unmanned, abandoned, their crews fled without firing a shot. Some of these costly new Soviet

T 51s are still coloured in the Russian forest grey; the Egyptians had no time to repaint them in the desert ochre camouflage.

This is how statistics come to life. The almost incredible figures of the destruction of the Arab air-force in that lightening pre-emptive strike becomes comprehensible now. Wandering over a captured Sinai airstrip, seeing the neatly arranged jet aircraft, each taken out with a pitiless precision that has left them little black heaps of debris in the middle of almost untouched ground, one only concludes that the Israeli marksmanship must be extraordinary, or they are using projectiles of a very unusual kind. They seem to have wasted hardly one cannon-shell or rocket. The whole thing has the appearance of an exact and clinically brutal surgery.

As I flew on south, the Canal looming on the starboard horizon, it became, if possible, harsher yet. Here the roads crawl through the red mountains whose razorback ridges make an unearthly foreground to the searing sun. And here they caught the convoys. A couple of miles of road suddenly looks like a thin strip of hell. Anything up to a couple of hundred vehicles, caught in the Mitla Pass, are trapped, burned, exploded, demolished; they are strung along in a caterpillar of ruination, upside-down, inside out, fragmented, terrible. Some – desperately leaving the road altogether – have been delicately picked out on the desert. They were heading home, but it was just that much too far away.

So down to Sharm-el-Sheikh, the remote pinhead of a place at the entrance of the Gulf of Eilat, which has a meaning for history only because this is effectively where it all began, when Egypt seized it from the United Nations – when? Last month? A generation ago? – and blocked Israel's traffic through the narrow straits, her only exit to the south and east.

I was here, on this very arid, austere and baking spot, some ten and a half years ago, when once before Israel had taken it from the Egyptians – and with me now, by the usual wild Israeli coincidence, was the man who had taken it then: Colonel Asher Levi, whom I know because until last week he was Military Attache round the corner from me in London, until he flew back here, to become like apparently everyone else in this country, a soldier.

The place has little changed; it is still one of the most unattractive and disagreeable locations in a campaign not noted for its easeful amenities. There was no battle here. The Egyptians had it manned by an infantry brigade and a squadron of tanks and auxiliaries, perhaps 5,000 men. They evacuated Sharm-el-Sheikh on Wednesday morning; the Israelis came in that afternoon. Sharm-el-Sheikh was taken by two torpedo-boats and a handful of parachutists, who didn't even have a parachute, somewhat to their annoyance, since they get a bonus for a drop.

The Egyptians took their artillery, but they left the hills around stored with ammunition and food – but of course no water; that has to be brought in by sea, and very precious stuff it is.

The new occupiers found the place commanded by no guns, the narrow turquoise waters un-mined. I wonder what, after all, it was all about? And then the most wry irony of all: the first ship that came knocking on the door of the Gulf for Israeli permission to enter was a Soviet freighter bound for Aqaba. The Israelis challenged it, noted it, and politely waved it on. The next day Russia broke off relations with Israel. It really needed only that.

WHO BREAKS A BUTTERFLY ON A WHEEL?

William Rees-Mogg
The Times
1 July 1967

There was both disquiet and amazement when Mick Jagger and Keith Richards were sentenced to prison for drugs offences after a private weekend party at a country house in Sussex. The sentences were quashed by the appeal court on 31 July. The event did nothing to enhance the reputation of the drugs squad, who were rumoured to be in league with a Sunday newspaper, but made Mick Jagger into a martyr and darling of the establishment.

This article was originally published in The Times *leader column.*

Mr. Jagger has been sentenced to imprisonment for three months. He is appealing against conviction and sentence, and has been granted bail until the hearing of the appeal later in the year. In the meantime, the sentence of imprisonment is bound to be widely discussed by the public. And the circumstances are sufficiently unusual to warrant such discussion in the public interest.

Mr. Jagger was charged with being in possession of four tablets containing amphetamine sulphate and methyl amphetamine hydrochloride; these tablets had been bought, perfectly legally, in Italy, and brought back to this country. They are not a highly dangerous drug, or in proper dosage a dangerous drug at all. They are of the benzedrine type and the Italian manufacturers recommend them both as a stimulant and as a remedy for travel sickness.

In Britain it is an offence to possess these drugs without a doctor's prescription. Mr. Jagger's doctor says that he knew and had authorized their use, but he did not give a prescription for them as indeed they had already been purchased. His evidence was not challenged. This was therefore an offence of a technical character, which before this case drew the point to public attention any honest man might have been liable to commit. If, after his visit to the Pope, the Archbishop of Canterbury had bought proprietary airsickness pills on Rome airport, and imported the unused tablets into Britain on his return, he would have risked committing precisely the same offence. No one who has ever travelled and bought proprietary drugs abroad can be sure that he has not broken the law.

Judge Block directed the jury that the approval of a doctor was not a defence in law to the charge of possessing drugs without a prescription, and the jury convicted.

Mr. Jagger was not charged with complicity in any other drug offence that occurred in the same house. They were separate cases, and no evidence was produced to suggest that he knew that Mr. Fraser had heroin tablets or that the vanishing Mr. Sneidermann had cannabis resin. It is indeed no offence to be in the same building or the same company as people possessing or even using drugs, nor could it reasonably be made an offence. The drugs which Mr. Jagger had in his possession must therefore be treated on their own, as a separate issue from the other drugs that other people may have had in their possession at the same time. It may be difficult for lay opinion to make this distinction clearly, but obviously justice cannot be done if one man is to be punished for a purely contingent association with someone else's offence.

We have, therefore, a conviction against Mr. Jagger purely on the ground that he possessed four Italian pep pills, quite legally bought but not legally imported without a prescription. Four is not a large number. This is not the quantity which a pusher of drugs would have on him, nor even the quantity one would expect in an addict. In any case Mr. Jagger's career is obviously one that does involve great personal strain and exhaustion; his doctor says that he approved the occasional use of these drugs, and it seems likely that similar drugs would have been prescribed if there was a need for them. Millions of similar drugs are prescribed in Britain every year, and for a variety of conditions.

One has to ask, therefore, how it is that this technical offence, divorced as it must be from other people's offences, was thought to deserve the penalty of imprisonment. In the courts at large it is most uncommon for imprisonment to be imposed on first offenders where the drugs are not major drugs of addiction and there is no question of drug traffic. The normal penalty is probation, and the purpose of probation is to encourage the offender to develop his career and to avoid the drug risks in the future. It is surprising therefore that Judge Block should have decided to sentence Mr. Jagger to imprisonment, and particularly surprising as Mr. Jagger's is about as mild a drug case as can ever have been brought before the Courts.

It would be wrong to speculate on the Judge's reasons, which we do not know. It is, however, possible to consider the public reaction. There are many people who take a primitive view of the matter, what one might call a pre-legal view of the matter. They consider that Mr. Jagger has 'got what was coming to him'. They resent the anarchic quality of the Rolling Stones' performances, dislike their songs, dislike their influence on teenagers and broadly suspect them of decadence, a word used by Miss Monica Furlong in the *Daily Mail*.

As a sociological concern this may be reasonable enough, and at an emotional level it is very understandable, but it has nothing at all to do with the case. One has to ask a different question: has Mr. Jagger received the same treatment as he would have received if he had not been a famous figure, with all the criticism and resentment his celebrity has aroused? If a promising undergraduate had come back from a summer visit to Italy with four pep pills in his pocket would it have been thought right to ruin his career by sending him to prison for three months? Would it also have been thought necessary to display him handcuffed to the public?

There are cases in which a single figure becomes the focus for public concern about some aspect of public morality. The Stephen Ward case, with its dubious evidence and questionable verdict, was one of them, and that verdict killed Stephen Ward.

There are elements of the same emotions in the reactions to this case. If we are going to make any case a symbol of the conflict between the sound traditional values of Britain and the new hedonism, then we must be sure that the sound traditional values include those of tolerance and equity. It should be the particular quality of British justice to ensure that Mr. Jagger is treated exactly the same as anyone else, no better and no worse. There must remain a suspicion in this case that Mr. Jagger received a more severe sentence than would have been thought proper for any purely anonymous young man.

William Rees-Mogg retired as editor of The Times *in 1981. He was made a Life Peer in 1988.*

MARY QUANT

—

Alison Adburgham
Guardian
10 October 1967

Perhaps because she so perfectly looked the part herself, Mary Quant, more than any other fashion designer, dressed the Sixties. She knew about fashion and created a new look, but she also knew the value of publicity, as evidenced by her wide-eyed admission that she trimmed her pubic hair into a heart shape.

'But I *love* vulgarity. Good taste is death, vulgarity is life.' I had asked Mary Quant whether she did not feel there to be an element of vulgarity in cut-out and see-through dresses which, giving an illusion of nothing beneath, can be regarded as an aspect of the permissive society.

'People call things vulgar when they are new to them. When they have become old they become good taste. The manufacturers who make my clothes and the people with financial interests in things I design never like anything when I first show it to them. The new thing is frightening. But the critical people, the people who understand fashion, they jump at the new thing, they're excited. In America, where everything is ruled by accountancy, they never make anything without first having a market survey to ask the public what they want. People only ask for things they already know about, so you don't get anything new that way. That's why American fashion is stuck.'

'You would agree then that a great designer is one who gives people what they want before they know they want it?'

'Yes, fashion doesn't really influence the climate of opinion, it reflects what is already in the air. It reflects what people are reading and thinking and listening to, and architecture, painting, attitudes to success and to society.'

'And attitudes to permissiveness? Do you in fact agree that this is a permissive society?'

'No, I don't. Or at least I would say it has only reached a reasonable level. And, of course, in some ways it is less permissive. We are less permissive to authority. The young won't be told now, they insist on thinking for themselves, they don't just accept things. This is more hopeful. And we are less permissive to violence. In the last war conscientious objectors were out on a limb, on their own. Now America has produced a million or more people who have refused to go and kill. If there were a war in Europe tomorrow, there would be millions of European conscientious objectors. The Beautiful People are non-violent anarchists, constructive anarchists.

They are the real breakthrough. But I have been worrying about the way they dress. It can't be called a fashion, because it's old clothes, and it's always depressing to wear clothes of the past. Whenever I see that happening I feel we designers have failed to supply the answer. It's always a valid criticism of designers if they fail to understand people's feelings and interpret them properly.'

Turning again to permissiveness, Mary said, 'People only see permissiveness in the sense of having more. But the young today are less materialistic and more intelligent than they've ever been. And they've got sex in perspective; they're not hung up on it any more; it's not difficult, they take it or leave it alone. They're the best lot that ever happened. They want money to spend, of course, but they don't want permanent possessions and super places to live in. They just want to be happy and to paint and write and do things, but not to *own* things. They're absolutely right. After all, every trouble in the world has been caused by envy, cupidity, material ambitions. The young today have no ambitions. It's sick to be ambitious – only the nutty ones like ourselves, the creative people, are ambitious and want to work. There will never be any trouble in filling the creative jobs, and far more people who have to do dull monotonous work could be trained to creative or constructive jobs. The competition in these will get stiffer and stiffer, but the result will be greater. It's quite unfair for people to have to do boring jobs that machines could do – there's nothing intrinsically good about work. There's a new climate of living now which was started by the young in the late 1950s and has been gathering momentum. And the young fashion explosion was part of it. We have taken the gracious living and snobbery out of fashion.'

'Was it you who triggered off the fashion explosion?'

'Not really. In the beginning I was just typical of the people who felt like that. Then the tickets followed. It was not happening because of me. It was simply that I was part of it.'

'Yes, you wrote in *Quant by Quant* that you just happened to start making clothes when that particular *"something in the air"* was coming to the boil . . . *"the teenage trend, the pop records and espresso bars and jazz clubs, the rejuvenated* Queen *magazine,* Beyond the Fringe, Private Eye, *the discotheques and* That Was The Week That Was *were all born on the same wavelength."* Now that it is twelve years since you opened Bazaar in the King's Road, do you still feel on the teenage wavelength? Don't you want to design now for people of your own age?'

'Fashion is for the time you're living in, not for your age. Your face has nothing to do with it. The elite young are ageless. You should wear the clothes that are right for your day. You're only old now when you stop being interested in new things and your views get stuck. People don't sign off so early now. But it's a bit terrifying really how pills are freeing women from all the things that used to age them . . . there's even a change-of-life pill now. We shall keep young much longer than men and that may lead to difficulties.'

'You have said that fashion reflects the age we live in, so you would agree that, just as there is brutalism in architecture, painting, the theatre, and music, there is an element of brutalism in fashion today? I am thinking particularly of the *presentation* of fashion, and most particularly of the work of some of our most influential fashion photographers. The intention is to shock, although the possibilities of shocking our present society without being pornographic must soon be exhausted.'

'Pornography is great if it's good.'

'What is good pornography?'

'Good pornography is erotic but pleasing. Only ugliness is obscene. Yes, I'm for pornography if it's good, against if it's ugly.'

Earlier we had looked at some of the photographs in a glossy magazine and paused at one of a model girl in knickerbockers lying on her back her legs straddled up in the air. 'You see,' Mary had said, 'this is a tremendously sexy picture, but in actual fact the girl is more inaccessible than she would be in any other period of fashion. Just look – she's got those thick tweed knickerbockers buckled tight under the knee, and she'll have stocking tights underneath and perhaps a pantie girdle as well. That's the thing about today's fashions – they're sexy to look at, but really more puritan than they've ever been. In European countries where they ban mini-skirts in the streets and say they're an invitation to rape, they don't understand about stocking tights underneath.'

She would not agree that to look sexy but to be unattainable was to go in for titillation, which is something one would expect a frank uninhibited generation to scorn. 'No, it's not *titillating* or vulgar because *she* decides. Unlike what happened in previous generations, the modern girl doesn't trade sex for material gain or marriage.'

'Have you any theory to explain why fashion has virtually abolished the bust? At fashion shows the model girls appear to have bosoms as flat as two pancakes.'

'The bosom is a motherhood symbol. In time of war, soldiers far from home yearn back to the comforts of mother and all that, and their pin-up girls all have big bosoms. Marilyn Monroe, Lollobrigida, Jayne Mansfield, they could all be considered by-products of the war. American men have a mother complex, it's a matriarchal society, so they always go for bosoms. In Italy, they say there is a sharp line across the country: to the north of it they go for bosoms and butter, to the south they go for bottoms and olive oil. It's probably something to do with the climate.'

'You know James Laver's famous fashion theory of the erogenous zone which shifts the focus of attraction in different periods from ankles, to hips, to breasts and so on . . . What is the erogenous zone of our present fashion period?'

'The crutch. This is a very balanced generation, and the crutch is the most natural erogenous zone. Clothes are designed to lead the eye to it. The way girls model clothes, the way they sit, sprawl, or stand is all doing the same thing. It's not "come hither" but it's provocative. She's standing there defiantly with her legs apart saying, "I'm very sexy, I enjoy sex, I feel provocative, but you're going to have a job to get me. You've got to excite me and you've got to be jolly marvellous to attract me. I can't be bought, but if I want you I'll have you." Now that there is the Pill, women are the sex in charge. They, and they only, can decide to conceive.' But there is an ironical twist to this that Mary Quant has noticed through employing so many young girls in her shops and studio. She says that in the days when parents were too shy to tell their daughters about sex, girls were brought up on purely romantic ideas and when they married it was often a shock. 'Now, when sex is discussed everywhere and girls are prepared for it at school or at home, parents are shy of talking about romance and true love . . . Girls simply aren't prepared for the real thing. Then when it hits them, when they suddenly fall in love, it bowls them over completely: they just lose their heads, and that's when they get deliberately pregnant.'

'Do you consider any kind of censorship of what people wear is justifiable?'

'On the stage, no. In the streets I suppose one must allow that one shouldn't expose one's body in a way that offends other people. But I think it's quite wrong for restaurant managers to define what clothes they will permit. We went to a night-club one evening to meet some friends there, and I put on a terrifically good velvet dinner suit and silk shirt. The manager simply would not let us in to join our friends.

'On the beach, there shouldn't be any censorship. It's absurd to put on clothes to swim in. For sunbathing it's more erotic and decorative to wear something – women always want to have something to take off. Bikinis have reached the minimum; there's really nothing more you can do with them, so they've become boring. So I've been working on ideas for decorating the body rather like a collage . . . it might be just three tiny triangular bits of adhesive fabric that can be stuck on, and then tattoo-like designs on other parts of the body – really decorative, rather Egyptian designs done with stencils and indelible cosmetic inks. Then you could have shift dresses to put on after the beach with cut-outs through which you would see these marvellous designs on the skin.'

'What other ideas have you for the future?'

'The body is a round thing, and it's absurd to go on making clothes with flat materials. They should be made with plastics blown out like glass – there will soon be no limit to what we shall be able to do with chemicals. Already my plastic boots that are, so to speak, blown into shape are in the shops; and in November there will be my tights with built-in shoes – just transparent plastic soles – you just wash the whole footed garment overnight like ordinary stockings. Next spring I have a complete body-stocking with plastic-soled feet coming on to the market; and I'm thinking ahead to just one fundamental garment which would be stretchy in some places and firm in others . . . firm for the soles of the feet and to give the support of a bra, stretchy where you want movement, and so on.

'Over it; I have a feeling for something that *wraps*.' Mary Quant stretched out her arms and then wrapped them slowly around her body. 'I don't know how it will go exactly, but I keep thinking all the time now of things that wrap.' She made the gesture again, this time including her head in the wrapping, bowing it down almost to her lap until she was sitting in a tight little huddle.

This could mean, I suggested, that the permissive limit of extrovert exposure has been reached, and there will be a retreat towards a more introvert, reticent way of dressing, a withdrawal from conspicuous attention-getting, perhaps a yearning for mystery – even romance?

'I don't know. I don't know. I just have the beginnings of this feeling for things that *wrap*.'

Alison Adburgham was the Guardian's *first fashion editor and worked at the paper for eighteen years. She also wrote frequently for* Punch. *More recently she has written books on British manners and fashion. Her latest book is* A Radical Aristocrat.

THE LAST JOURNEY OF CHE GUEVARA

—

Richard Gott
Guardian
10 October 1967

When Bolivian troops shot dead Ernesto 'Che' Guevara they created a Sixties hero, although recent biographies describe a man more an opportunist than revolutionary. Born in Argentina, Che Guevara had been a close friend of Fidel Castro until the Cuban leader suggested he move on.

The body of Che Guevara was flown into this small hill town in south-eastern Bolivia at five o'clock last night.

From the moment the helicopter landed bearing the small figure strapped in a stretcher to the landing rails, the succeeding operation was to a large extent left in the hands of a man in battledress, who, all the correspondents here agree, was unquestionably a representative of one of the United States intelligence agencies.

He was probably a Cuban exile and so Che Guevara, who in life had declared war almost singlehanded on the United States, found himself in death face to face with his major enemy.

The helicopter purposely landed far from where a crowd had gathered and the body of the dead guerrilla leader was hastily transferred to a van. We commandeered a jeep to follow it and the driver managed to get through the gates of the hospital grounds where the body was taken to a small colour-washed hut that served as a mortuary.

The doors of the van burst open and the American agent leapt out, emitting a war cry of 'Let's get the hell out of here'. One of the correspondents asked him where he came from. 'Nowhere,' was the surly response.

The body, dressed in olive green fatigues with a zippered jacket, was carried into the hut. It was undoubtedly that of Che Guevara. Ever since I first reported in January that Che was probably in Bolivia I have not shared the general scepticism about his whereabouts.

I am probably one of the few people here who had seen him alive. I saw him in Cuba at an embassy reception in 1963 and there is no doubt in my mind that this body was that of Che. It had a black wispy beard, long matted hair, and the shadow of a scar on the right temple, probably the result of an accident in July when he was grazed by a rifle shot.

On his feet he wore moccasins as though he had been shot down while running fleet-footed through the jungle. He had two wounds in the lower part of the neck and possibly one in the stomach. It is believed that he was captured when seriously wounded, but died before a helicopter could arrive to take him out of the battle zone.

My only doubts about the identity arose because Che was much thinner and smaller than I had recalled, but it is hardly surprising that after months in the jungle he had lost his former heavy appearance.

As soon as the body reached the mortuary the doctors began to pump preservative into it, and the American agent made desperate efforts to keep off the crowds. He was a very nervous man and looked furious whenever cameras were pointed in his direction. He knew that I knew who he was and he also knew that I knew that he should not be there, for this is a war in which the Americans are not supposed to be taking part. Yet here was this man, who has been with the troops in Vallegrande, talking to the senior officers on familiar terms.

One can hardly say that this was the factor with which Che failed to reckon, for it was his very purpose to provoke United States intervention in Latin America as a way of bringing help and succour to the embattled Vietnamese. But he certainly did fail to estimate correctly the strength and pervasiveness of the US intelligence agencies in this continent, and this more than anything else has been the cause of his downfall and that of the Bolivian guerrillas.

And so he is dead. As they pumped preservative into his half-naked, dirty body and as the crowd shouted to be allowed to see, it was difficult to recall that this man had once been one of the great figures of Latin America.

It was not just that he was a great guerrilla leader, he had been a friend of Presidents as well as revolutionaries. His voice had been heard and appreciated in inter-American councils as well as the jungle. He was a doctor, an amateur economist, once Minister of Industries in revolutionary Cuba, and Fidel Castro's right-hand man. He may well go down in history as the greatest continental figure since Bolivar. Legends will be created around his name.

He was a Marxist but impatient of the doctrinal struggles between the Russians and the Chinese. He was perhaps the last person who tried to find a middle way between the two and attempted to unite radical forces everywhere in a concerted campaign against the US. He is now dead, but it is difficult to feel that his ideas will die with him.

Always an open Marxist, Richard Gott resigned as literary editor of the Guardian *in 1994 after allegations that he had, without his newspaper's knowledge, accepted minor expenses from the KGB.*

HOW DO YOU PLEAD, MRS. JOHN BULL?

Irma Kurtz

Nova
February 1968

Fifty years after British women won the right to the vote, and with feminism about to become the most fundamental of political movements, the magazine Nova *looked at what it meant to be an Englishwoman in the late Sixties.*

Some of my best friends are Englishwomen and their own worst enemy is, I suspect, being Englishwomen. It doesn't help them either that they often marry Englishmen and have, perforce, English sons and daughters. To be English with style demands a full-time performance, to be a woman is a full-time job; to be both is probably more than any person should be asked to endure. Fortunately, unlike being American, which is a neurosis, or French, which is an appetite, the English part of being an Englishwoman is just a habit and therefore breakable. You need only unstiffen the upper lip, forget you ever played field hockey, not teach your daughter to preserve her dignity in Britain and abandon it on any Italian beach and, for heaven's sake, stop overboiling vegetables. Don't be nationalistic females, join the big sorority. Like the rest of us, you are a woman; and that, dear sister, is inescapable. That is a damn sight more than a habit. There is no breaking away from that, and there is no holiday from it. We were all born into a compulsion; we are compelled to be women.

We are not better than men, as east-coast American women and some lady novelists maintain; nor are we inferior to men, as most Englishwomen, deep down under their brave struts and corsets, really believe. We are, of course, different from men, but not so different as we and the men want to think. Like men we want a measure of joy, a measure of security, like men we want to exercise talents, and like men we cry out for freedom; but unlike men, who look to themselves for liberty, we keep looking to men for our liberty. Having begged them to make slaves of us, we then blame them for holding us in bondage. Having agreed to be their little mice, we then object to their baiting of traps. We blame the astronaut for the chastity belt, we blame the knight errant for the Second World War, we blame our husbands for our boredom, we blame our fathers for our confusion, we blame any convenient male for our strait-lacing; and we never blame ourselves for anything.

'It's a man's world,' we say, and then we complain about everything they will not let us do, instead of doing everything we can do, and doing it well. After our heartrending shrieks for the vote, we vote for the man who seems to love his wife most; we talk of the Common Market as though it were a Grand Bazaar somewhere in Belgium while we weep because our sons must go to war; we direct traffic without learning how to drive a car. We call ourselves emancipated, but we're not so sure we know how to be, we're not even sure we want to be. And that emancipation we yowled for was given us a lot faster and more willingly than it is given most under-developed peoples; yet, having got it, we have done very little with it.

Now, marriage is a thing that most of us have a chance to do and do well and yet many of us do so badly. It's no good talking about equality as long as we are still chained to the belief that marriage – any marriage – the very act of marriage, is the only target a woman should have. To be satisfied at nineteen with a wedding, to think of marriage as an end and destiny in itself, is not to be free. That radiant tigress of nineteen, clinging to the arm of her man, will be the dissatisfied matron of thirty-five, overmothering her offspring and over-feeding her husband while she blames him for taking away the freedom she never really allowed herself to have. Probably it is not freedom from marriage which women need, although many people might disagree, but it is freedom inside the marriage, a freedom which must be of the woman's own creating. Nobody else will give it to her. She cannot swallow her personality at the altar, throw herself with that great sigh of relief – 'I do' – into his wake, and then blame him for all her frustrations. Long after the rice has been thrown, there is still thinking to be done, reading to be done, work to be done with dignity by married women, friends cultivated. Any married woman who says 'she doesn't have time for any of that' has no idea of what freedom is and doesn't deserve to be untied from the Hoover.

When those two horrid little creatures crawled out of the mud, one probably turned to the other and said, 'Darling, do look at me. I'm different from you. I'm prettier.' In vanity she emerged, and to the slave ship vanity she committed all of us. Not just to physical vanity, a weakness which leads us all into the most ludicrous postures and attitudes, but also to an unwholesome delight in our own quaint foibles.

We say we want to walk with the men, but we adore being out of step. We love to be complicated, to talk about our intuition which, except for a quickness in spotting other people's love-affairs which is due entirely to our jealous interest, is non-existent. We are pleased when famous French wits waste their time cataloguing our little quirks, we want witches and warlocks to study our feminine mystique, and we like to have special doctors who are devoted to our entrails. 'Oh well,' we say when a man fails to follow a muzzy argument, 'you wouldn't understand anyway. It's because I'm a woman.' While we are being enthralled by our own differences from men, we blame men for treating us as if we were different. Although by this time we have possibly convinced men that there lies a gulf between us, the truth is we aren't nearly so different from them as it is convenient for us to believe. For when we admit our similarities, we shall really be on equal ground and women will have to begin acting like intelligent people freed from their obsession about the differences between them and that sort of person.

There is no reason why we can't make the dash up that hillside to equality while wearing our favourite high-heeled shoes. Englishwomen especially, it seems to me, have a grotesque tendency to imitate men in appearance and trivia. The county lady, so badly turned out at Glyndebourne, sits her horse like a man and thinks like a schoolgirl. The political lady has her hair done short and carefully over a head too often filled with pompous chat and wisps of her husband's comments on the morning papers. The Fleet Street lady, who curses like a man and drinks her whisky neat, is a mass of neuroses and clanging chains when her lover comes to call. It wasn't, after all, for the freedom to smoke cigars that all those bloomered darlings raised such a fuss. Emancipation isn't supposed to turn us into shadowy men, it is supposed to free us into becoming adult, responsible human beings who are women. It is enough to be a wife, to be a mother, to be a daughter or a sister, to qualify for womanhood, but it takes a degree of wit and some courage to qualify for emancipated womanhood.

'I shall stop,' says your husband, 'being an accountant today. I don't want to be an accountant any more. I have decided to give you and the children a decent income while I go to an island where I shall paint women clad only in poinsettia petals.'

'Your husband,' says the family friend, 'is an unusual man who will paint magnificent women in poinsettia petals.' 'Well and good,' you say. 'I have decided to stop menstruating, ovulating and all that. I don't want to love my children or ever sleep with a man again. I shall shave my head and be a Buddhist monk.'

'You,' says the family friend, 'are mad as a March hare.'

When we weep for getting the tatty end of the stick in our fantasies and the humdrum fate in life, we forget that as few men go off to dusky islands as women go off to sunny ones with tubercular pianists. We and our brothers are born with the same adventure potential, but rarely does either sex explore it. We don't live in a very adventurous society, but any girl who wants to can hoist her skirts, like a Victorian lady traveller, and take off for the Himalayas. Most of us, however, men and women, stay right where we have been stuck. And if some men, who have no intention of doing so, look as if they could go wandering more easily than we, it doesn't mean that we, who have no intention of going anywhere, don't have our chances too.

Down the length of five decades now, since emancipation, there echoes a high-pitched wail: 'I'm bored! Do something! I'm bored!' Whatever made us think that freedom would be fun? Did we honestly believe that having the vote would be entertaining on long winter nights? Were we promised that the dish-washer, washing machine, floor polisher and our husband's swelling income wouldn't fail to fascinate us? Freedom is, potentially, dreadfully boring and the whole point of having it is to learn ways not to be bored with it: learn Spanish, learn French cooking, petit point, knitting; contemplate an unwinking navel, learn to read again, or empty your mind before the telly. Learn anything, do anything, but don't be bored because being bored is a terrible admission of having failed as an emancipated human being. When we are bored we are failing ourselves, our families, and those dear fire-balls of energy who squealed fifty years ago for emancipation. Boredom is not, as lady journalists like to tell suburban housewives, a kitchen and nursery malady. Heaven knows how many of your husbands are bored: with their jobs, with themselves, with you. Boredom is failure and failure is boring, and if you're bored you are boring and if you are boring you will bore, and it is all a very tedious circle which exists only to be broken.

All the noise the suffragettes made would be but a sigh compared to the outcry which would arise if anyone suggested that women should be deprived of their role as mothers; and those who would fight hardest might well be the very females who are always ruefully excusing themselves from progress because they are pregnant again. No woman in the world is the only woman in the world who can bear children, and mothers shouldn't hide behind their daughters' skirts. To bear children is simply not enough to merit anyone's respect and love; least of all that of the children who have been borne, and women must emancipate themselves from the belief that anyone is grateful to them just because they have done the most natural thing in the world and time. Childbearing, like marriage, is a bad place to imprison oneself; it is no more an end in itself than the wedding ceremony was. Instead of seeing the births of our children as restrictions of freedom, as another reason for becoming just a mammal – simply a warm container for the future – we must bring up our children as we would have them raise theirs, not as an excuse for unsung operas, unwritten novels, unloved Russian princes, but as something we have chosen freely and dearly wanted to do. We have nothing to lose, ladies, but our umbilical cords and the fact that we are attached to them at two ends hardly matters at all.

American-born Irma Kurtz finally became a British citizen in 1994 after living for thirty years in London. She currently has an advice column in Cosmopolitan.

INSIDE KHE SANH

—

David Leitch
Sunday Times
18 February 1968

After North Vietnam's Tet Offensive of January, 1968, Americans suddenly began to realize that the United States might not win the Vietnam War.

Stuck up on the red-mud wall of the trench, just above the grenades, there is an amateurish photo of a girl. She is not a very special girl, except she is naked to the waist and has a rather touching look – an amalgam of shame and determination.

Evidently she is not in the habit of posing for semi-nude pictures but her expression says she is determined to do this, and anything else, if it will help her boyfriend while he is in Khe Sanh. All we can do now is to hope that it did help because it certainly is not helping any more.

My Marine friends found the picture in the wallet of a dead soldier whose charred body they dragged, at great risk, out of the wreck of the Hercules C-130 transport plane which now lies in three spiky heaps fifty yards away. They also found the girl's address and they say they'll send the picture back, with a letter of thanks and condolence – if they ever get out themselves.

Looked at from this trench, the likelihood of girl and photograph ever being reunited seems remote. A Marine captain, keeping his head well down, indicates Hill 950 with its jungle-covered tip half-buried in the low cumulus. From this position the North Vietnamese troops can, if they wish and the weather abets them, lay down a murderous fire on the airstrip only yards from our bleak trench.

It is only one of the half-a-dozen positions from which they dominate this pathetic little rectangle, preventing anyone coming in or running away.

We know that there are two divisions of them – say 20,000 – and possibly two divisions more. There are only 4,800 Marines within the meagre Khe Sanh perimeter, and all of them are waiting for the *coup de grace*.

There has been a good deal of armchair speculation about whether or not the North Vietnamese army intend to attack Khe Sanh. Some people, even experts in Saigon, believe that General Giap is not primarily concerned with achieving another Dien Bien Phu, but is using Khe Sanh as a decoy.

Giap, according to this theory, simply wants to immobilize the US troops, while he skirts them. This may make sense in Saigon or Washington, but when one is huddled inside a flak-jacket, trying simultaneously to watch for troop movements in the scrub on the other side of the wire and listen for the incoming mortar shells, General Giap's intentions seem only too immediately obvious.

Every day this week, the NVA (North Vietnamese Army) troops have moved closer and there seems to be no way to stop them. Every night you go to sleep in Khe Sanh expecting to be awakened by an ill-intentioned North Vietnamese with his Chinese-manufactured automatic weapon. On St. Valentine's Day the Marines received their second 'red alert' – troop movements had indicated that the enemy was massing for attack.

Colonel Davie E. Lownds, the forty-seven-year-old commander of this daily diminishing Marine group, has no doubt in his mind. 'Of course, they're coming,' he says in the command bunker. 'But I don't want to put any time frame on it . . . I wish I knew.'

So do his men, in their vulnerable foxholes. (There are perhaps two bunkers in Khe Sanh where men would survive after a direct rocket hit. The rest would crumple under a mortar, and their protection value is as much psychological as anything else.)

When you see the NVA troops outside the wire, you see brisk, eager little men in jungle kit, going about their jobs with frightening impassivity.

Sergeant W.W. Trottino, a large dead-pan Oklahoman who had kindly offered me the hospitality of his bunker, picked out an advancing section through his binoculars. 'Jee-sus,' he said, 'there's Charley, just like he's going out on an Elks picnic.'

'What does he look like?' asked Private First Class Steve Adrio (an amateur photographer who had been bitterly disappointed that I was what he called a 'writing correspondent' and therefore not carrying any colour film).

'Baby,' said Trottino, declining to relinquish the binoculars, 'he's a small, yellow-looking kind of guy and he speaks with an accent. You'll recognize him by his gun.'

At this point we all heard an agonized, hollow cough from somewhere about 1,000 yards away and lost interest in the cross-talk as we flattened on the red, probably highly fertile, soil which is peculiar to Khe Sanh.

As the mortars come closer, the sound becomes shriller, straighter and faster; you have quite enough time to ponder over your sins of omission and commission between discharge and the arrival. On this particular occasion the nearest explosion was a clear fifty yards away, a dull booming thud, which leaves one with a headache if nothing worse.

Trottino got to his feet with dignity and continued his visual reconnaissance and running commentary. A Negro Marine who had been lying next to me tried to pick mud off his flak-jacket and broke into a huge and deeply frightened grin. 'Kindly get me out of here,' he said. 'I'll go on a chopper, I'll parachute, if you insist, man, I'll walk, but just take me out of this place.'

He was one of the more rational people I spoke to on St. Valentine's Day. Talking, in fact, is rather difficult. This is not because the Marines are taciturn, for everyone in Khe Sanh is so acutely aware of their intermingled destiny that strangers become intimate acquaintants in minutes. It is the noise that inhibits chat – the rippling thud of helicopter blades, the irritable cough of mortars, the fluttering inexorable whine of artillery.

And the sky, on the good days, is black with aircraft – the Skyraider ground-attack planes, jet fighters, and tiny delicate spotter planes, which the Marines talk about like pet dogs as they run through their subtle little arabesques. The spotters are trying to locate gun emplacements beneath the jungle canopy, which comes so near you are aware of it physically, like someone nudging you in the Tube.

These aircraft are delaying the outcome of this battle, taking suicidal risks to help the muddy, frightened men on the ground. But they also have a disturbing message for the Marines in the foxholes because it is clear they are operating each day a little closer to the perimeter.

There is no doubt that the North Vietnamese are moving in, painfully, agonizingly, but still a few yards farther each day. A US Skyraider we watched came swooping in above us, so low we all ducked. But he had not made a mistake.

He dipped down across the perimeter in an arc that seemed inevitably to be leading him to crash, straightened up, and hugging the ground discharged from his belly what looked like a cluster of yellow flame which bounced and swooped, moving perhaps fifty yards parallel to the ground before exploding in a burst of white smoke so close it tickled the throat and made us cough.

'Napalm,' said Trottino. 'Oh, decent, man, isn't that the most beautiful sight you ever saw . . .' The Marines, disregarding the retaliation that had to come, were jumping up and down, clapping their hands.

The Skyraider wiggled its tail in a half victory roll and gained height for another sweep. We had been looking due east but now there was a deeper rumble dominating the cacophony of lesser sounds coming from the north-west. 'Arclight,' said Trottino, by now an old friend, who had shown me pictures of his children, and asked me to send a message to his wife.

Arclight is the USAF code for the terrifying B-52 bombers which dispense their own kind of justice, God-like, from 55,000 feet, homing in by radar, and destroying an area roughly 1,000 metres long by 400 wide. When their bombs, 500 and 750 pounders (sixty-five tons or thereabouts in all) hit the ground, we were all shaken. The sand started to leak out of the sandbags. The wooden supports of the bunker teetered. And across the valley, just north of the gap that lead to Laos, the jungle began to ignite.

There is a lot of argument about the B-52 'kill potential'. The efficiency of the raids in military terms may be high or low but psychologically they are crucial. When the Marines see the piles of smoke rising across the valley they feel that someone is remembering them. For the rest of the time they just sit here like so many clay-pigeons, forgotten, they believe, by their leaders, waiting to be sacrificed.

But the air-strikes, the only tactical factor that makes Khe Sanh tenable, tend to be double-edged. If you are dug in even reasonably well – and the Marine trenches and bunkers are now adequate though by no means brilliant – then there is a fair chance of surviving a determined bombardment. As long, that is, as you can hear them coming. An experienced soldier hearing the sound of an approaching rocket, something like the barking of an enormous dog, can get under cover fast enough to be protected from anything other than a direct hit.

But with the aircraft circling overhead one can hear nothing. It is necessary to leave the bunkers to work, to get something to eat, to consult a senior officer. And every time one walks even twenty-five yards on the mud tracks like 'Buchanan Road' which runs through the base, one is playing a game of Russian roulette. The rockets and mortars come in without warning. They either have your number on them or they don't.

But this is the kind of risk the Marines are happy to live with. Their casualties at the moment are averaging something in the region of forty a day, which they believe is acceptable.

The real problem is what happens when the weather gets too bad for air support. So far God has been on the side of the United States, and in this situation they badly need supernatural support. The usual torrential monsoon rains have been tardy, and three days in four the weather has been good enough for the support planes to fly from their bases in Da Nang, Saigon and elsewhere. But what is going to happen if the weather changes and a great quiet descends over this valley for two or three days? I asked this question of a section of Marines, who were playing five-card stud poker with military scrip in a trench on the extreme north-east of the Khe Sanh position, uncomfortably close to the ammunition dump. 'If the planes can't come any more then the Reds are going to attack,' said a cheery corporal. He had just noisily won forty-five cents by producing three sevens – 'sevens is always been mah lucky numbah' – against a shattered top sergeant who had drawn two aces and a pair of nines. 'What are they going to do? You don't have to ask that question, friend. They just have to start running over that wire when it's dark and we kill a few of them and they keep coming and then we say goodnight. No problem there.'

As long as the planes are there, the North Vietnamese troops are forced to dig in, keep their heads down, and concentrate on avoiding either being roasted by napalm or pulverized by B-52 strikes. But once the weather makes it impossible for these friendly birds to make their complicated passes, fending off the evil day, it all comes down to a question of numbers. There are not physically enough Marines to keep the North Vietnamese out if they are really determined to come, without bothering about the size of their losses, and this has never been something that worried them in the past. At Dien Bien Phu Giap did not try to demonstrate he was a general who kept his losses down.

Khe Sanh is eminently takeable. If Giap decides to take it he can, though it will cost him men. If he waits until weather conditions are better it will be that much easier.

Meanwhile the Marines can do nothing except endure with as much dignity as frightened, potentially defeated men can muster (which, one should say, in their case is a great deal of dignity). As Major Joe Donnelly, the officer who is running one of the hill outposts supporting the area, says, 'The game is now completely in their hands. We wait – it's up to them to move.'

This has been all the more true for the last couple of weeks. Before that the Marines were at least able to send out patrols to spot enemy concentrations and give the command some idea of what they were doing. This is no longer so. Patrols have become too costly. First you send three men, and if they don't come back, you have to support them with a section. If the section too disappears into this unfriendly landscape there is nothing for it but to send a platoon.

The Marines are used to taking heavy losses, indeed they almost glory in them, but this is something else. At the moment Colonel Lownds is trying to preserve as many men in his command as he can. His men sit around and listen to 'Hanoi Hannah' on their expensive transistors – she is the Vietnamese equivalent of Lord Haw-Haw – or play cards, look at their *Playboy* pin-ups, and pray to God something is going to happen.

Most of them would prefer the NVA to launch a major attack. At least this would be preferable to lying in the red mud and trying to calculate how long you can go before the rocket scores a direct hit. The Marines here are poor boys, ex-truck drivers, labourers and, at the top end of the scale, counter-clerks. They do not have education to help them but their spiritual resources are considerable. They are surviving on companionship and humour.

It makes them the most sympathetic American troops in this country. If you get stuck in Khe Sanh, they automatically accept you as one of them, and talk about newspaper proprietors in the same way they go on about the general staff, forgetting that journalists, unlike soldiers, have a choice about where they go, and do not have to stay to the end of such affairs.

They insist that the people back home do not know what they are suffering. 'I write my parents and my big sister a lot,' said a Negro PFC. 'The first week I was here I wrote eleven letters, would you believe that? Do you think any of them will get there?' Another Marine said: 'I write my wife all the time. Naturally I couldn't get away with telling her what's really going on – nobody Stateside knows that, and if they did know they'd blow their minds.'

My own view is that he is absolutely correct. No Government, one thinks cowering in the trenches of Khe Sanh, has the right to exact this kind of sacrifice from its boys – most of them are boys, literally. The average age of the troops I talked to, perhaps sixty of them, was certainly no more than twenty-two.

They all seemed to be patriots, insofar as they hated the Communists at least. But they combine this hate with a deep and all-abiding cynicism about their leaders, both generals and politicians. The repetitive Marine expletives make it impossible to repeat much of what they say in a newspaper that people will read over their Sunday morning eggs, and they are anyway not very articulate. There is no Wilfred Owen to describe this war.

(It would have to be an Owen. A Rupert Brooke in the age of napalm and revolutionary war would need to keep extremely quiet.)

Many of us are making plans
Of what we will do when we hit our homeland
Much as it hurts, it must be said
Some won't hit home for some will be dead.

This poem was read out in a bunker with the sign above it: 'Friendly place.' Everybody listened, and then went back to their card game, trying at the same time to reserve a measure of concentration for incoming mortars. I asked the dealer whether he liked the poem or not and he grinned: 'Play your cards while you can.'

The one thing that will raise any enthusiasm in this ghost camp is an air strike, not so much, as far as I could make out, because of pleasure at the damage the wheeling planes were doing to the NVA, but rather because it suggested someone was trying to help them, somebody knew they were there.

Most of these people, I feel, have never enjoyed a sense of solidarity with people of their own American generation, except perhaps in gangs. It is sad that it takes a situation like this to turn them into social animals. It is appalling to imagine, after the youthful commitment to violence, how those who survive will react to the world outside.

'You aren't going to believe this, but I volunteered to come here,' said a twenty-one-year-old corporal. 'They told me about the sixty-five dollars a month additional combat allowance. I was in Oakland, California, so bored you know. I thought with that money I could get a tape recorder and so on but of course I didn't know what I was going to buy it with – naturally, in this kind of place all that stuff comes kind of expensive.'

The corporal had made a map pinpointing the mortar and rocket explosions within the camp in the last week. He was hoping to deduce a pattern which would help him to avoid the dangerous sections, though they all looked equally bad. He gave me the map as a souvenir to send to his girlfriend, on the assumption that I would get out (which on St. Valentine's Day with the clouds closing in seemed fairly unlikely) and that he wouldn't.

Getting into Khe Sanh has been extremely difficult for two weeks and is now becoming more so. Despite all the US air strikes, the NVA mortars and rocket fire, zeroed on the runway which at some points is no more than thirty yards within the perimeter, continue unabated.

At the south-east end of the runway, where the incoming planes touch down, there is an NVA .50 calibre machine-gun, or a group of them, which have managed to survive all the rockets and napalm from the air. Now that this gun, which destroyed a C-130 transport last Saturday, is calling the tune the Communists appear to have the potential to dominate the situation.

The C-130s no longer fly because they are reckoned to be too easy targets: instead they have been replaced by smaller C-123s, which have to make more runs to bring in the same amount of supplies. These are slow, awkward planes and their approach run involves them hugging the surface of the innumerable knolls and rises which surround the Marines' camp on all four sides.

This ground-hugging goes on for perhaps five miles on the run-in and the passengers have the impression that this lurching, juddering cow of a plane could be knocked off by someone on the ground with a strong arm and a cricket ball, let alone rockets.

When you finally hit the runway you are encouraged by the wreck of last Saturday's C-130, parked in three pieces on the perimeter. And when you actually come to a stop all hell breaks loose. The apron section of the runway, where the aircraft turn round, is known as 'the Mortar Magnet'. The NVA have now had weeks to zero in on this area and if you survive the machine-gun bursts at one end of the runway you find yourself faced by the mortar fire at the other.

The C-123s keep their engines going all the time, spill cargo and passengers out of the back, taxi and take off within three or four minutes. In this time, under the sound of the engines, the mortars – if you are lucky – and rocket – if you aren't – rain in on the apron. The NVA have been sufficiently harassed from the sky for their fire to be rather erratic.

The plane I came in on attracted one mortar fifteen feet from the tail after standstill, which was the best try, and a fusillade of mortars and rockets that came screaming in to land from anything up to seventy-five yards from the turning area. They naturally achieved casualties but the plane itself got away.

The worst job in Khe Sanh is unloading these arriving planes which carry either fuel or ammunition, and loading them with wounded. Twenty-year-old Howard Hunt from Atlanta, Georgia, explained the job to me in a ditch where we spent twenty minutes after the C-123 I had arrived in had made its battered, cumbersome way back up the strip towards Da Nang for safety.

'Every time I go out on the strip my mind goes blank,' Howard said. 'Sometimes the ammo boxes get stuck and I scream – you can't hear it for the noise of the jets and the guns but it seems to make me feel better. I don't do it on purpose, you understand. I just seem to find myself screaming.'

Hunt and his nine friends doing the same job are all in a state of advanced mental exhaustion. 'You know those planes have got to get in here,' said PFC Jim Veron. 'But all the same you get to dread seeing them come because of the fire. It's funny because you know that the plane is the most dangerous thing, the real mortar magnet. But once you get inside it to pick off the cargo you tend to linger, like it's protecting you.'

Once the planes stop flying even for forty-eight hours, Giap will probably launch his attack. If he really has four divisions in the area, say 40,000 men, as some observers believe, and not two divisions only, there can be little doubt about the NVA's ability to over-run the strip. He is rumoured to have a dozen tanks, but it is not certain that tanks are within striking distance of Khe Sanh. The Marines fear they are – the plane I flew in on was carrying anti-tank rockets.

The Marines are bitter when they say, 'You tell them they're using us as bait.' But the anger they feel at their own situation is directed at the Communists as well as the world in general, and there is no doubt they will fight well when the attack comes. Most of them say things like: 'It's time Uncle Sam lost his patience. We ought to drop the big one on Hanoi and put an end to all this.' Most of them think America should withdraw from Vietnam, but initiate a kind of scorched earth policy first. (After seeing the damage to Hue last week one wonders whether, in effect, such a policy is not being carried out already.)

At the 'mortar magnet', the apron where supply planes turn round, a brawny military policeman crouches in a bunker checking that in the general confusion no Marine decides to hop on the plane for Da Nang and leave Khe Sanh to sort out its own problems. So far there has not been a single case of this happening. The only Marines leaving are the dead ones in rubber bags or the wounded on stretchers.

Departure is even more terrifying than arrival because getting the wounded on board up the slippery ramp in the C-123's tail is an awkward and slow performance. The noise of the engines drowns any 'incoming'. Helmets are blown off in the slipstream and sometimes the plane starts to taxi in its eagerness to take off before everyone is on board.

I went up the ramp hanging on to one end of a stretcher carrying a quiet and patient Negro who looked uncannily like Cassius Clay. There were two other stretcher cases – one a comparatively minor shrapnel case, the other a soldier so covered in bandages that he looked like a white mummy. God knows what wounds the bandages concealed or how the medical orderly managed to attach the saline drip during the flight.

The plane had been strafed by the usual .50-calibre machine-gun on the way in but for some reason got off the ground without attracting a single shot. The stretchers on the floor lurched crazily, the engines screamed and we were above Khe Sanh.

None of the fifteen walking wounded on board showed any emotion, or spoke a word, partly because the noise level was too high, partly because they were just past speaking. At one point the man who looked like Clay indicated he was cold and as there were no extra blankets was given a couple of combat jackets. A Korean Ranger, who had taken a shrapnel burst on his left arm, side and leg removed the cellophane from a cigar with one hand and after long consideration put it in his mouth the wrong way round. He proceeded to smoke it gingerly, the cigar held between swollen black fingers.

With great gentleness a sallow corporal, probably from the Philippines, was fitting a filter cigarette into the small hole in the bandages that must have been the mouth of the Marine in white. I don't know whether he died during the flight but by the time we reached Da Nang he was no longer managing the tiny puffs.

He was carried off, his bloodstained medical card pinned to his bandages, his helmet fastened to the stretcher. On it was written his name, blood group ('A'), a calendar of his service in Vietnam, and a couple of slogans. 'Kill all Gooks' and 'Make war not love'.

The walking wounded followed him still not speaking. They had got out of Khe Sanh, the hard way, but seemed past caring.

David Leitch has written for the Sunday Times, The Times, *the* Guardian *and* New Stateman. *His autobiography* God Stand Up For Bastards *was followed by* Family Secrets, *the discovery of the family he never knew. He has also written three investigative books including* Philby: the Spy who Betrayed a Generation *with fellow* Sunday Times *writers Bruce Page and Philip Knightley.*

MY NAME IS IVY BENSON, I'M THE LEADER OF THE BAND

—

Arthur Hopcraft
Sunday Times Magazine
24 March 1968

The Sixties wasn't, of course, a period in isolation, and the All Girls Orchestra which Ivy Benson ran owed more to World War II than Ready, Steady, Go! Fashionable London may have moved on but change is never uniform – things take a little longer in English seaside resorts.

The balloons are blown up and piled in their basket in the centre of the dance floor, ready to be hauled to the ceiling for release as the climax of the evening after the funny hats, the paper streamers and the palais-glide. Tonight is to be carnival night with Ivy Benson and her All Girls Orchestra.

The sharp sun of late afternoon slants acutely through the windows of the West Park Pavilion, St Helier, like a forgotten spotlight. It glows on a strip of wood-block floor and some faded, end-of-season paintwork. Ivy is in the shade on the bandstand, shaping an elaborately chorded *Lady Be Good* at the piano, a big smile held across her left shoulder for us, photo-call style, as we walk in. 'Just tinkling,' she says, and she bobs up and comes chirruping off the stand and across the floor, both hands held out. She is tiny and pert in a knee-length dress, a Forces' favourite of the Forties, startlingly still girl-like in figure. We sit in a corner of the ballroom and talk about afternoons at the Mecca and garrison theatres and shady agents and the changing fashions in dance music. But most of all we talk about GIs.

How many of her girls married GIs last year? Ivy ticks off names on her fingers. 'Five marriages last year,' she says, 'and so far this year it's two marriages and two engagements.' The American serviceman may not be able to buy his fun with nylons and chocolate nowadays, as he could twenty-five years ago; but for Ivy's girls he's still got every other uniform beaten out of sight. 'They're very fast workers,' Ivy says. Who, the girls? 'The GIs.'

Some of these romances have all the unlikely drama and frantic urgency of the ones in the old war-time films which were weepy with twenty-four-hour honeymoons and stagedoor farewells. Ivy remembers the torrid affair of the piano player and a guy named Skip. 'We were playing Stuttgart. Suddenly, in the middle of a number, she shouted, "Ooh, there's Skip." And jumped off the stand and vanished into the crowd and I never saw her again.'

Others have the sad comedy of all those old jokes about the fast-talking Texans, whose ranches and oilfields turn out to exist only in lines learned from the Hank Jansen-Micky Spillane school of Romeos. 'I had one girl with stars in her eyes over her GI she was going to marry, and he had a wife and two children in Mississippi.'

Ivy was a GI bride. She married Top Sergeant Bradley Calloway, who was in charge of a servicemen's club in England, in 1958. He was her second husband, and they were divorced last year. She tells her girls that as soon as they marry they should leave the band. 'I say to them, "This is farewell to romance. Take my advice and put your sax in the fridge."'

There has never been another girl's dance band, either in Europe or America, which has lasted like Ivy's. Marriage is the first reason why the band is seldom composed of the same girls for longer than six months at a time. The line-up in Jersey of twelve musicians and two singers had four girls who had been with the band for six years, but few stay for more than one year or two. The constant factors which keep Ivy in business are her own professionalism, her girls' musicianship and the sustained deliberate appeal to the armed forces.

Ivy was a clerk in Montague Burton's in Leeds in the late Thirties, adding to her eighteen shillings a week by playing a clarinet or a saxophone in other people's dance bands for only seven shillings and sixpence a night. The meanness of the pay offended her Yorkshire spirit, and she was not encouraged by the Musicians' Union resentment of girl players. The start of the war, when the bandstands were suddenly stripped of male musicians, gave her the chance she needed to form her first band. 'But even then Mecca wouldn't buy me as a band. They hired the five girls at five guineas a week and me, as bandleader, at six pounds ten shillings.' But the work was regular, and soon she had a bigger band with a regular radio spot.

The band's link with the Services was established almost from the start. 'The rule was that an artist who did six weeks entertaining the troops wouldn't be conscripted for war work. At least, that was what Jack Hylton told me. But it didn't always work. One of my girls still got put into a factory on a capstan lathe.'

Ivy talks about the Forties and early Fifties with clear memory and obvious pleasure, but without any excessive relish of nostalgia, always insisting that dance music is a business for her. The girls have come and gone, along with the jitterbug, jive and the samba. Her music pad now has the pop world's Top Thirty, as well as the swing of her early days. But she touches the nerve ends stingingly all the same. She recalls shows in makeshift theatres in the Middle East.

'All those tin huts. I remember one particularly, because of the bats. We used to open in the pitch dark. We'd play a fanfare, and then all the lights would come on. There'd be this terrific sound, and then, zoom-zoom-zoom, all you'd see were the bats flying round the girls' heads.'

The highest fee that entertainers could charge for troop shows was ten guineas. Ivy spent most of her first ten years as a bandleader playing to servicemen. 'I've never regretted it. I'd got a tremendous following in England when all those boys came back home.'

A young waiter delivers some coffee. He is extra polite. 'He's in love with one of my girls,' Ivy says. 'Oh, it happens all the time. Everywhere we go.' Immediately she is reminded again of servicemen and their enthusiasm for her girls. 'In the War Office there used to be a chart showing who the most popular entertainers were with the troops. No matter what anyone else might tell you, it was my band that was right up at the top.'

Since the war she has played in a dozen countries, but never yet lost a musician to any foreigner except an American. 'Strange, isn't it?' she asks, sounding as if she has never given a thought to the traditional appeal of the affluent GI to the English working girl. 'No Germans or Swiss. Funny, isn't it? Of course, you've got to remember that my girls speak English. It's a real event at an American service base abroad when we arrive. All the German girls are interested in is getting to the States.' Here and there, in conversation, an American nasality intrudes in Ivy's voice.

Her girls are well-off nowadays, paid between £30 and £38 a week. Most of them drive cars. Boyfriends take them out a great deal, buy them presents and pay for their meals. They save money. Mostly they are in their late teens and early twenties, easy mannered in self-confidence, living far too instructive a life to evince any girly-girly sweetness, collectively or on their own. Ivy says she lists no rules for them to follow, but they know what kind of behaviour would cost them their jobs. 'I won't have any drunkenness on the stand, or arriving late. And they've got to be clean.'

All through the year girls write to her, telephone her and travel to see her, asking to join the band. They are often as young as fifteen or sixteen, and alarm her by their readiness to travel long distances on their own. 'I try to persuade them to wait a bit, unless they've been recommended to me or I know their parents. But they still come from all over the place. The young ones are so sure of themselves these days.' She does not pretend that she has never had promiscuous girls, or drinkers, but says she is surprised she has not had more problems of delinquency than have come her way over the years. 'I've only had one girl who was pregnant before she joined. It was a few days before I realized. I had to send her home right away.'

The band is capable of a splendidly brassy sound; as Ivy says, 'Just as strong as any men's band.' Musically, the girls are clearly entirely earnest, absorbed while they are playing and able to manage a full-bodied *In the Mood* as well as a tricky *Puppet on a String*. A dark, solemn clarinetist says she chose the band in preference to scholarship English.

Ivy's trumpeters and trombone players are nearly always northern girls, from the brass band towns, where dads teach their little daughters to tootle wavering first notes on Sunday afternoons in a flush of fondness and post-practice beer. 'They just don't seem to exist in the South,' Ivy says. In more than twenty-five years she has had one coloured girl, a singer.

A drummer left her to form her own group of five, and was away for three years. 'When she came back she was as thin as a rail and sick with worry. It's not an easy way of making a living, when you've got to look after girls as well as money. I try not to get too tensed up. All the railway porters know me. They say, 'Oh, don't you worry, Ivy; we'll get 'em all on board for you'.' She taps her handbag. 'I've got an offer to tour South America in here. But I'm not sure about it. It's a long way to walk back, isn't it?'

Ivy's hair is auburn, and she has a trim, self-possessed vitality; it is a distinctly northern personality, the natural frankness not much corrupted into obtrusive showbiz gush. 'Let me be mother,' she says, pouring coffee, and adding with an ironic wistfulness, 'as always.'

There is something of the bold, all-girls-together character of the factory bus or the chorus dressing-room about the band. Girls who leave often keep contact for years by letter, and often in sassy style. Ivy quotes from a letter from a singer, gone solo, who says she is doing well in London but thinks 'What's helping me really is my boobies'. She's forty round the chest, Ivy says.

The band's uniform for Jersey was a light and twinkly trouser suit. Ivy says she re-dresses the band four times a year, 'and it costs a bomb'. She regrets that mini-skirts are not suitable for girls sitting on a bandstand. Even if the clarinets and saxophones were safe from the voyeur, in their place at the front of the stand 'there would always be the drummer high up at the back'. Other considerations intrude. The band played for ten successive summer seasons in Douglas, Isle of Man. 'Very cold in the Villa Marina gardens,' Ivy remembers. 'I put the girls in woollen suits.'

The physical setting of the dance hall has changed hardly at all since Ivy first started playing professionally. The West Park Pavilion is white-stuccoed on the outside and it has the indispensable crystal ball shimmering up aloft, dead centre above the dance floor. In the first half-hour of the dancing, only the serious couples are in action, swooping and jerking with their elbows up high and their eyes fixed on some mesmerizing object moving high up round the walls. But, ballroom bronze medallists apart, the customers behave very differently from the days when they used to mass round the stand to applaud the music, Ivy says.

'On beat nights it's fantastic. Boys come on to the floor and just dance by themselves. Everyone sticks to their own little square foot of floor, just moving in time to the beat.'

But tonight the band are playing mostly for an older generation. There is no group of lads back-combing each other's hair, as Ivy says was the case the night before. Tonight the holiday-makers are keeping the waiters busy on errands to the bar, are clapping the singers and are shouting snatches of *Jeepers Creepers* and *Gypsy In My Soul* in each other's ears. Ivy says that we are invited to join her with sixteen lady publicans and licensees' wives from Bermondsey and district, who are on holiday without their husbands.

By midnight the coloured streamers and the bits of burst balloon are thick around the dancers' ankles, the band has stepped up the volume and lines of bulky people are lurching, glazed in the eye and slack in the mouth, through the conga. This could very well be 1945. Bald and plump men keep going up to the stand to introduce Ivy to their wives and ask for favourite songs. The landladies, in a fuss of fur stoles and their hair in voluminous curlicue, are raised above the dance floor on a secondary stand. Their jewellery glints in the lights, and they are wearing little paper hats. Drink has given them a brief immobility in their chairs, so that they have a curious, brilliant stateliness as they gaze in detachment on carnival.

In the cocktail bar of their hotel a little time later, they receive Ivy in strident, competitive adoration, surrounding her with drinks, then warning her that there are people about who'd like to see her tiddly. They have sprung to life in a pastiche of Cockney knees-up. Two of them pound upstairs and re-appear draped in candlewick bedspreads and lavatory-seat covers, doing a cod Easter dance. Another, blonde and dumpy, is seated on a bar stool in her pink nightie. 'Ive,' they keep shouting, 'play for us, Ive. Be a sport, Ive.' They offer her a guitar. Ivy strums *Your Cheating Heart*.

In all this noise and knockabout she maintains a warm decorum, effortlessly treading the tightrope between reserve and unseemliness. She might be an exotic sister, home from somewhere glamorous abroad for a family reunion. She is regarded fondly here, and she is not having to work at it. Foreign place names decorate her conversation, and there are knowing winks between the laughs. 'Do you know?' she says, 'this is the first night out I've had all the season.'

A MULE CORTEGE FOR THE APOSTLE OF THE POOR

by Alistair Cooke

Guardian
April 9 1968

American Civil Rights leader Dr. Martin Luther King was assassinated at a motel in Memphis, Tennessee, on 4 April 1968. His murder provoked riots in black areas of several US cities. On 11 April President Johnson signed the Civil Rights Bill, making it illegal to refuse housing on the grounds of race.

Once before, the ninth of April was memorial day throughout the South. One hundred and three years ago today Robert E. Lee tendered his sword to General Grant and was granted in return the release of 'your men and their mules to assist in the spring ploughing'. Today, on a flaming spring day, with the magnolias blooming and the white dogwood and the red sprinkling the land, they brought a farm wagon and its mules to stand outside the church on the street where Martin Luther King was born and, after the funeral service to carry his body four miles to his college and lay it to rest. The 'mule train' is the oldest and still most dependable form of transport of the rural poor in the Southland. And somebody had the graceful idea that a mule train would be the aptest cortege for the man who was the apostle of the poor.

From the warm dawn into the blazing noon, the black bodies wearing more suits and ties than they would put on for a coronation, moved through the Negro sections of the town towards the street of comfortable, two-storey frame houses where the coloured business and professional men live and where, across from Cox's Funeral Home, the Rev. Martin Luther King lived and preached, in the Ebenezer Baptist Church, a red-bricked nondescript tabernacle.

Thousands of college students had volunteered to act as marshals to hold the crowds; but though there was a tremendous push and jostle of people before the service began, there were enough police on hand to stem the crush and hand the visiting celebrities through like very pregnant women.

The bell tolled out the tune of 'We Shall Overcome' and big cars slid up to the entrance, and out of them climbed the Attorney General, Ramsey Clark, and Mrs. John F. Kennedy, and Richard Nixon and Senator Eugene McCarthy, Governor and Mrs. Romney of Michigan, and Governor Rockefeller and John Lindsay of New York, the new Roman Catholic Archbishop Terence Cooke, Sidney Poitier, the Metropolitan Opera's Leontryne Price, Eartha Kitt, Sammy Davis Jr., Bobby and Ethel

Kennedy and brother Edward, and Dr. Ralph Bunche, U. Thant's man and Dr. King's friend.

Over the breaking waves of street noise and the tolling bell, the strong baritone of the Rev. Ralph Abernathy, Dr. King's heir, chanted from time to time: 'We will please be orderly now . . . let us have dignity . . . please . . . there are no more seats in the church.' Somebody lifted a squalling baby and passed it out over the tossing heads to safety.

It is a small church, and shortly after 10.30 the last cars and the last mourners were slotted in their places. First, Mrs. King and her four children and the dead man's brother, and Harry Belafonte. Then at last an alert squad of aides and Secret Service men surrounding Vice-President Humphrey. The conspicuous absentee was Lester Maddox, the Governor of Georgia, a segregationist whose presence could upset a coloured funeral any place North or South.

The inside of the church impressively belies its outside. It is a pleasantly modern room with a single oriel window, above a white cross over the choir and the pulpit. The flanking walls have two simple Gothic windows decorated alike with a single shield bearing a cross and surmounted with the crown of Christ. Tiny spotlights embedded in the ceiling threw little pools of light on the famous and the obscure equally. The warm shadows these shafts encouraged gave an extraordinary chiaroscuro to the congregation, making Bobby Kennedy at one point look like the captain of Rembrandt's 'Night Guard' amid his lieutenants slumbering in the shade.

It was a normal Baptist service with Southern overtones of gospel singing and solos, by black girls in white surplices, of Dr. King's favourite hymns sung with impassioned locking of the hands and closed eyes. Through it all, Mrs. King sat back at a sideways angle with the carved, sad fixity of an African idol. Dr. King's brother covered his face with a handkerchief once and others dabbed at their eyes; and the youngest King daughter sagged over in deep sleep like a rag doll. But Mrs. King was as impassive as Buddha behind her thin veil while the prayers were given, the hymns, the eulogy by a New York dean as white as Siegfried, who had taught theology to Dr. King. Once there was a suspicion of a glitter in her eyes when the Rev. Abernathy told of the last meal he had with Dr. King, an anecdote as simple as a parable.

'On that Thursday noon in the Lorraine Motel, in Memphis, Tennessee, the maid served up only one salad, and Martin took a small portion of it and left the rest. Then someone reminded the girl that she had brought up one order of fish instead of two. And Martin said, 'Don't worry about it, Ralph and I can eat from the same plate', and I ate my last meal that Thursday noon. And I will not eat bread or meat or anything until I am thoroughly satisfied that I am ready for the task at hand.'

There was one innovation that was nearly forgotten at the end. Both the casket and the family were ready to go, but there was a quick whisper in the Rev. Abernathy's ear and he announced that Mrs. King had requested a playback of one of Dr. King's last sermons.

It was the premonitory vision of his inevitable end, and his voice resounded through the hushed church: 'I think about my own death, and I think about my own funeral . . . and every now and then I ask myself what it is that I would want said and I leave the word to this morning . . . I don't want a long funeral, and if you get somebody to deliver the eulogy, tell him not to talk too long . . . tell him not to mention that I have a Nobel peace prize – that isn't important. Tell him not to mention that I have 300 or 400 awards – that's not important . . . I'd like somebody to mention that day that Martin Luther King tried to give his life serving others. I want you to say that day that I tried to be right and to walk with them. I want you to be able to say that day that I did try to feed the hungry. I want you to be able to say that day that I did try in my life to clothe the naked . . . I want you to say that I tried to love and serve humanity.'

Then the doors were opened and the family went out and all the parsons, and the mule team bore its flowered casket and moved towards the many, many thousands that had gone on before to Morehouse College.

Veteran journalist and broadcaster Alistair Cooke continues to send his Letter from America *once a week to the BBC. He was knighted in 1973.*

SOMETHING ABOUT A SOLDIER

—

Alan Coren

Punch
24 July 1968

As every schoolboy of the Fifties and Sixties can testify, World War II produced its fair share of boasters. What schoolboys couldn't know, however, was that those exploits so carefully recounted had probably been rehearsed ad nauseam *at the local golf club . . .*

'A team of investigators has shown that of all the men who wear regimental ties, six in ten are probably imposters.' *Daily Mirror.*

Thomas Breen laid his green leatherette sample-case carefully in the boot of the company Cortina; shut the lid; locked it. You couldn't be too careful, not with the electric toothbrushes. Valuable items like that, and the country the way it was, no morals any more and much of it black. He crossed the carpark, gravel grinding under his brogues, a march step, firm and dependable, can't beat good real leather on your soles, none of your pansy composite, and stepped, smartly, through the saloon lounge door, masculine stride across the figured pile, shoulders fat (but square), belly held in, small smile beneath the smaller moustache, and the wide green goldstriped tie trumpeting on his chest.

'Good morning, sir.'

'It is, indeed! Bright. But not sunny. It'll be taking spin.'

'Sir?'

'The wicket. Bit green after the rain. Taking spin. Definitely. Skittle 'em out by tea. Or soon after.'

'What can I get you, sir?'

'Pink gin. Large.'

Thomas Breen sniffed, twitched his bristles, cleared his throat.

'Ice?'

Short nod, chins interfolding briefly.

'Tight cap this, sir. Can't remember the last time I had to unscrew the pink. Customers don't seem to drink it these days.'

'Old habit,' said Breen. He chuckled. 'Medicinal. Not,' he added, leaning slightly towards the barman, humorously, 'that there's much beri-beri round here, eh?'

Breen slid the bitterness down his throat, and pushed his glass back across the counter.

'Army joke. Same again. Gin for the malaria, Angostura for the beri-beri. That's what we used to say. Bit before your time.'

'I dare say, sir.'

'White man's grave, Burma,' said Breen, allowing his eyes to glaze. 'But a clever little devil, your Jap. Get him in a corner, fights like a rat.'

'Really, sir?'

'Like a ruddy rat. Have something yourself. Yes, many's the time I had to go in with cold steel and finish off some yellow Johnny fighting on with half a dozen rounds still in him. Wouldn't lie down.'

'Amazing.'

'Wouldn't lie down. Once – I'm not boring you? – once, down near the Foonsang Delta, rainy season, my chaps were pinned down under a withering . . .'

Breen's voice frayed, and stopped. Beside him at the bar, a tall bony figure had materialized, grey-suited, with a tangerine rose in his buttonhole, yellow gloves. And a green goldstriped tie. The two men looked at one another, and the pupils ran around their eyes like trapped ants.

'I say!' said Breen.

'Ha, ha!' said the newcomer.

The barman smiled, with all the bonhomie of his calling.

'Here's a turn-up,' he said. 'Same regiment! This gentleman,' he continued, drawing a beer for the newcomer, 'was just telling me about your lot in Burma.'

'Burma?' said the newcomer.

'Only there a week or so,' said Breen quickly. 'Didn't get much chance to meet anyone, ha-ha-ha! Went down with trench foot second week.'

'Trench foot?'

'Mouth. Flown back to Catterick right away.'

'Catterick, eh?'

'Only for the day. Baffled Medical Corps. Didn't see a soul I knew. Driven straight to an isolation unit.'

The new man drank half his beer and put down the glass. 'Never saw Burma,' he said. He took out a handkerchief and mopped his forehead, despite the coolness of the day.

Breen unclenched his hand, and licked a bright bead from his moustache.

'Really?' he said. 'Ah, well, they shipped me back there, soon as I'd recovered. Hardly saw anywhere else.'

'Weren't in Libya, then?' said the new man.

'Libya?'

'Or do I mean Palestine? I mean, I do. I say, I reckon the old wicket's due to take a bit of spin this morning, don't you? Not that I think the Australians have sent us much of a –'

A third man entered; took off his coat; revealed a wide green goldstriped tie.

'Palestine, did you say?' he asked, looking at them uneasily.

'Libya, actually,' said the second man quickly. 'I was shorter then, of course. Sprang up after I was thirty. Fingleton,' he added desperately, extending a wet hand.

'Breen,' said Breen.

'Wittle,' said the third man.

'Not Charlie Wittle,' said Fingleton, 'by any chance?'

'NO!' shouted Wittle. 'I mean, no. No, they sent *Charlie* Wittle to Libya, I suppose,

I mean yes, they did, I remember that on the postings, yes, he went to Libya, and I went to, er, Burma.'

'There's a coincidence!' cried Fingleton. 'Breen here . . .'

'Just missed you!' exclaimed Breen. 'I remember, it was the day they were flying me home with foot and mouth, and they came in and said, there's a new chap just been sent out, chap called Wittle, pity you've missed him. That's what they said.'

'Breen went back, though,' insisted Fingleton, 'after he was well.'

'I would have been gone by then,' said Wittle, hurling a large Scotch down his gullet, somewhat erratically.

'Yes!' shouted Breen, 'I remember, I got off the plane, and they said, you've just missed Wittle again, he's gone. That's what they said.'

'Did they?' enquired Wittle, staring at him. 'Oh. Yes, well, I got posted back in time for Salerno.'

Breen and Fingleton breathed out. Everyone smiled.

'Parachuted in,' explained Wittle.

Everyone nodded. Fingleton bought another round.

'One of our regulars was at Salerno,' said the barman pleasantly. 'With your lot.'

Six eyes fixed on him from the rims of their drinks.

'Major Moult. Often mentions – well, talk of the devil!'

'Breen,' murmured Breen.

'Fingleton.'

'Wittle.'

'Moult.'

'I was telling the gentlemen, Major,' said the barman, taking Moult's pewter tankard from its hook, 'about Salerno.'

'Yes,' said Breen happily, 'Wittle parachuted in, you know.'

Moult looked at Wittle. 'I didn't know there were any parachute landings at Salerno,' he said.

'Ah, well, you wouldn't, old man,' said Wittle, laughing lightly, despite a shoeful of beer. 'Typical RAF cock-up, ha-ha-ha! Wrong prevailing winds. All baled out over the jolly old target area, and landed forty miles away.'

'I suppose you managed to make your way back to rejoin the regiment, though,' said Fingleton, 'didn't you, Wittle?'

'I would have been out of it by then,' said Moult. 'Got taken prisoner first day, shipped out to Deutschland, chop-chop.'

'Not a POW of the Jerries, were you?' said a new voice.

The four men turned, to find a short wiry man in a camelhair coat and a brown fedora. Between the smooth lapels of the former gleamed two gold bars, on a green ground.

'I escaped almost immediately,' said Moult, very loudly. 'Why did they get you, Mr . . . '

'Binns. Didn't they get any of the rest of you, then?'

The others shook their heads.

'They got, me alright,' said Binns confidently. 'In Libya.'

'Fingleton was in Libya,' said Wittle.

'Yes,' said Fingleton, 'I came after you were captured. Got sent out from Palestine to replace you. Jerry's got Binns, they said. You'll have to go out to Libya. That's what they said.'

Binns looked at him.

'You sure they said Binns?' he said.

Fingleton eased his tie-knot.

'Er, yes,' he muttered. 'Go out and replace, er, Erasmus Binns.'

A shadow lifted from Binns's face.

'Different chap,' he said. 'I'm *Arthur* Binns. Not, of course,' he added hurriedly, 'that I haven't heard of Erasmus Binns.'

'Have you?' asked Fingleton.

'Of course, he wasn't in Libya at the *exact* time as I was,' said Binns. 'I think he was in Burma, then.'

'That's it!' cried Fingleton. 'He was in Burma before he went to Libya and got captured and put in a POW camp.'

'After I'd escaped,' said Moult.

'He was probably in Burma about the time you were,' said Fingleton to Breen.

'Just missed him,' said Breen. 'I remember, it was the week I got dysentery, after I got back from Catterick and missed Wittle again. You've just missed Erasmus Binns, they said. As I got off the plane. They've sent him to Libya, they said.'

'Terrible thing, Burmese dysentery.'

'Who said that?' shrieked Breen, knocking over his fourth gin.

'I did.' The group was joined by a large bald man in a black jacket, set off with green and goldstriped tie. Breen grabbed his sleeve.

'They cocked up my diagnosis!' he shouted. 'What I actually had was phosgene poisoning. Not like you at all. Nothing like it.'

'I wasn't in Burma,' said the bald man carefully.

'None of us were in Palestine,' offered Moult.

'I would have seen you if you had been,' said the bald man. 'I was there for the duration.'

'Fingleton said he'd been in Palestine,' said Breen. 'Didn't you?'

'No! Libya. With the other Wittle, not this one. Erasmus Wittle. If I said Palestine, I meant I'd *passed through* it. At night. On the train.'

'I recall that train,' said the bald man, licking a dry lip. 'I remember someone saying, Fingleton's on that train. Going to Libya.'

'That's it!' cried Fingleton. 'That's exactly it!'

The bar clock struck three.

'Time please, gentlemen,' said the barman.

The six, as one man, flung themselves at the door, bound for their cars and freedom. Their escape, however, was cut off by a group of four men, waiting quietly outside the saloon bar: two had lost a leg, a third had an empty sleeve pinned across his chest, and was playing '*Tipperary*', one-handed, on a harmonica, to the banjo accompaniment of the men on crutches. A fourth man held a white stick in one hand, and a collection box in the other. All wore campaign stars; and wide green goldstriped ties.

Fingleton pulled Breen towards him.

'Look at that,' he muttered. 'Begging!'

'Disgusting!' said Breen. He felt for his car-keys. 'Don't know what the Regiment's coming to.'

Humourist Alan Coren is virtually a one man industry of journalism. After being editor of Punch *and the* Listener *he currently has a twice-weekly column in* The Times *and writes once a week for the* Sunday Express.

AT MIDNIGHT IN BRATISLAVA

—

P.G. Cerny
Guardian
23 August 1968

Several thousand Soviet troops, along with those from other Warsaw Pact countries, crushed the Prague Spring of liberalism within the Communist system in the early hours of 22 August 1968. It was to be twenty-one more years before the Soviet grip on Czechoslovakia was broken.

Czechoslovakia goes to sleep early as a matter of habit, and Bratislava was almost deserted when the first tanks appeared in the streets around midnight.

We were munching hot dogs in the main square when a soldier near us spotted three tanks at the far corner. Something was certainly amiss; in Czechoslovakia tanks are not permitted in the streets as a matter of policy. And these particular tanks were acting most strangely.

They took up strategic positions on the street corners and threw out leaflets in Russian, calling on Czechoslovak soldiers to support their Russian brothers in their struggle to liberate Czechoslovakia from the counter revolutionaries and imperialistic elements which had taken control. The point was made. 'This is the end,' said the soldier.

In the next hour and half all the city centre was strategically occupied, and convoys of tanks, armoured cars, and personnel carriers began to deploy to the outlying districts. A telephone call was made to the Slovak National Council, and another later to the Ministry of the Interior, but nobody knew anything. The surprise was complete.

Was Czechoslovakia's 'bloody autumn' about to begin – that prediction so feared by the people when made by a clairvoyant in July, and yet considered 'impossible' even this morning when the fact was accomplished.

For the next three hours the streets of the city were filled with the noise of the rumbling tanks, but only a few people woke and came down to watch. Czechoslovak policemen, their clothes hurriedly put on, and their briefcases swinging rather absurdly at their sides, ran or walked swiftly to work. The Russians remained quiet, simply taking up their positions in complete oblivion of the frantic scurrying, not seeming to care. The tactic was effective. 'We can do nothing,' said a bystander.

In the main square, however, things began to hot up. Long columns of Russian vehicles continued to pour through on their way to new positions beyond the city, but a sad and bitter crowd began to form. Most of the people were young, but all ages and types were represented.

One girl raised her skirts and wiggled her behind at the Russians. Then, as the main column of supply lorries came to a momentary halt, two or three young people sat down, Gandhi style, to block their path. Although the fear was great, especially as the trucks began to move again, more people joined the protestors.

The lorries stopped again. Slovaks began clawing at the door handles, locked from the inside. Headlights were broken, and a boy sat in several obscene positions on the bonnet of the leading lorry. More people joined the blockade, singing the old Slovak national anthem, the 'International', and other patriotic songs.

Many people tried to speak with the Russian soldiers, to convince them that they ought to go home; their listeners remained stonily silent. One Russian soldier, however, spoke up to a small group of Slovaks. Russian soldiers, he said, were intelligent; they sympathized with the argument of the people, but their officers and politicians were stupid and the soldiers could do nothing.

In the ensuing hissing, the soldier lost his hat, but the Slovaks gave it back to him. But the pressure-point was getting ever greater. The Russians decided to move. The lorry-drivers, ordinary soldiers, began to drive but stopped – causing a minor collision – when the crowd began once again to sit down.

The tank-drivers were not so charitable. They drove straight at one boy who had stretched himself out across the road. At the last instant, he turned sideways and passed beneath the treads, scrambling to safety after it had passed him. What relief! Nobody was in any mood for martyrs; the tragedy would have been too great.

A man of about thirty-five standing next to me began to sob and one could not help recalling those famous photographs of the crowds – crying, jeering, and waving their arms in despair – when the Nazis occupied Prague in 1939 or Paris in 1940. The crowd at most counted only about a hundred people, perhaps 200 at its peak; a feeling of helplessness pervaded the atmosphere. Should they cry 'Fascist,' as some did, or should they just say 'Please go home, and leave us in peace,' as most did? At most, the acts were symbolic.

A few attempts were made to increase the resistance. Paving stones were torn up and either placed beneath the tyres of the lorries to block them – which they did only momentarily – or thrown at the tanks, along with litter bins. Like shooting elephants with cork-tipped darts!

The best opportunity came when a supply tank loaded with spare parts and oil drums drove by. Several boys managed to clamber aboard and threw two oil drums into the street, one of which was set on fire. But it did not burn well, and the tanks just brushed it aside.

By this time, the main column had already passed and people were following them up the street. Some shots rang out – about three rifle shots and two machine-gun bursts – but they were over in an instant and nobody seemed to have been injured.

Now and then a Czech army truck or jeep appeared, to be roundly cheered. Smiling, confused Czech policemen began to turn up, and the big events of the night seemed over by four o'clock, until the morning, at least – after a few hours for reflection, discussion, or, if one has iron nerves, sleep. In the morning, solemn faces queued up at the shops; hoarding became the order of the day. The occupation had begun.

The impossible had happened – the last death struggle, the final groping for life, of a form of communism long since relegated to the dustbin of history. Stalinism triumphant, but for how long? And for what? A military coup is one thing; a turning back of the political clock to the days of Jan Hus and the blindness of ideologically based power is another.

The Czechoslovak people have lived most of their history under some form of subjugation; their reflex mechanisms are well developed. That their efforts turn away from social productivity to personal entrenchment and self preservation on the one hand, and to intellectual and artistic endeavour on the other, is a fact of history. They are accustomed to oppression, but that does not excuse the Russians for their action. That the Czechoslovaks will endure is certain; that they *must* endure is injustice.

TRAINING FOR ARMAGEDDON

—

John Mortimer
New Statesman
6 September 1968

In August, 1968, Basil d'Oliveira, England's Cape Coloured all-rounder, was omitted from the English cricket team to play in South Africa, resulting in protests from anti-apartheid groups. When he was later selected, South Africa banned the English team, anyway. They were, in South African Prime Minister Vorster's words, 'a team of troublemakers'.

The fact that those responsible for selecting the English cricket team should be accused of cowardice, trucking to racial prejudice and injustice comes as no surprise to me. Neither am I amazed that football should give rise to uncontrollable violence and the mass destruction of British Rail's lavatories, or croquet to a mean cunning in otherwise generous and open characters. I remain calm at the revelation that even those unfortunates who spend weeks crouched over their handlebars sweating up the mountainsides of industrial France are secretly chewing dope in place of fruit-gums. I expect fast bowlers to be greeted by a shower of beer bottles, tennis players to accept defeat with hysterical resentment and rugger forwards to hack furtively at each others' vital organs and sing embarrassing songs in the shower-room afterwards. War, political upheaval, even marriage and divorce sometimes, cause human beings to give rise to uncontrollable violence and then behave well. Games bring out the worst in everybody.

When I first went to school, I noticed that the time was divided almost equally between work and play. The hours of work were tolerable enough. It was possible to lean on the radiator, drop off to sleep whilst the masters, shell-shocked veterans to a man, ramblingly accounted for the bits of shrapnel still lodged in them as a result of the 1914 War. As we were too young, in those days, to write, our mothers would come to the school once a term and have us dictate our exams to them. For the rest of the time, placidly illiterate, we stared out into the Square, made small wind instruments or framed reproductions of the Mona Lisa in passe-partout. The hours of work were protected, considerate and safe.

Not so, I soon discovered, the periods of games. Presumably designed as times of rest and recreation, games were a daily and dangerous nightmare. It was as if every whistle blew with a sickening call to go over the top after all-too-short periods of leave. Then the shell-shocked masters underwent a terrible change. Rallying to their memories of Passchendaele, they would charge uncontrollably amongst us children, urging us, with blows and abuse, to tackle each other low, to bring each other slithering to the ground and to receive cheerfully each others' boots in our faces, to have our heads crushed between the small and bony buttocks of those with whom, left to ourselves, we might have made perfectly good friends.

The Square was also fatally close to Chelsea Barracks. Looking back down the long Chamber of Horrors representing my past's alarming, despairing and sickening moments, one tableau – forever embalmed and lit with a special green light – stands out vividly. A giant boxing ring, designed for stalwart troopers to batter each other insensible, stretches round me as far as the eye can reach. In the middle, insignificant as flies on Everest, I and my friend Swanson, great balloons of gloves lashed to the ends of our pale, matchstick arms, land Lilliputian blows on each other's scarlet faces, terrified of showing any lack of enthusiasm for this unkind task. Between rounds, two moustached, bullet-headed sergeants flap us with towels, pummel our stomachs, pour water down our throats and mutter 'Next round Sonny, go in for the kill.'

Both Swanson and I survived this encounter, but only just. After it we avoided each other's eye, each filled with the implanted guilt of having allowed the other to survive. I stood by the War Memorial on Poppy Day in heavy rain and heard the headmaster say that it was the habit of playing games on his soggy fields that taught his old boys, when called upon, to fix bayonets and play until the last Armistice whistle blew. Then I knew what games were about. They were about to get me killed.

It was to be expected that games and battles should become as confused as they did in the mind of Lord Montgomery when he offered to hit the Germans for six. At a later school, on alternate football days, we went on manoeuvres. Dressed in puttees and peaked caps, we would scatter across the country round Aldershot. I remember in full uniform, settling down behind a bush to read a good book. In a little while, an officer rode up on a white horse to tell me I was dead. From then on, I decided that, when games were afoot, it was best to move stealthily away and hide in the hope of being pronounced a non-contender.

The cracking boredom, the aimless contest and triviality of most of our games was justified on the grounds that they taught us 'team spirit' and kept our minds off sex. Our individual personalities (all our education was calculated to make us regret the fact that we were not identically alike) might at least be sunk into a corporate Fifteen or Eleven, pursuing, as one automatic many-legged monster, a small flying object. This, we were told, was to be an invaluable lesson for life. I must say, I have never found it so. Achievements of value have, in my experience been the result of individuals working alone and not encouraged by anything but their fierce determination to be like nobody else but themselves. Only Hollywood film-scripts, television commercials and cabinet decisions have the flavourless quality of team-work.

What is sad is that an educational system which has left the average Englishman with most traces of foreign languages, mathematics or poetry drained from his mind, has also given him an exaggerated reverence for games in which, happily for him, he need no longer participate. Asking for the score all the summer becomes a sort of religious salutation, a way of showing that we really inhabit a purer, less materialistic world than the bank or the doctor's waiting-room. Politicians believe, I think wrongly, that they never appear more sympathetic than when they jokingly confess that the tedious business of the Budget has made them miss Wimbledon on the telly.

The pretence is usually unconvincing: nobody believes that Harold Wilson is really more interested in the batting averages than the by-election figures. No one knows now with what trembling hands, and at the expense of how many sailors, Drake played that last intolerable game of bowls.

The truth is that games produce scenes of international disharmony, rivalry and dissension quite unjustified by their importance or interest. The Olympics have a fine imposing sound, evoking photographs of alabaster discus throwers in a thousand headmasters' studies, and vague feelings of universal and masculine love. In fact the political wrangles as to who shall take part in this distant Mexican Sports Day seem to have lasted as long, and been conducted with as much bitterness, as the run up to a major war.

But the myth that sport takes place in some sane, healthier, altruistic world in which we are proud to share, if only at second hand, persists. To be knowledgeable about Arsenal makes the most aloof critic feel at one with the masses; even with that great majority that never goes near a football match. If he's not careful a touch of sport may infiltrate into his prose, so that he may be seen as the complete man. 'A Macbeth,' he will write, 'who after a couple of uncertain overs rose to the bowling splendidly in the murder of Duncan, and snicked "Tomorrow and tomorrow and tomorrow" to square leg in a manner which I haven't seen equalled since the P.W.W. Bulstrode made mincemeat of the Aussie bowling all one long hot Manchester afternoon in the great days of yore.' If that's what it's like, it's the sort of acting from which I'd rather stay away.

I don't have to play games any more: but I can scarcely live through an English summer day without remembering looking up at the sky to pray that a thunderstorm might cancel the match. When I hear that magical phrase 'Rain stopped play' I feel the relief of the cricketers who can sit, as I imagine, all the happy afternoon, munching jam sandwiches and reading old back numbers of *Whitaker's Almanack*, the welcome rain thudding on the roofs of their little pavilions. As an item of news, as an object of international tension and national aggression, might not rain stop play indefinitely? Haven't we got enough on our plates? If we must learn to live with the Russians and the Americans, should we be called upon to cope with cricket as well? These last weeks I spent driving through Africa looking at, amongst other animals, lions. There is much to be said for lions. They don't attack their own species, nor do they play organized games.

John Mortimer was a barrister. He is now a journalist, playwright, novelist and television writer – his most enduring creation being Rumpole of the Bailey.

JANE FONDA'S CURIOUS MENAGE IN ST TROPEZ

John Sandilands
Nova
November 1968

In movies the late Sixties was generally a period of soft-focused extreme silliness. Few films were more absurd than Barbarella, which starred Jane Fonda and was directed by her husband Roger Vadim.

The new films of Roger Vadim are always accompanied by a certain excitement. His first picture, *And God Created Woman*, made at St Tropez in 1956, starred in great anatomical detail his wife Brigitte Bardot. Its release was accompanied by the rumours of impending divorce through Bardot's relationship with her leading man in the picture.

The divorce was confirmed in December 1957, and the following day a young Danish actress called Annette Stroyberg gave birth to Vadim's baby. They married and Annette became the star of Vadim's next picture, *Les Liaisons Dangereuses*.

At the time of the film's opening it was reported that she was having an affair with a French guitarist called Sacha Distel who had come suddenly to fame as a boyfriend of Brigitte Bardot. A divorce followed.

The release of that picture outside France was delayed for two years by censorship difficulties but when Vadim came to New York for the delayed opening he was accompanied by a new protégée, an eighteen-year-old French actress called Catherine Deneuve. Their friendship received considerable publicity, as did the birth of Vadim's son to Catherine although neither was considering marriage.

The presentation of Vadim's first film with the American actress, Jane Fonda, daughter of Henry Fonda, was enlivened by news of their romance. The film was called *La Ronde* (The Roundabout), but Vadim went on to marry Jane in 1965.

Their latest picture together, on general release this month, is a highly erotic science-fiction fantasy called *Barbarella* in which Jane appears nude and in a variety of futuristic sexual dilemmas. A few weeks ago, just before the London opening, she gave birth to her first baby, a daughter.

She is eight-and-a-half months pregnant and she is looking absolutely lovely. She is tall so that her imposing front makes her stately and she can still glide a little when she walks. It is blazingly hot at St Tropez and she is wearing an embroidered Tunisian *djellabah*, ankle-length, as a maternity gown. Nothing else. The sleeves are wide and cut to the waist and when she raises her arms to push back her mane of blonde hair it is possible to see her bare breasts which are remarkably shapely, even at this late date.

She seems wonderfully happy. Everybody seems happy. There are guests at the villa, an Italian prince and princess and their baby boy. On the low wall along the terrace above the sparkling Mediterranean the princess is reading a book, lying on her stomach with just the bottom half of her bikini between her olive skin and the brilliant sun. The boy baby is naked, plump with contentment and rude as a cherub.

Two dogs, an Alsatian and a golden spaniel, are panting companionably together in the shade and in the kitchen the good-looking Italian boy in his tiny shorts is preparing lunch, moving methodically but lazily, the exact pace for working when it is very warm and nobody really cares about the time. It is a late August weekend in the Vadim villa at St Tropez and nobody seems to care much about anything except just *being*, pleasurably, in the Mediterranean sun.

Jane Fonda, the third and current Madame Vadim, is discoursing amiably about the state of maternity which has now overtaken her, at thirty, for the first time. 'I think,' she says, 'that it would be nice if you could have babies by all the men that you love and respect. There are a few of Vadim's friends that I would love to have babies with but the trouble is that it all takes too long. Christian Marquand, now, who is Vadim's best friend, said to me once, 'I'd like to have a baby by you,' and it would be wonderful to have a son of Christian's but, I mean, nine months . . . If a pregnancy lasted two months, say, it would be different but I don't think I could consecrate nine months to anything that wasn't Vadim's.'

She gazes with her huge, innocent, blue-grey eyes out across the Golfe de St Tropez and it is possible to wonder if this is the latest small-talk of Riviera villas but she is thinking about it seriously in a fond, rather wistful way. 'If I weren't married to Vadim I'd be very sad not to have his baby,' she ponders. 'He has such extraordinary children, you know.'

Vadim is out there somewhere in the gulf in his speedboat, one of the stream of craft that pour out of the famous harbour to sport like dolphins, aimlessly, on the spangled water until the lure of St Trop draws them home again. He is absent but overpoweringly present because it is his unique lifestyle that has created this wondrously insouciant scene.

For more than a decade Roger Vadim has stood as a symbol of male emancipation – a man with the ability to ignore convention and, much more importantly, to make beautiful women ignore it with him. There should stand on the celebrated quai at St Tropez a large bronze statue of Vadim, frozen in some noble pose, a resting place and occasional convenience for passing sea-birds and a permanent memorial to the marvellous skein of movies and marriages, parting and paternities, schemes and scandals that he has woven over the years with St Trop as their sunny setting.

In the beginning was Brigitte Bardot, whom he married and casually handed over to the world in a celluloid package, smile, bosom, legs and incomparable behind.

Next there was Annette Stroyberg, a Nordic replica of Bardot, a baby, then marriage, then more sizzling film stock devoted to her naked charms. Next there was Catherine Deneuve, a baby, no marriage but the inevitable *Paris-Match* pictures in which this pale, Parisian beauty had suddenly come to look amazingly like her predecessor and Bardot.

Somehow St Tropez has always remained the maypole round which this complex combination of flesh and flouted morals, casual wedlock and off-hand fatherhood has circulated and now there is another Vadim consort there, pregnant and seemingly quite comfortably attuned to this curious *modus vivendi*.

Even bow-fronted, without a trace of make-up, she looks with her high cheek-bones and flood of careless blonde hair again a good deal like Bardot but it may be an illusion brought on by St Tropez. Jane Fonda is different from her precursors, she has come from another mould. She is not a Vadim invention but a film star in her own right, the daughter of a famous film star, a beautiful woman with her own stock of intelligence and poise. She is aware of all this and she tries, politely, as if it is a duty, to explain.

'I guess,' she says, 'I'm a kind of slave type. I seem to function very well when someone puts me in a framework and Vadim always knows exactly where he's going. His marriages, you know, don't end because he's impossible to live with. He's a very understanding, easy going, intelligent sort of person, the complete opposite of everything you hear about him before you know him. He has the ability to make a woman blossom. He brings out qualities in her that may have been there already but were never going to come out without Vadim to help them along.

'He seems to be attracted to complicated, impossible people, myself included, but he is never the one who makes the difficulties. When I first got pregnant, for example, I was the world's worst bitch. I was really terrible. It got to the stage of saying very calmly: "Look, we won't get divorced yet, while I'm having a baby." For a little while there it was all over and I was terribly unhappy.

'Some time later when I was very relaxed and contented again I mentioned all this business to Vadim and he'd completely forgotten the whole thing. He'd forgotten and to me it was this awful drama!' She opens her eyes even wider and smiles showing all her pearly, quaintly protuberant teeth, astonished at the saintly detachment of Vadim from the idiocies forced upon him by beautiful women. Fondly she recalls how easy it was to misjudge him without the privilege of closer acquaintance with him.

'You know, I first met Vadim in Maxim's when I was seventeen years old and I was studying painting in Paris. He was with Annette Stroyberg who was very pregnant with' – she pauses only momentarily to assimilate the implications – 'well, my step-daughter, and I'd only heard the bad things about him. How he was cynical, vicious, immoral, Svengali-type character. I was very aggressive because I'd only heard the legend. Later on he sent for me to come to see him at the Beverley Hills Hotel in Hollywood, to talk about a film, but we had nothing to say to each other. I thought that all the charm and the softness were just an act to cover up for all the other stuff. One of the reasons for the flip-over' – she demonstrated the flip-over with her long, brown hands – 'was the discovery that he is so utterly different from his public image.'

She is quite plainly, to use an old-fashioned expression, in love with Vadim but discovering his many remarkable qualities is no longer exactly an original exercise for a lovely girl who has the world at her own feet. 'Look,' she says, 'I know there is a pattern that repeats itself with Vadim and women but it's not something he works at, it's just the way he is. He has his friends and his way of life here and we are constantly running into people who knew him then, but if you're married to someone like Vadim and you were jealous of his past you couldn't go on living, could you?

'I'm not jealous because I find that men who have lived a full life and known a lot of beautiful women are no longer trying to prove themselves. The mystery and glamour of every new woman that comes along has gone for Vadim because he knows it all. The French have an expression for the way he is which is something like "he is at ease within his skin".' She lowers her eyelashes and drops her voice at least an octave. 'Besides, the kind of life he has had has made him a good deal more interesting.'

There would seem to be a danger, alongside a personality so accurately adjusted and well-defined, of a certain loss of identity even for an actress who has become one of the biggest box-office attractions in the whole of the film industry. Jane Fonda shook her head so violently that she had to go through the fascinating process of pushing back her mane. 'I have my identity more than ever before because when you are happy you become so much more what you are. Most women, with Vadim, become more definite although it's not something he tries to create. When he's not there I feel less of a person, not more. He was away in America a while ago and he stayed away just a few days too long and I began to feel very lost and unhappy. When you are very contented with somebody it seems to give you a kind of aura. I think I have become much more attractive to men since I married Vadim.'

Vadim has been missing again for some time now and there is building up a certain air of expectancy about his arrival that is strengthened by the fact that promising signs of lunch have appeared. The plump housekeeper who, in the convoluted manner of a Vadim *ménage*, turns out to be the mother of the Italian cook, has set a table on the terrace loaded with wines, salads, long loaves and interesting sauces, and the spectacle has magnetized a sudden crowd of people, all of whom introduce themselves by saying: 'Where is Vadim?'

There is the prince who belongs to the princess and a sultry girl in a bikini who turns out to be the baby's nursemaid instead of a contessa and Serge Marquand, who is Christian's brother and thus, evidently, Vadim's second-best friend. With him there is an enigmatic American girl who confesses later, and mysteriously, that she used to date both Serge and Vadim when she was fifteen and in Mexico of all places. She too wears a bikini and the uniform olive tan.

They all sit down at the table and look hopefully towards Jane who, in turn, looks hopefully out towards the sea which at present, somewhere and presumably contains Vadim. The villa is in the Parc de St Tropez, an expensive enclave with a guard at the gate, out on the headland past the village where the tourists endlessly turn over the clothes at *Choses* on the quai and scramble for the status of a table in the front row, far right at the *Cafe Senequier*. The seagoing traffic is now all streaking back to St Trop, because it is the hallowed French luncheon hour, and Jane watches the white wakes for a time. 'You know,' she says, 'I hate St Tropez.' There could be so many reasons why. It was Vadim and Brigitte Bardot who invented all that wonderful nonsense about the importance of slacks from *Choses* and certain seats at Senequier, the whole satire on *chic* and *le snobbisme* that is the best of St Tropez. The actual, immortal villa of Bardot at Cap Pierre is only concealed by a large rock, just out of view.

It emerges that what Jane dislikes are merely the huge crowds which flock into what was once no more than a tiny fishing village. 'We have this big car and sometimes when I take it into St Tropez to do the shopping the traffic is so awful that I just burst into tears. I leave the car right there in the middle of the road and walk away.' She makes a weary housewife face as though St Trop were Surbiton instead of the scene of her husband's most picturesque forays.

There may be a subtle association of ideas, however, for she says suddenly, 'You want to know something very funny? Sometimes when I go into St Tropez with Vadim people call me Brigitte. They're standing right up close to me and they call me Brigitte!' It sounds a thoroughly disagreeable experience for someone with a name as famous as Jane Fonda's but she doesn't seem to think so. 'I mean, I just find that puzzling. I don't know how people can make that mistake.' There is no suggestion that she is the least bit troubled by being part of a small procession. 'Bardot,' she says, shaking her head in honest awe, 'she's a real phenomenon. She can be in a room filled with powerful personalities but you are still constantly aware that she is there. I've met her but I can't talk to her – she scares me to death.' She thinks about that for a moment then produces a tiny spark of rebellion: 'Of course she has made a series of very bad pictures.'

The acting career of Jane herself has not taken its major strides through the movies she has made for Vadim, for in Vadim pictures the volume and quality of sheer flesh that he favours tends to out-weigh such a shy nuance as acting talent. Her professional reputation rests, at this moment, with *Barbarella*, Vadim's latest creation based on a pseudo-science-fiction comic-strip. In it she is required to say little more than 'Good heavens!' as she is continually confronted with an astounding spectrum of sexual occurrences, both pseudo-science-fictional and distinctly earthy in every respect.

On the topic of her career there is just a hint of something less than euphoria, a defensiveness that she displays nowhere else. 'If I have anything as an actress,' she says, 'I have variety. Why not go out on a limb and do something like *Barbarella*? It's *fun*, it's something new and different. Maybe making the picture wasn't as rewarding to me in the acting sense, day by day, but I *like* taking a chance like that.'

The honesty that exists permanently in her blue-grey eyes exerts itself. 'I guess that if I had just received a letter from Dino (Dino de Laurentiis who produced *Barbarella*) I would have thrown it away. I would never have done *Barbarella* with anyone else but Vadim. He convinced me that it was right for me and I'm very glad that he did.

'Of course I know that in America everybody is going to go "Eeeeek" and say that it's just another Vadim nudie picture. I'm sure that, back home, my grandmother is going to say, "Jane, how could you do it?" but I don't think of it as an erotic film. It's just funny and free and nice. You know Vadim only has me *completely* nude behind the opening titles? He said, "Everybody will be waiting for that so why don't we get it over with right away and get on with the picture?" That's how *he* thinks about all that.'

More time has passed and a measure of desperation is beginning to emanate from the guests at the table. They are now nibbling with increasing vigour at the salad and the bread and the bravest among them have actually started on their hors d'oeuvres. Conventional instincts long bred in Jane from her birth in respectable, mid-western

Nebraska and encouraged during her further education at Vassar finally prove too strong and she rises and sweeps towards the table in the classic hostess manner.

'Meals in this house are *such* a problem,' she announces brightly but unnecessarily. 'Vadim is always *hours* late for everything.' This news is received so mournfully that Jane loses her nerve and whispers to the cook's mother who almost sprints out of the kitchen with the main course, a gigantic fish lying on its side like a bombed battleship. 'Vadim caught this fish at five o'clock this morning!' Jane prattles on sociably. 'We didn't get home until dawn. Vadim's way with a dull party is to stay right to the very end in the hope that something will happen. He just doesn't use the same clock as other people.'

Her audience is not attentive and the fish's huge bones are showing as if it had been attacked by piranha when a loud whoop is heard, theatrically, to seaward. 'That's Vadim!' says Jane, igniting as to a mating call. She hurries into the house and is back with her eye make-up on by the time the Titan appears, walking slowly up the steps which lead from the rocks to the terrace. He is tall and strongly built, broadening quite a bit at the waist of his bathing suit and wearing thick-rimmed library glasses. He looks older and more impressive than the lean, slightly wolfish figure of his early St Tropez period.

The guests, in much better heart now, greet him like a hero. He has a loud voice, deep and heavily accented and his manner is lazily boisterous. He envelops Jane in an embrace then peers down her revealing sleeve while patting her bottom with his free hand.

After examining her noble stomach he tells everybody: 'I am sure that it is really full of water and there are seven little red fishes swimming around in there. I am so certain that I am preparing an aquarium for them instead of a nursery.' He heaves a big mock sigh. 'One night of pleasure and nine months waiting for seven little fishes!' Undeterred he sits down to the remains of his morning catch. 'He has been through all this pregnancy thing before,' Jane explains fondly, 'but he forgets. It's just as though it's the first time. You know he has even had *cravings*?'

After lunch Vadim sits next to Jane on the wall, thrusts his hand up her sleeve and fondles her breast while promoting a discussion on whether childbirth leaves a faint white line on a woman's abdomen, extending from the navel due south. The American girl has had a baby recently and Vadim pursues his researches down into her bikini without relinquishing Jane's flesh.

The controversy continues for some time but it is very hot on the terrace and it is decided that an expedition will be made to Pampelone beach, so much more favoured than the Tahiti *plage* nowadays. Vadim manoeuvres the riva, that most status-laden of Riviera power boats, up to the small jetty below the house and Jane makes the tricky progress aboard just like everyone else, without benefit of solicitous hands or noticeable concern from anybody over her unwieldy condition.

Vadim revs up mightily and buckets across the waves around the headland while she reclines, a thought precariously in the circumstances, on the rear decking. Presently Vadim hands over the wheel and takes to water skis, performing expertly while the boat is hurled through a series of back-breaking arabesques which make Jane's position seem even more temporary.

She is quite unworried and turns round to watch her husband and, by shifting slightly in the well of the boat, it is possible to conjure up a highly symbolic optical illusion. It can be made to appear that Jane is holding Vadim on a leash of brilliant orange nylon rope, but a very long leash which in no way restricts his freedom of movement. It seems a reasonable moment to wonder why Jane and Vadim took a step so oddly conventional as actually getting married.

'Mostly,' says Jane, 'because of the child.' This, too, appears rather formal reasoning for such a liberated couple. 'Not this child,' says Jane, patting her stomach. 'We took my stepdaughter to America with us and you know how they are there. Kids used to say to her: 'Oh, your mommy and daddy aren't married are they' and there was all that nonsense with hotels and things like that. It was just easier to be married, that's all.'

The subject is making her slightly more uncomfortable than her seat on the back of a bucking boat. She is vehement for the first time. 'Vadim and I have been together for five years but I honestly can't remember if we've been married for two years and lived together for three or if it's the other way around.

'Our wedding was on the twenty-first floor of a hotel in Las Vegas. The judge was seventy years old and we went out afterwards and gambled all night. I can't even remember the name of the hotel. Maybe it was the Sands.' It was the Dunes and the casual nature of the ceremony has been established, but Jane continues, 'I'd formed a very definite view about marriage – that it's silly. It just doesn't make sense to me. That people form a couple seems perfectly natural. Marriage is something else again, something superfluous like the human appendix. I'm sure that in the future, like that organ, it will be eliminated because it certainly doesn't protect anything as far as the couple are concerned. We're all fickle, why have the added burden of marriage? Maybe women do need the security, I don't know, but two days before the wedding I went into a complete panic and I wanted to call the whole thing off. Now I feel better about it. I believe that, in the end, if you're careful, marriage needn't really spoil anything.'

On cue, Vadim performs a final sequence of spectacular gyrations and disappears abruptly beneath the waves while Jane winds in the empty towing line. She makes her own descent, heavily, into the surf at Pampelone beach and everybody gathers at a small bar which blossoms magically out of the golden sands. Within moments, and from nowhere, whole segments of Vadim's life manifest themselves. Vadim's mother appears, a tiny, bespectacled grey-haired lady, Vadim's sister, big-boned like Vadim, and Vadim's brother-in-law, one of the several he has acquired in his time. There is Vadim's daughter by Annette Stroyberg, Nathalie, a tall, lissom ten-year-old who exactly resembles her mother, plus Vadim's slanting Tartar eyes. Jane sits amongst them all, very contented, talking as volubly as everyone else in her fast American-accented French.

By the time it comes to leave, the news of a Vadim visitation has spread right along the beach and a crowd of people has assembled outside the bar. Jane makes a majestic progress back to the boat with the throng falling back in front of her like awed savages, their faces covered with cameras as if in respect. Thus each of her predecessors, pregnant or otherwise, have made their departures from the beaches of St Tropez, but her smile is generous. She seems quite happy with her position in the line of descent.

Back at the villa the Vadim entourage disappears to change into the vivid kaftans and pyjama suits and tight *Choses* trousers which constitute evening wear at St Tropez and Vadim alone remains in his bathing shorts on the darkening terrace. He has made himself a large Scotch and he is in a mellow mood, looking out across the velvety gulf. He is prepared to divulge a little of the philosophy that has enabled him to dispose of so many of the stresses which bedevil almost every other husband and father on earth, a few of the secrets of the care and maintenance of such a carefree *ménage*.

'I am asking a lot from life when I am living with a woman,' he says. 'What is important for me is to trust and to trust is not to protect a woman too much and never to put her in situations where she has no temptations to face. To protect your wife too much is to be like a stingy man with money. It is a sick thing. In life beauty must be seen and it is a terrible conception that if that beauty exists in your wife it must be hidden.

'I would not be jealous if my wife was naked in our garden and she was seen by someone for whom I have respect – someone who would appreciate her beauty on a normal, intelligent level. I would not mind a bit. If a man has an intelligent wife he will not hide her, will he? I do not have the slightest sense of sin so far as sex and the body are concerned. Why should I pretend that I do for the sake of narrow, stupid, bourgeois thinking?'

He smiles charmingly, showing his big, horse teeth. He is immensely attractive, infinitely persuasive because his face is guileless and pleasant except for a hint of secretive humour around his wide-set eyes. With an effort now, however, he manages a stern expression. 'It is respect that is important between a man and a woman. Here, at the house, we may be playful with each other and our friends but at a party, at a club perhaps, if my wife starts to flirt and dance lasciviously I don't like that because it is vulgar and does not show proper respect for the relationship. You will *never* see me kiss and caress a woman in public,' he concludes with a conviction that brooks no possibility of argument.

It remains mildly puzzling that, in his films, his womenfolk are so ardently addressed and undressed by other men before a public of varied intellect and numbered in millions. Vadim considers the question, an old friend whom he met after his very first picture and the suggestion of humour around his eyes becomes a statement. 'It is strange, isn't it?' he says.

He is forty years old, a father, at last, in wedlock; was there any chance now that his way of life might change, his taste as a movie-maker progress to properties more recognizably serious, and certainly more adequately clothed, than *Barbarella*? 'You change a little at adolescence,' says Vadim with endless tolerance. 'Sometimes that adolescence lasts a very long time but you never learn anything really new after you are twenty, except perhaps in a relationship with a woman. I think that Jane is sensitive and intelligent and evolved enough to understand that which is why, at the moment, we are very happy.'

He is interrupted by the ringing of the telephone inside the villa and Jane emerges in the beautiful white maternity smock that she wears for evening. 'C'est Brigitte Bardot qui t'appelle,' she says casually. Vadim thanks her politely and goes to answer the call.

John Sandilands was probably the best profile writer on Nova. *He has also made television programmes and, with Lavinia Warner, wrote* Women Beyond the Wire, *an account of women held in Japanese prisoner-of-war camps in the Second World War. He is currently writing a book on the French Foreign Legion.*

A GROUPIE'S VISION

Germaine Greer
Oz
February 1969

The concept of the groupie, the fan who bestows sexual favours on her favourite rock stars, became a growing service industry in the pop boom of the Sixties. Some groupies achieved a a certain notoriety at the time. One or two took the longer view and married their heroes.

Musicians, like other men, have always had women, but something in their way of having them was different by virtue of their being musicians, like it would differ again for airline pilots and lighthouse keepers. In the years BB (before Beatlemania) there were two kinds of musicians' birds – the musos' old ladies and the scrubbers. The rock-and-rollers picked up and put down the local goers like meals, perhaps storing a little woman at home, protected from the knowledge of her husband's promiscuity and the lunatic fringes of his sexuality. The scrubbers suffered all his aggression, all his loneliness and self-doubt. The jazz musicians had a different scene. They toured less often and less spectacularly and played to a discriminating clientele that came to listen. They were deep into their music, and so perforce were their women. Marriage was not common, but monogamy was the rule. It was a hard life for the birds, because they never went out at night except to listen to the old man's sets. There wasn't much money so they worked in the daytime, and fought fatigue and loneliness sitting in a dark corner where the club owner would not find their presence intolerable. They came to listen instead of waiting at home in bed because musicians were not often verbal in those days of separated media, and the only way they could hear the message of love was through the music. But cool jazz was cool. The message was often cold, inner-directed, and musos often lost their birds, not often to each other. Some of them took up a pose of embitterment, and took it out on the scrubbers. Lots of them drank or pilled up. One or two kept a wife in the suburbs. And took that out on the scrubbers, too.

'The first boyfriend I ever had,' said Dr. G, the Daytripper, 'was a jazz drummer, the best. I was with him for a year, and I never danced with him, that was one of the things it meant. I couldn't even dance to his music in front of him. Seems like I sat that whole year. In the end I became the hat-check girl in the club. Then he took a long gig in another state. On his last night in the club he sang a blues song just for me, about having a girl ten foot tall, and I cried myself blind in the hat-check room. The rag merchants talked all through it and then they all clapped their hands.' She knitted her brows. 'Then somebody told him I had been with somebody else, 2,000 miles away, and he just dropped me cold without another word. Can you imagine that?'

But the post-Beatle era was dawning and the media were drawing closer to each other for the fusion which is now. Music became commercial and creative, not only notes but words, not only sound but physical onslaught, sigh, movement, total environment. The jazz musician's love affair with his instrument moved out of his hand and met the rocker's violent cruel sensuality at tenderness junction, and the girls sitting wiped out against cold nightclub walls in quiet clothes arose with their listening eyes and danced alone, opened out their beauty in the various light and sex flowed back into the scene and lapped all around them. Where all the currents intersected and flowed forward and back, there he was, the musical revolutionary-poet calling all to witness the new order and achieve the group grope, astride his thousands of volts, winding his horn while the mode of the music changed and the walls of the city fell and everybody burst out laughing. The women kept on dancing while their long skirts crept up, and their girdles dissolved, and their nipples burst through like hyacinth tips and their clothes withered away to the mere wisps and ghosts of draperies to adorn and glorify, and at last the cunt lay open like a shining seapath to the sun.

So who did it happen for? Not for everybody. For the musicians it happened, and for those same girls who dragged out their lives flattened against a leaf of sound, for their sisters and their daughters, the women who really understand what the bass guitar is saying when it thumps against their skin, a velvet-hard glans of soundwaves, nuzzling. To understand and face the possibilities of annihilation OM without flinching. To be limitless. Infinite. Bounty as boundless as the sea, and love as deep. Here's how it happened for one: 'I was very slow to turn on to pop. I turned down an invitation to a party for the Beatles. I moved from jazz through blues, skirted folk music, and ended up with Bach and Buxtehude, Monteverdi and the great madmen. Hobnobbed with guys who were called *composers* and wrote operas and ballets and stuff. Started to go to concerts of contemporary music and talk about it. Sang Carl Orff. The song that made the difference was "I Can't Get No Satisfaction" and the original resensifiers were the Stones. I pay attention. The walls of the city begin to shake.

'It was evident that there was a pop conspiracy to blow the minds of my generation. I was interested but not involved. I only began to understand the group symbol when I met Simon Dupree and the Big Sound in a TV studio. The place was full of smoothies and groovers using cool and calculating every move. The sounds of sucking filled the air, when these little guys blast off, singing what was really an old number, "Reservation", I remember, and his underpants showed. And he sweated a lot. And his sound blew out all the crap and BBC gumshoes, and I knew I was on his side. You know what it's like; all the technicians regard rock stars as freaks, the management regards them as charming, grubby, mental defectives. They do their thing and don't give a fuck. The message is sent. When I was being dressed for some change or other in some tight little thing that squeezed all my boobs up, I looked up and they were all looking at me with a kind of hot innocence, and I suddenly realized that groupiedom was possible. But the stitches were still in. Just say, it occurred to me. They all went off and took a train to Aberdeen or somewhere, some gruelling bloody awful tour.

'The first pop star I actually pulled was an entire accident. I was at this ball in the country (the best scene for a calculated 'hit' now I come to consider it) and I was having a dreary time because my bloke was utterly spaced out, so I made myself mildly conspicuous [we should point out that Dr. G's six feet and other freakish attributes make inconspicuousness a more significant achievement] and sure enough, in the first break the lead singer of the group turned up next to me and stayed there, which was all right except it was a nowhere group who were not getting it together and I didn't dig him. I started to kind of edge away and I walked into the lead singer of the star group and we went into this crazy improvised routine, as if we'd known each other for years. When it's right that's how it is. You recognize each other and you play in tune. Because you start that way there are no hang-ups, no ploys, well, no ways of exploiting each other. If you fuck, you do it with the carnal innocence of children or cats or something. When you've watched a man calling his call and you've heard it and know what it means, there are no limits; the night you spend together is limitless too . . . you might go off for a few days to a few places, but it's immaterial if you're still together . . . Sounds like a poor line in cheap mysticism, but that's how it can be. Usually you separate quite soon, because there are things to do, more things to have and do, and maybe it happens again a few times, maybe months apart. It's a bit like a jam session I suppose. Or a supergroup. Maybe he's married or got an old lady: that's like his regular scene. He knows he can blow good things when he's without, sometimes things he can only blow with you, so you get together. That's how I like it. Monogamy is death for me.'

She's laughing but she means it. She explains that she's very promiscuous but out of the hundreds of guys she's made, relatively few are pop stars, but most of the pop stars are names to conjure with.

'I guess I'm a star-fucker really. You know it's a name I dig, because all the men who get inside me are stars. Even if they're plumbers, they're star plumbers. Another thing I dig is balling for the greats before the rest of the world knows about them, before they get the big hype. Because I have to follow my judgement, not the charts, you dig? Now take Magic Terry, he's a star which your telescope hasn't picked up yet. We met at a party in New York and he said he wanted to come and read poetry at my apartment. I believed him, although it seemed unlikely, and he came and he did this amazing thing, this ENORMOUS poetry, which he's going to do soon (if he doesn't die or something) with the best hard-rock backing money and his judgement can get, and that is the best. When it happens it will all happen to me, too, whether I'm there or not. The great thing about star-fucking is that every time you play a record, or just dig his thing again, it's all there, like he was there.'

I spy on her by looking through the records scattered round the turn-table: they are the names I expect, with a few notable exceptions. I had seen her sharing Jim Morrison's spotlight at the Doors concert so I asked why there were none of their records there.

'I suppose I went there to get some Jim Morrison. I never know until I experience the thing properly whether it's a good thing or not. Jim Morrison was a terrible bring-down, I mean, he was there coming on like a fucking sex kitten, pouting and wiggling and slipping out of his clothes. He thought he was singing to teeny-boppers and kept throwing them the drumsticks and stuff and everyone froze with embarrassment. The vibes were so bad that he started to have trouble getting it together. He went upstage and tried to bring himself on jigging the maracas up and down with his elbow down here so he'd have a stand to show the customers, and then he goes leaping down to show it to everyone and it's gone.

'Most commercial groups are a terrible bring-down: it must be like fucking a whore, you know. You watch them standing there slapping their instruments with these terrible fixed expressions. Can you imagine sex with Andy Fairweather-Low or that podgy guy from the Amen Corner, or is it the other one? Jesus, I never know which is which. That night, the Doors communicated their impotence to all of us, and we sneaked home furtively, separately, ashamed of liking that LP so long ago. What a disgusting hype they are.

'But do you know I find Engelbert very horny-making. He's so evil you know, getting all those lonely housewives to cream their jeans, with his tight high-fronted shiny mohair trousers with just a touch of rubber hose. So fucking evil.'

She's still laughing, and I start her off on a different tack and she stops.

'I don't know, I mean everybody uses the sacrament acid, most people some of the time. I only ever once went with anyone on horse, and I remember it as absolutely magical, I nearly turned on myself. He was as strong as a hawk, as light as a feather. His breath was as sweet as a child and his skin was hot and smelled like sunlight. He slept and woke and made love and slept as easily as if it was happening every day instead of every hour. He was amazingly high energy, and unutterably tender. I thought it would be all monkey-on-my-back stuff, but it was unbelievably potent and delicate. I still feel very involved with him although I never see him. I heard he fell off a bandstand the other day and cut his head. He gets sick a lot and he's unhappy I think. That's a drag, not being able to help. I guess it's unemancipated or something but I won't call him. I only hope if it gets really bad he'll think of me . . . I love him you know, him and a thousand others as they say.'

She is laughing again, but I am glad when the phone rings, and I put on a record while she talks.

What a bring-down . . . when she comes back, I ask my last question. I phrase it awkwardly and the Doctor squeezes her fleecy hair up in her hands and laughs again.

'It's not a matter of *minding* balling the whole group. They're not like the ton-up boys who'd hold a girl down while they all fucked her: that's the fascist sort of homosexual kick, like where the leader fucks the girl in the glare of their headlights and they all jack off and stuff. I'd never be likely to wind up in that situation. But I'd love to be one of a group in a loving sexual situation. I just don't know very many groups who can get it together. The Airplane seem in love and listen to each other a lot, but *Rolling Stone* tells me they get uptight about sharing birds. Now *RS* is not always right, any more than a penis is always called a Hampton Wick, but I haven't often come across a group that were so together that they could make that scene. Probably the MC5 are near it. I had to go to sleep in their hotel after Elektra had had to ring me up to get Rob Tyner to a conference, and they slept two to a room with the door open and everyone walked through. I found out I really *really* liked being able to hear other people balling close to me while I was, and I was very pleased; you see, the group fuck is the highest ritual expression of our faith, but it must happen as a sort of special grace. Contrived it could be really terrible, like a dirty weekend with the Monkees!

'When you asked me that question, you made like you thought that it was a kinky sort of thing, well it isn't you see, because kinkiness . . . it's the great British disease. Kinkiness comes from low energy. It's the substitution of lechery for lust. You don't really feel desirous so you turn yourself on with cute variants like rubber mackintoshes and nuns' habits . . . Lots of pop stars run a sort of playboy scene where they lie about, being the rich tycoons, having skilled whores go to work on them, sort of refining sensations like learning about caviare. Look at the image Tom Jones puts out on his TV show, a sort of fat, noseless Hugh Hefner, real consumer sex in self-seal plastic wrap. But the groups I dig, and who are likely to dig me, are high energy, high voltage tenderness! There are no taboos, you can do anything anywhere, from excess to excess. *Rolling Stone* speak true when they say The Happy Nation sucks. Frank Zappa's an odd case though. I fancy him like mad. Have you seen the photo on the American sleeve of Ruben and the Jets? Here they made it too little, but the big photo reveals that Frank Zappa is a Grade-A-High-School-Prom-Heart-Throb!

'I dig everything he does, except when he goes into his paranoid why-am-I-explaining-you-don't-care-or-understand routine, but I'd think twice about balling him, because Ed Sanders told me that he has the same perversion as Tyrone Power in *Hollywood Babylon* and somebody else told me that that means he's a shit fancier! How can you get that together for God's sake? I don't really believe it. It's probably meant to frighten off all but the brave and resourceful. Still, maybe I'm not that brave and resourceful. Nevertheless, because I really respond to his vibes, I want him, shit or no shit, because that's how it is if your body and soul and mind are hooked up. I'd fuck Shakespeare, except that he specially asked that his bones not be disturbed.'

She jumps up to get ready to go eat at the Macrobiotic (because she likes it!) and rattles on while she fluffs out her hair, about the *café-au-lait* groupies of New York, brittle and loveless, but beautiful and entertaining, or the softer girls who still hunt among the minstrels the familiar lineaments of a husband and cry by silent telephones in lofts along the Bowery of the necessity of being into your own thing; of getting back into your body so if you understand or admire an artist, your nipples erect when you read a line of him or hear a bar of his music (like berries under the brown gauze of her long dress whipped with old lace) so Norman Mailer's penis blossoms in her head, stopping suddenly to swoop and kiss me on the mouth, with her hand cupping my breast as naturally as a nest a bird, a kiss full of promise of a 'day when we shall come to life among the flowers of Beulah, sprung in unity in the Four Senses, in the outline, the circumference and Form, forever in the Forgiveness of sins which is Self-Annihilation', and notice that she has changed her record.

'I'm so glad
I'm so glad
I'm glad
I'm glad
I'm glad.'

A year after this article Germaine Greer published The Female Eunuch, *a worldwide best seller. Until recently a columnist with the* Guardian *she has now joined* The Times Magazine.

THE STONEHENGE HEAVY ACID TEST

—

Ray Connolly
Evening Standard
10 May 1969

By the end of the Sixties the drug LSD had become a staple hallucinogen for those of the psychedelic culture.

You don't meet too many men with the Stars and Stripes painted in enamel on their false teeth. Truth to tell Ken Kesey is the only one I know. Every time he smiles, which is pretty frequently on a good sunny day, the zip in his mouth breaks apart and his upper right incisor says a pepperminted 'God Bless America' in red, white and blue.

We're rolling and waltzing, and power jerking and swanking and feeling good behind the blue, anti-glare windscreen of his maltreated Cadillac – Kesey and me and a New York girl disciple, all doe eyes and sweeping adoration; around we go along the edges of Hampstead Heath, down the lanes and under the blossom, and Kesey's telling us how he came to be the one guy we know with an American flag printed on his tooth. And he's talking in that down-home cowboy way that he does:

'You see I was running from the FBI when I crashed into my lawyer and wrecked my car. And somehow I caught my head, so that my tooth was hanging out by the nerves. But I had to keep hiding. So I waited in a laundromat for a while. It's funny how you can just sit in a laundromat and no one ever thinks of looking for you there. But the pain was terrible, so I finally made it over to a dentist I know. But he also happened to be an acid-head. And while he was fixing me he said, 'Hey, d'you want a tooth with the Stars and Stripes on it?' and I said, 'Yeah, that'd be nice' and so here it is. You never think these things can really happen.' And he unplugs his plate with its garish token and waves it around for all to see.

Ken Kesey, the man who began the LSD fascination of hippy California, who believes he invented the word 'trip', to describe the sensation of that fascination, and then introduced psychedelia to provide a form of it, who turns on Hell's Angels, and went on the first Magical Mystery Tour ever – years before the Beatles – is here in London, in a borrowed flat, en route for Stonehenge, the Wailing Wall and the Great Pyramid.

Here in London with his three children, his wife Faye, his friend Spider, and now some new followers like Dilly Disciple from New York who's sitting here with us saying how we ought to stop and get some of Dr. J. Collis Browne's Chlorodyne on account of how it has some opium extract, and rabbiting on about this trip and that trip and whatever kind of trip a man can imagine.

And then there's this other girl, too, who's staying with the Keseys, 'like she's a Wasp', says Dilly Disciple, 'with the hair and the turned up nose, and she's very virginal and all that'. And I get the idea that there's no love lost between the Wasp and Dilly Disciple. But what a household it must be.

Kesey is thirty-three, and was born in Oregon. Faye, who is a woman of remarkable yet passive tranquil beauty, was his childhood sweetheart, and they married in their first year of college. After college they graduated to a beat generation community, where Kesey wrote his first two novels, one of which (One Flew Over the Cuckoo's Nest) was considered brilliant by some reviewers, and who then sold his body to a local clinic for their experiments into a drug called lysergic acid diethylamide – LSD. Under the surveillance of the white-coated clinic staff Ken Kesey had become the world's first acid-head guinea pig.

Soon he was turning-on everyone in his community, and when the bulldozers came to remove the community they up and went and bought a bus, 'an old 1939 International Harvester yellow schoolbus', wired it and taped it for the thousands of watts of sound needed to play their rock and roll music, aerosolled it in Day-Glo mandellas and took themselves off on a long cross-continent acid trek of the United States.

Back in California on various narcotics charges, he faked a suicide to give the FBI the slip, slipped over the border into Mexico, and was eventually captured when, with a degree of contempt bordering on the foolhardy, he went back to San Francisco and appeared on television.

Considering the mischief he and his followers had created in the eyes of the police he was lucky to get off with six months on a work farm. But by this time he was beyond acid. The LSD, he said, wasn't necessary.

'No I haven't taken acid in quite some time,' he says in his Hampstead flat, pulling on his socks, one bright red, one brighter orange, and snorting up his cold. He had come to the door just in his trousers, big as a bear, chest coated with blond curls, hair almost gone on the top but thick as a rug down the sides and round his ears.

He pulls on a T-shirt and the inevitable Indian token around his neck and finds a leather jacket: 'I shot this elk with a bow and arrow myself. And had Mountain Girl make it up into this jacket for me,' he says.

'We're now into other things. There's not a great deal of energy in dope. It's moved now to the occult or militancy.'

Since he first came to Britain last December with the Grateful Dead and Hell's Angels and those Harley Davidsons and egg-nog, he has become quite an Anglophile. England is the 'holiest' place he's ever been, and Stonehenge is the 'heaviest', he says.

'We've traced our way back right from the West Coast to the New England colonies and right back here, and Stonehenge is the oldest place we can find. We're going down there for the summer solstice, to see the sun come up between those great pillars that are as big as two Buicks.

'And then we'll get my bus over here and go off to the cathedral at Chartres and on to Dachau and the Wailing Wall and the Great Pyramids. I haven't seen those places but I figure that any place that took so much in human endeavour to build must be a very heavy place to be.'

He goes on rapping: 'One of the troubles with all that drop-out scene was that at the same time as throwing away all of the bad things of the past and the environment, they also turned loose a lot of the good stuff, too.

'But right now I think that a lot of young people are just sitting around and waiting and watching. Most people think that whatever's going to happen will be a bad thing, but I don't believe that. I think something is going to happen and it will be a good thing.' Something like the millennium, or cargo cults?

'Maybe a cataclysm that will sink California and New York by earthquakes and blow out all the old tubes,' he answers.

He's also here to make a record in a spoken word series for Apple. But since their economy measures he's found himself without an office or co-operation. He's a little bitter about it, but he's carrying on with making the tapes anyway.

'I write a lot. I just haven't written anything that pleases me for a long time. Nothing I've done communicates as well as tape does for me.'

He's a great Peter Pan of a fellow, quick witted and very funny, and driving around London in his cowboy hat and windcheater he looks like some leftover from Bonanza.

And later when Dilly Disciple is still on about her Dr. J. Collis Browne's Chlorodyne we go to find a chemists. Down Finchley Road into a side street, and there's nowhere to park. Without a moment's hesitation Kesey charges the pavement. The great Cadillac bucks and jumps on its hydraulics and down the pavement we charge between shops and lamp-posts, coming to rest half on and half off the road and lodged at a forty-five degree angle to the kerb.

A little old butcher carrying a meat chopper rushes from his shop and makes insane motioning gestures towards the Cadillac's twin wafer-thin fins. 'Shall I chop a bit off?' he says. And Kesey laughs. He always laughs.

Ray Connolly is the editor of this anthology.

WHEN THE BULLETS STARTED FLYING

—

Max Hastings

Evening Standard
15 August 1969

After generations of anti-Catholic discrimination, large-scale sectarian violence returned to Ulster in 1969.

The province of Ulster was today facing a crisis that has ceased to be moral, religious or even political. It has become the brutally simple problem of dealing with thousands of inhabitants of all backgrounds and beliefs who are now thoroughly roused for battle.

Four men and a nine-year-old boy were shot dead and hundreds injured in last night's rioting. The child and one of the men died when bullets came through the windows of their homes.

In the Belfast trouble, in which four people died and more than 120 were injured, forty-two by gunfire, a terrifying number of those involved were visibly enjoying themselves.

Protestants from the Shankhill Road area turned up with every sign of enthusiasm to watch the police slashing machine-gun fire through the Catholic Falls Road area for several hours.

I saw B Special Reserve police cutting loose with their revolvers at anything and everything that took their fancy, with street lights a great favourite; and Catholics in the huge Davis Towers block of flats on Falls Road crouched under the balustrades, surrounded by scores of primed petrol bombs, apparently envisaging themselves as the heroes of some beleaguered fortress saga.

In the next few days, there is going to be a great deal of accusation and counter-accusation about who fired the shots which caused at least forty-six gunshot wounds in the battle. No one can say for certain, because in a major street battle you don't step into the line of fire to have a look.

What is agreed by all observers, however, is that only a handful of shots can be attributed with complete certainty to hostile sniper or rioter fire.

For the rest, one must record that while the Belfast police insist that automatic weapons were being used against them, evidence to this effect is very scanty.

What everyone around Falls Road witnessed last night was a barrage of fire from the sub-machine-guns and heavy machine-guns of the police. Armoured cars sprayed bursts in the general direction from which they thought themselves attacked.

Police, sure that they were being fired upon from the Davis Towers flats, put down heavy fire towards that building, although it is officially stated that most of the shots were aimed in the air.

I was moving past Davis Towers when a man ran down the stairs shouting that a child had been shot. Running into his flat I saw a fair-haired nine-year-old, Patrick Rooney, cradled in his father's arms on the bed. He had been hit in the head.

The floor of the room was hideously blood-stained, the child bleeding profusely, and yet the father was too terrified to carry the boy across the Falls Road to an ambulance without arranging a truce with the police, who were covering every movement.

There had to be a hasty dash across the firing-line and a shouted conversation with the police before one could signal the father to bring his son across. The ambulance could not come to him.

Father and son were eventually driven away, many minutes wasted. But then it probably made no difference. The boy died anyway.

Chatting to an armoured car crew, drinking tea up a police-guarded sidestreet in between their dashes through a hail of petrol bombs to machine-gun possible trouble centres, I heard a driver make a remark that explains much of the Catholic mistrust of the police.

'Of course,' he said, 'Dr. Paisley has been telling us this would happen for the last nine months, but none of us had the sense to listen.'

In among the police in the front line, young Protestants were waving petrol bombs, dustbin lids and sticks they were obviously itching to use, and the police seemed to welcome them among their ranks.

'After all, they've got to think about protecting their homes,' said one police officer with a shrug of the shoulders by way of explanation.

To avoid any misunderstandings, one must say that the regular police on duty showed no sign of either deliberate brutality or unpleasantness. Instead, and in many way more alarmingly, they seemed unable to judge the situation in any kind of perspective.

Their fear of the Catholics is at least as great as that of the Catholics for them. When a police officer with medical experience was requested under flag of truce from the Davis Towers flats, he walked across Falls Road obviously as doubtful as his colleagues as to whether the Papists would send him back intact.

There is no doubt, however, that it was the Catholics who started last night's battle. Soon after 10 p.m. some 300 to 400 mostly young Falls Roaders were massed in the middle of their area, unashamedly limbering up for a fight.

They were equipped with petrol bombs, they ripped up paving-stones for missiles, and they built bonfires and barricades behind which to do battle.

Police surrounding the area sent in occasional armoured cars to tear along the street scattering barricades and mobs, although neither firing nor using gas.

Every car was met with a hail of petrol bombs, the form of local welcome which if it goes on will most certainly end by incinerating a police crew within the next few days.

I saw two boys, neither of whom could have been more than sixteen, fighting for possession of one petrol bomb which each was equally determined to have the honour of using. In the end, the victor succeeded in lighting a fire on one of the cars as it roared past, which it took several minutes to douse.

The rioters' early armoured car encounters were followed up by fire-bombing and house-wrecking along the length of the road. A bulldozer left by building workers was started up, moved towards police, and then diverted to smash down telephone-poles.

When the bulldozer finally stalled it, too, was fire-bombed and set alight, along with adjoining shops and buildings.

It was then that the first shots were fired. Some observers say one of the mob cut loose, others say it was the police. Either way, within half an hour a kind of massive Siege of Sidney Street scene had developed.

In dark streets and alleys in which many of the lights had been broken or shot out, frightened but mesmerized householders hung out of their doorways, although keeping always in shadow, while on every corner groups of police crouched with their weapons, firing intermittently at something – or nothing.

Behind each group of police lingered a handful of Shankill Road Protestants, watching and chatting. Every roadway was littered with rocks, broken glass and bottles, uprooted paving stones.

Positions changed frequently as senior officers reported threats of fire from some new direction.

As supposed sniping positions were spotted and isolated, officers with SLR rifles checked their magazines and waited for a clear shot. Sometimes they seemed to become too impatient to wait for the clear shot.

On the roof of one building, a silhouetted figure appeared. A B Special, looking strangely 1920-ish in his old-fashioned helmet and out-dated uniform, jerked out his revolver and took aim. Then he decided 300 yards was too tough a range for him, and called for a rifleman. As the rifleman took aim, however, the figure disappeared. A few seconds later, someone suddenly remembered that there might be nightwatchmen, not snipers on that roof.

But it was the merest chance that bullets were not cracking against the building before anyone bothered to have their doubts about who the target might be.

Some say that if gas had been used early in the evening, the mob could have been dispersed and control restored long before rule by sub-machine-gun took over. One's attitude to gas must depend on whether its effect on the many innocent people in the area seems to outweigh the possible loss of life by gunfire.

This has been a melodramatic night because whatever one's feelings, it is a melodramatic experience to move through a British city at night at a running crouch, flattening into doorways and hurling oneself for cover as armoured cars roar past, blazing fire from their turrets while a column of black smoke rises from a blazing building.

The first light of dawn found the same groups on the same corners, begrimed and very dirty now, watching firemen quelling the last of the half-dozen major blazes that had sprung up, which for hours they had been unable to tackle in the face of the constant struggle around them.

Houses and shops, pubs and businesses, have been wrecked in plenty. Falls Road is a blitzed area.

It is a futile exercise to try to apportion blame for what has happened, although many people in Ulster are going to try. Sufficient to say that this was the moment when this province totally and horribly lost its head, in a way that makes last week's events in Derry seem like a nursery outing.

The loss of life and the casualties, so many of them among Catholics, have escalated the situation, have raised the ante so suddenly that these next few days promise nothing but terrible misery.

Max Hastings is now editor-in-chief of the Daily Telegraph.

THE WORLD OF CHARLES ATLAS

—

Philip Norman
Sunday Times Magazine
19 October 1969

Pumping iron: before young men went to the gym there was always Charles Atlas . . .

Charles Atlas puffs out his cheeks and chest like an ebony bullfrog; at seventy-six he is sensationally fit and brown against the leg veins and coffee-coloured straw hats of people his age who go to West Palm Beach, Florida, to die. He swims in the salt-water pool on South Ocean Boulevard or runs by himself along the endless, booming beaches. When his wife died four years ago Atlas almost gave up his body-building business. 'I thought "maybe I'll join a monastery. Devote myself to study and give the monks or brothers some callisthenic exercises; spend my life like that".'

But he is still at such a peak that Nature seems to be holding him there at pistol-point: cantering at the edge of the surf, eating vastly, talking in his earnest mixture of Palermo and Bronx. Although his bathroom cabinet is filled with patent medicines, Oil of Camphor, Bromo, Seltzer, Pepto Bismol for the wind, the most severe illness he ever has is the sniffles occasionally, after exercise. 'My one habit is chewing – helps to keep the wrinkles off my neck.' And he has discovered, to his distress, that he is still highly attractive to the blue-rinsed, dollar-rinsed widows of Miami. 'I've had proposals, sure. Here and in New York City. One of these ladies wanted me to go to Europe with her as her companion. "Forget the business," she said, "forget your pupils. How much you want? Fifty thousand?"

'I went to an engagement party over there in Miami and it was full of these widows, the poorest worth maybe ten million dollars. Suddenly this pair of arms grabs me and a voice says, "Boy! What I could do to *you*!" And then three of them took me upstairs. They say they want to show me something; I thought it was a picture or a work of art. That wasn't it in the least. "Ladies!" I said to them, "but ladies, I am seventy-six years old!"'

That kind of thing has troubled Atlas deeply ever since the 1920s and the foundation of his muscles-by-post empire; since the days when he did, in all probability, own the finest physique in front of a plate camera. Impotent fathers often approached him to sire perfect babies in exchange for money. One of the offers was two thousand dollars. 'And I said No, I could not betray my dear wife, not for ten thousand. I was a virgin man until I met my dear wife. As a young boy I used to have these nosebleeds and the doctor told my mother "sometimes the body makes a little too much blood; when he is married that will take care of it". I never went with any other girl. When I was married the nosebleeds stopped.'

He *exists*. Three generations of the back pages of pulp comics have carried his advertisements; a strong man with a big smile that seems to touch the innermost nerves of flabbiness and cigarette addiction; a keg of muscle, legs planted wide apart in hot, white sand, asking only a five-day trial to turn a sprat into a tiger-man; a big brother abruptly serious as he stands above the strip cartoon, the enduring parable of the runt on the beach who had sand kicked in his face. Those who believed in his existence have always been assailed by rumour – that Atlas was helpless in a wheelchair, for example. Or that the muscles of his seventeen-inch neck became so big that they choked him to death.

He is still in effective control of one of the world's original and most successful mail-order businesses, with the smallest overheads. And he promises, 'I'm going to live for a long, long time'. Despite the old-fashioned big drum manner of his advertisement, all the exclamation marks, slogans ('You Too Can Have A Body Like Mine') and skilful, unsubtle imagery suggestive of chiselling brawn from weak fluid, the vital thing is that Atlas's system of exercises *does* improve the body; at least, it does so given supreme patience, application and stamina on the part of the student. The Atlas Dynamic Tension method is simply the basis of isometric exercise, the matching of one muscle with another of equal force. Mr. Atlas had the good fortune to copyright the name before science approved officially of the method.

A commonwealth of moral teaching goes with it. 'Live clean, think clean and don't go to burlesque shows.' The advice, like the big smile, is timeless. Until quite recently the Atlas course of lessons warned against listening to too much jazz or ragtime and urged 'Banish all evil thoughts from your mind'. Atlas himself believes passionately in a world of golden innocence created by muscles judiciously applied. 'Nobody picks on a strong man. England and America . . . we must keep ourselves strong. I do the course myself, religiously – Sundays, every day. Now if I don't keep myself well, how can I take care of my pupils? They say, "Ah what the Hell that guy! He's a has-been."'

He is careful to do most of his exercises when the other residents of his apartment block, faltering in Bermuda shorts, have gone indoors for the evening. 'If they ask me for advice, I tell them, don't overdo it. What the Hell, they are my brothers and sisters. I'm not showing off by this. It's my religion. We are created in God's image and God doesn't wanna be a weakling. Jesus held a tree on his shoulders. Sure, he dropped it a coupla times but nevertheless he carried it. He was pretty well-built, Jesus Christ.'

Atlas feels very close to his students: up to 45,000 new ones a year, a third of them from the United Kingdom. They are said to have included Rocky Marciano, the heavyweight boxing champion; and Joe DiMaggio, the baseball hero; even a member of the British Royal Family who wanted to avoid having sand kicked in his face. Atlas says this was the Duke of York, which would mean George VI: Charles Roman, his partner and the source of the brilliant slogans, says it wasn't – 'He's getting his dooks mixed up'.

Letter-writing machines in the New York office controlled by Roman deal with the bulk of the student enquiries, easily classified under headings like Bad Breath or Dirty Acts. Questions of a more intimate nature are dealt with by the strong man personally. He has intervened over many a fallen young girl and seen her properly married. 'And young fellows – some things they won't even tell their fathers, they ask Mr. Atlas. They won't even tell the local physician. They get to maybe sixteen, seventeen years old and they get gonorrhoea so they write to Mr. Atlas: "I dunno what to do, I'm despondent." I say "Tell your father. He was a young man like you one time. Maybe he was in the same category."

'I make a fine living. I do as good as any lawyer or judge, but I'm very economical.' He has an apartment on Long Island, as well as the one in Florida where he spends the winter by himself. On the verandah, where the surf wind blows the brocade drapes out, he keeps a fixed bicycle. Otherwise, his surroundings are strangely impersonal – brocade chairs, a huge TV set he seldom watches, a huge, gold-brocaded, lonely-looking bed.

His past feats of strength included lying on a bed of 700 nails, eating a banana as three men stood on his chest (women fainted), pulling a railcar or string of automobiles or – his speciality – bending a 100-pennyweight steel spike into a U. 'I haven't tried that feat of strength for many years now. I wonder if I could still do it. Only I don't wanna strain myself. We lost a lot of strong men that way – Hackenschmidt, Eugene Sandow.' At the same time his physique was once so classically perfect that sculptors competed for his services as a model: the Palm Beach apartment has a bronze statue of him in his forties, still with a thirty-two-inch-waist. Atlas liked modelling and is sorry he missed Michelangelo. 'Yeah, he was a fine artist, it's too bad he's passed away.'

In Florida he seemed a little isolated, but his telephone rings constantly. When it is not bodybuilding students it may be members of the Mafia, who have a boom town in Miami, recalling that Atlas was born Angelo Siciliano and asking him to parties. This is no new vexation either. In the 1930s he had to decline a Mafia credit card. In the 1920s, when he was staying in Chicago, Al Capone sent him a case of champagne and an invitation to dinner. Atlas pretended to have a bad cold and the hit-man sent to fetch him was most sympathetic. It happened again recently; a social call from a noted Mafioso. 'This guy drove over to see me. I thought he was a movie star. Soft hat, thirty-dollar shirt – and two guns he had.'

His advertisements are correct in claiming that Mr. Atlas himself started life as 'a seven-stone weakling'. Brought to New York from Italy by his mother when he was ten, he was considered too sickly even to ride a bicycle. They lived on Front Street, Brooklyn, and he was kicked around by Irish bullies. After school he worked in a ladies' pocketbook factory where the superintendent, a Mr. Welch, could pick him up with one hand. 'He was six foot seven. "Charles," he said to me, "you got a lotta talent." He was the only man I ever met who looked good with whiskers, although I wore some myself in later years to distinguish me from F.D. Roosevelt. Some of the framers at the factory didn't like it when Mr. Welch put me over them. One day he picks up a chair in his hand and remarks, "Anyone who harms this boy I'll beat his brains out".

'When I'm still at school I went with some of the children that had been well-behaved to a museum. And I sat down amazed at the statues of Diana, Apollo, Hercules, Atlas. I asked Mr. Davenport, the teacher: "Mr. Davenport, did these guys really live? Do you think a skinny kid like me could get like that?" Mr. Davenport took me to the YMCA but I thought "Jeez, how am I going to afford the fees?" So I started to go and do a lot of stuff in my own room. I saw the cat in the morning doing all kindsa tricks – stretching back and forth. I thought maybe I'll go to the zoo and see what the lions and tigers do.

'I got up very early as I had to walk all the way to the Bronx, Prospect Park – it was five cents car fare then. And here comes a lion out of his cage, stretching himself and rolling and yawning. The tigers did the same thing. I thought I should apply this to the human being. So I hit on this idea of pitting each muscle of the body against the other. The beauty of this is that, the stronger you grow, the more weight you can add. These muscles whirl around, you know.

'Next thing I know is, Jeez, I'm looking good. I changed my name from Siciliano to Atlas after the Atlas Hotel in Rockway, Long Island. In 1920 I was on Coney Island. I had bought myself a nice green bathing suit which was cut to show my chest muscles. Suddenly a guy starts going after me, following and watching me. His name was Mr. Arthur Lee; he had talent you know, good sculptor.' Subsequently Atlas posed for works including Energy in Repose, Patriotism (outside the headquarters of the Chicago Elks), and the water centaur in the fountain outside the State Capitol of Missouri. 'I posed for Mr. McManus, who was carving The Arms of Civic Virtue and for Mrs. Payne Whitney who was sculpting the soldiers, sailors and marines for the Fifth Avenue Triumphal Arch. Mrs. Whitney had a son. His name was Sonny Whitney, and she says to me, "Mr. Atlas, can you do anything for my boy? He's so lean." I says, "Now what you do is, to build him up, give him a good breakfast every morning, like I have. Two soft-boiled eggs, big glass of milk, a coupla slices of home-wheat toast and I'll give him some callisthenics."'

He always had a deep horror of violence. One of the studios he used to visit had a handyman who baited Atlas for two years before he turned. 'I said "Listen. I'm gonna be sorry for what I do to you, you're gonna go to the hospital, I'm gonna *hoit* you." ' He clouted the man and felt sick for two weeks afterwards. Thereafter he made a point of apologizing when people trod on his toe. He was a dandy, in spats and expensive suits, carrying a cane with a dog's head handle on which the jaws used to move. The only violent incident he remembers after he hit the studio porter was on the subway, when Atlas offered his seat to an old lady and a big truck-driver sat there first. He picked the trucker up and shook him gently. 'There's an old saying, the tongue is mightier than the sword. I reasoned with him. You can do anything if you got a good lingo.'

He then became a Coney Island strong man. 'I worked for a Mr. Henry Brill who had the finest show on Surf Avenue. I bought myself a pair of tights and a leopard skin and I had to ballyhoo outside, myself: "Come see Atlas do feats of strength, see the magician, see the boxing midgets." I did a kind of muscle dance. There were many thousands of people there; nevertheless some men were stronger than me. Mr. Henry Brill would offer 500 dollars to anyone that could bend the railroad spike like me. One night – I think it was in Binghamtown, New York – this fellow got up, and by golly the platform creaked you know. He was an Indian weighing 250 pounds. He thought it was a straw to bend. But he stopped bending half-way and the metal cooled: he couldn't do it. When I bent it in a U this guy took me on his shoulders. A lotta people kept those spikes for paperweights.'

He won the title The World's Most Perfectly Developed Man in 1921. The competition was sponsored by *Physical Culture* magazine whose owner, Atlas says, still owes him nine dollars. 'These young fellows today think all you need is muscle to get in the magazines. In those days you hadda be perfect inside and out.' Atlas took the cash prize of 1,000 dollars instead of a test to play the first screen Tarzan. He began his course in a tentative way: it was almost a disaster, thanks to his habit of giving lessons away for nothing.

Charles Roman – 'a very very fine young fellow' – intervened. He was an advertising executive, newly graduated and assigned to make something of the Atlas account: he went on the strong man's payroll in 1929 and the punchlines he subsequently composed have become engraved on the medicine ball of history. The story of the man who had sand kicked in his face has passed into the literature. Roman, however, is very modest: 'The success of that strip simply demonstrates that the public is the best judge of a slogan. They invented the line "Quit Kicking Sand In Our Faces". Originally the caption to that strip was "The Insult That Made a Man out of Mack".'

Roman, as slim as a fox, does the Atlas exercises himself every day. He is nearing sixty but has kept a thirty-two-inch waist. He runs the paper warehouse side of the business: America and most of the world's land masses are handled from his office in East 32nd Street, New York, where the foyer, with its ersatz Greek columns and statues of Atlas, looks rather like a long-lost stage set for *Oedipus*. This office and the one in London, established in 1936, are staffed mainly by middle-aged women. They are just big stationery stores – endless shelves of the Atlas course in the seven languages in which it appears. The best customers are New Zealand and Latin America, where a former Peruvian War Minister is now among those who won't have sand kicked in his face: the only serious failure was in Africa, where Roman tried to give the course away to the natives, an altruistic gesture he now much regrets. The method is entirely postal; no salesmen. 'I can't think of who it might not suit,' Roman says, 'unless somebody isn't well. It's for everyone. Another profitable market that springs to mind is Newcastle-upon-Tyne.'

Though the beach-bully in the strip cartoon no longer wears a chest-high swimming costume, Roman has kept the advertisements virtually the same as they were long before the last war: Atlas at his oldest, in white trunks, is about forty-four: some of the shots, in a leotard, date back to about 1930. Atlas himself would like to have some current snapshots printed – 'show that an old guy of seventy-six can still be in good shape' – but Roman firmly disagrees with that. 'To whiten his hair would not be meaningful because he is almost a living trademark.' Roman also refuses to print the more ecstatic testimonials from Atlas students, because he thinks no one would believe them.

A further legend persists: that Atlas will eat only fish, prunes and gruelly substances. In the warm bath evening at Palm Beach he put a gigantic dinner away, his teeth champing on most of a London broil of steak, hot biscuits, mashed potato and asparagus, in which he praised the sulphur. He refused salt, warning that it could cause impotence. He drank root beer and diet cola and a single glass of skim milk to keep his waist trim – once he would consume six quarts of milk a day. If he catches a chill he treats it with hot water and lemon juice, a remedy to which he was introduced by Dr. Harvey Kellogg, health expert and offshoot of the cornflake family. 'Fine gentleman, Doctor Kellogg. He lived to be ninety-two. He dressed all in white and took a snow bath every day: fine gentleman.'

The true measure of his fitness was his ability to talk for eight hours practically without stopping: he guffawed and preached and banged my knee with his fist. He has an extraordinary memory for names. He truly did once have sand kicked in his face, on Coney Island: the girl he was with was called Bella Marr. Outside, the first pink sheets of a Florida storm lit up the palms on the boulevard before the wind howled them down into bow-shapes. The ancients in the apartment building called in their poodles. Atlas stood out in the downpour to say goodbye. 'I don't mind the rain,' he said. 'It does my hair good.'

'Some people say I should get married again; some say I should marry Miss Lucas [a friend of his daughter who was helping him close the apartment this summer]. I think I'll read a few books on astronomy and try to look into the future. I don't know what it will hold, but without Jesus Christ you can do very little,' he said. 'I've had a clean life: it couldn't have been any cleaner.'

Philip Norman is a novelist and journalist. His latest novel is Everyone's Gone to the Moon.

MILADY

—

Neville Cardus

Guardian
1969

The story of a love affair.

I met her by sheer chance. In the summer of 1929 I was writing some 8,000 words weekly in this paper about cricket and music, stationed in Manchester, but nearly every week I went to London to cover a concert, or a game at the Oval or at Lord's. One day I described a Lord's Test to the length of 1,500 words, then on the evening of the same day I rattled off 1,200 words about Covent Garden Opera.

During the Canterbury Festival of that year, when I was coping with Lancashire and Yorkshire at Old Trafford, a letter came to me, my first from her. It was written in pencil, on a page torn out of a notebook. It informed me that she had strained an ankle, was lying 'prone' in bed, and unable to go to Canterbury to see Woolley batting. 'You,' she wrote, 'will surely understand the deprivation I am undergoing.' I couldn't ignore the tone, the charm, of the letter, so I replied, suggesting that one day we might meet.

A month or two later, I had to go to London for a Kreisler recital. We arranged, by post, to meet at the bookstall in Charing Cross Station. We described roughly our individual appearances. On 8 October 1929, I positioned myself at the bookstall in Charing Cross Station. For ten minutes I waited; no sign of anybody who answered to her self-identification. Then, as I was about impatiently to depart, she emerged from the ladies' waiting room, where she had been, as she put it, 'carefully inspecting me'. Frankly, I was disappointed by her appearance and dress; she looked pale and might have been the next suburban office girl.

We walked from the station across Trafalgar Square; and while we were dodging the traffic she asked me if I would lend her ten shillings. She had laddered her stocking, and had come out without her purse. I gave her a ten shilling note while we were having coffee in a café in the Haymarket. After an hour's more or less conventional talk I told her that I had to leave for an appointment, which wasn't true. I could have taken her to lunch, spent the whole day with her, with dinner and a theatre in the evening.

I got rid of her on the pavement opposite His Majesty's Theatre, where I called for a taxi. I asked her if I could give her a 'lift' anywhere. She said, 'No, thank you, goodbye.' Before the afternoon was over no stronger notion of her remained with me than of a pleasant young women with beautiful eyes and a large generous mouth.

Next day, or the day after, she sent me a ten shilling note, and letter of one sentence: 'I really did leave my purse at home.' A month afterwards I met her again; I hadn't the heart to let her think that one look at her had been enough for me. I arranged to take her to dinner one Saturday in the Howard Hotel, near the Embankment. I waited for her in the lounge. She came through the swing-door on the minute. In my dying hour I shall remember the radiance which now emanated from her. Her eyes were more lustrous (and alluring) than any I had ever seen. Her high cheekbones were vivid, her natural colour. Her lips were rose red, also by the dowry of nature. She walked with a suggestion of a swaying side-way motion. Later, when Richard Strauss came to know her, he said, 'She walks to the music of the "Dorimene" movement of my *Le Bourgeois Gentilhomme* suite.'

This time she was simply but charmingly dressed; a small grey hat, which followed the shape of the back of her head, her hair coiled in wheels about the ears. When she uncoiled her hair for me – but not yet! – it fell to her knees. She was thin, or rather, slender; and not too tall. Her head fitted perfectly into my shoulder. When I took her arm to lead her into the restaurant I felt the life in her trembling. I had known this sensation only once before, when I held a bird in my hand. At dinner she talked as if she had known me for years. I asked her why at our first meeting she had looked – er, 'so different'. 'Engine trouble', she replied.

She burned a flame of sex and being. She had found my wavelength, and it was a flame blown about fitfully now and then. Between her eyes a line would sometimes appear, a straight thin wrinkle. I guessed that she had gone through some troubles, not to say endangering experiences, one time or other. She sensed what was passing at this moment through my mind, and in a low voice with her chin resting on her hands, said: 'Yes, I have been naughty, but I was educated in a convent in France, and always help with the harvest festival at our church.'

I do her no wrong, this wonderful girl, if I write that whenever I introduced her to anybody redolent of English middle-class flavours, I would stand aside to note their reactions to her. I could almost hear them asking themselves: 'Who – what is she, *really*?' But abroad, in Germany and Austria, men such as Huberman, Schnabel, Stefan Zweig, Arnold Rose, and Weingartner, at once fell under her spell. She could, as she would put it, 'produce' herself, given the occasion. In London she was admired by Sir Thomas Beecham; and C.B. Fry invariably addressed her as 'Milady'.

We were together in Salzburg during the festival of 1932. Deep in conversation we crossed the road, near the Stein Hotel, failing to take note of a prohibited sign to pedestrians. A policemen charged after us, crying out officiously, *'Durchfahrt verboten!'* With a regal toss of her head she said to him, *'Durchfahrt* yourself,' and we proceeded on our way.

At Salzburg, this same year, if I remember well, Anton Weiss of the Vienna Philharmonic Orchestra insisted that we should go on to Vienna, at the end of the festival, to hear Weingartner conducting *The Ring*. Weiss assured us that he would give instructions at the secretary's office of the Staatsoper that tickets would be waiting for us, reserved seats for the performance of *Das Rheingold*.

So, on to Vienna we journeyed; and on a golden September afternoon I entered the secretary's office, to pick up the promised tickets, leaving my beauteous one waiting on the pavement outside. But there were no tickets for us, no seats reserved, the performance was *ausverkauft* – sold out. I protested – 'But Herr Weiss promised.' No avail; there had been a mistake. I departed from the office and, outside, told her about it all. 'It doesn't matter,' I said, 'I don't particularly want to hear *Rheingold*. I'd much rather we went to Hartman's for dinner.' But she expostulated. (And how she *could* expostulate, eyes and mouth.) 'I'd like very much to hear *Das Rheingold* in Vienna. Besides, we were promised. *I'll* go and see it.' Through the imposing doors she walked, in spite of my protestations that it would be useless for her to argue.

For nearly an hour I stood in the street; opposite was a jeweller's shop bearing the name of 'Hugo Wolf'. I paced up and down. I furtively peeped into the corridor leading to the secretary's office. No sign of her. Then she reappeared, holding in her hand a card of admission that evening to the Director's box – *du lieber Himmel*, to the private box of Weingartner! 'Good God,' I exclaimed, 'but how – how did you get this?' 'I persuaded them to take me to Dr. Weingartner,' she said. 'And,' said I, 'what then?' 'I was NICE to him,' she replied. And I find it necessary, for the purposes of true and living communication, to have the word 'nice' printed in capital letters.

We proceeded that evening to the Director's box, armed with our imperative card of admission. When we arrived at the Director's box it was crowded – crowded with civil servants, hangers-on of the Staatsoper staff. They were all cleared out, every one of them, and we sat there alone throughout the performance, opera glasses in plenty digressed from the stage to look at her. Next day the Vienna press printed inquisitive paragraphs about '*die schöne Engländerin*'.

After this *Rheingold* performance, we went to Hartman's restaurant, and soon Weingartner himself entered, accompanied by one or two famous artists, himself straight from the conductor's desk. He was wearing a long cape, and before divesting himself of it and seating himself with his guests, came to our table. He took her hand and kissed it and, with accent and intonation of an aristocrat, hoped she had enjoyed the performance. Then he kissed her hand again, clicked his heels, bowed to her, and departed to his own table, taking not the slightest notice of me.

There was no artificiality about her. When she projected herself it wasn't to impress others, but to get the best out of herself in a given situation or scene. I would watch her when she wasn't aware that I was watching. Like a young girl she would review herself in front of a wardrobe mirror, swirling around, showing herself to herself.

She pretended to no wide culture: and whenever she was with those who knew their subject, she was discretion itself. But she was a good and careful reader, with so sure an instinct for the best music, poetry, and literature, that often, while formally educated people were talking nonsense, I could feel that, as she quietly listened, she was thinking devastating sense.

She never ceased to surprise me by her contrasts of extrovert enjoyment followed by abrupt transitions to a quiet self-indulgent seriousness. She could achieve a crisis which would ruin a day out with her. If she caught a chill she at once wanted her temperature to be taken. A tight shoe would put an end to a walk in the country almost before we had gone a hundred yards.

The irony of these imagined maladies is that she was victim of the most cruel asthma, which at nights would overwhelm her until she terrified me by her gaspings for breath. She never suffered this way in my presence; she would go into another room, assuring me that the affliction wasn't dangerous, just something she had to go through, like 'the curse' every month. In the adjoining room she would burn some medicinal paper, inhale the fumes, and wait patiently for the paroxysm to pass. Next morning she was as fresh with the bloom of life as ever.

At the height of a riot of an enjoyment of herself, with a laughter which, in an English restaurant, invariably provoked pained glances towards our table, she would make a decrescendo worthy of Furtwängler and ask, 'Do you think that *Hamlet* really is two plays patched together?' If I affected to exhibit on any subject a more expert knowledge than truly I possessed – and to tease her I frequently did so pretend – she would say, 'That'll do, my dear: save it for Sir Thomas.' Always she told me to 'save' my blarney for Sir Thomas Beecham.

As I say, she wasn't a systematic reader, but had the gift to get to the core of a book as though intuitively. Her sense of words was gorgeous. She savoured them on her tongue, licked them with her red lips. She had no time for primness in writing, and she went so far as to cast Ernest Newman out of her court, much as she admired him as critic, because he persistently used the word 'commence'. One day I wrote a cricket article in which I referred to a batsman's 'vivid hook'. She was at the other end of England, but next morning, as soon as she had seen the *Guardian*, she sent me a telegram – 'I like vivid but isn't it a bit highfalutin'?'

She knew much of Shakespeare by heart, revelled in Dickens, delighted to read from Montaigne to me, and chortled at the Sitwells – 'all dutifully writing every morning in their different apartments, like a sort of writing-sewing guild'.

She was certainly born for the theatre. James Agate repeatedly, and with irritation, said to her, 'Why the hell didn't you go on the stage?' Her wit was a constant joy. One autumn day we went to Windsor for an outing. We were walking along a narrow street, and I stopped to look into the window of a bookshop, while she went a few paces ahead. Then, suddenly, I saw her objectively; I was often trying to look at her with detachment. Now, on this autumn morning of ripe sunshine, I saw her as though anew; she was wearing a scarf loosely tied.

I looked at her like a painter inspecting a canvas brush in hand. And I flew to her, embraced her, kissed her. She received the kiss with the whole of her indulgent mouth. And, at this crucial moment, a line of small Eton schoolboys came round the corner and saw us. 'My God!' I exclaimed, 'what an example we have given to them. So young and innocent.' And she said, 'Let them begin with the classics . . .'

At a theatre or a concert she was a perfect companion, never saying the wrong thing. During a performance of *Tristan und Isolde* she would have tears in her eyes when Kurvenal died. In the intervals of the same opera she would be saying, 'Oh, these bloody shoulder-straps!' When she was present at Noël Coward's *Bitter Sweet* (or whatever it was) and the hero was suddenly and fatally shot or stabbed, she cried out, from her seat in the stalls, so that the entire audience around her could hear, 'Crikey!'

She was Eliza Doolittle before and after Professor Higgins had taken her in hand. But I never grew accustomed to her face; it constantly changed, responsive to her volatile mind and temperament. Even in her sleep her face didn't have repose; she was alive in her dreams, 'producing' them, herself the principal and endearing character. She came out of the same stable as Mrs. Pat Campbell; but was gentler. She had the voice of Mrs. Pat. In my last moments of this life I shall hope to hear her reading, *not* reciting

> *Go not, happy day,*
> *From the shining fields,*
> *Go not, happy day,*
> *Till the maiden yields.*
> *Rosy is the West,*
> *Rosy is the South,*
> *Roses are her cheeks,*
> *And a rose her mouth.*

All in a tone as soft and low, and as beautifully modulated as the viola of Lionel Tertis. Life in her was too abundant and self-consuming. It couldn't last. She died, suddenly, still young, a rare gift to the gods, rare and premature.

Neville Cardus started working for the Guardian *in 1916 as a general reporter but became known for his writing on cricket and music. He was knighted in 1967 and continued writing until his death in 1975.*

MPs HEAR A VOICE FROM THE BARRICADES

Norman Shrapnel

Guardian
May 1969

Bernadette Devlin, a civil rights worker and psychology student at Queen's University, Belfast, was elected to Parliament on 18 April 1969, with a majority of 4,211 over her Unionist opponent.

It may be too late to cure the deeply festering ills of Northern Ireland. Several authoritative speeches in the Commons last night took this pessimistic view. But the emergency debate was a great occasion, at least, for youth, for women, and for maiden speakers – all embodied in the small but modestly triumphant person of Bernadette Devlin, the new Member for Mid-Ulster.

The baby of the House sounded alarmingly wise, and her own words were far from hopeful. So perhaps the joy of her parliamentary christening was less hers than Westminster's.

For joy and admiration were undoubtedly there. Miss Devlin spoke within minutes of making her ritual entry into the Chamber, usually in itself a sufficient ordeal for newcomers twice her age. The tiny figure moved steadfastly between Mr. Paul Rose and Mr. Gerry Fitt, both looking like political giants, and was given a roof-raising cheer. Order papers were ecstatically waved by Liberals, Nationalists, and a good many Labour back-benchers. Tories, including Ulster Unionists, were more restrained. Dr. King, the Speaker, shook hands as warmly as the occasion merited and instructed the House not to be jealous.

However, many a promising entrée has been let down by the main dish. Miss Devlin turned out better than her most ardent backers could have anticipated. There was more here than curiosity value, and the MPs who crowded at the bar and round the Speaker's chair got more for their discomfort than most standing-room-only occasions provide.

It would have been a good speech from a veteran. For a twenty-one-year-old newcomer it was superb. Without obvious rhetoric, Miss Devlin managed to combine the orator's most conflicting arts. She was straightforward yet witty, quietly charming without the least hint of self-admiration, unassuming, and utterly assured. Most of the time she ignored her copious notes. And the way she took Mr. Chichester-Clark apart aroused, at one point, what must have been a pale smile of admiration even from him.

Mr. Chichester-Clark's speech was reasonable for an Ulster Unionist – which would not be saying much in Miss Devlin's opinion – and he had made the tolerably unprovocative remark that 'the Englishman has yet to be born who understands Ireland or the Northern Irish'. She seized avidly on his text. In Miss Devlin's view no Ulster Unionist, even the Member for Londonderry, could have the least understanding of the oppressed people she represented.

Next she echoed his phrase about the 'stark human misery' caused, as Mr. Chichester-Clark had told us, by the window-breakers on Saturday. She was with him there, but her own view was from the other side of the barricades – 'not one night of broken glass, but fifty years of stark human misery'.

She resented the false images he imposed, as she saw it, on the civil rights movement. First it was said to be purely a Catholic uprising. It was in the interests of the Unionists to say so, just as it was in the interests of the Member for Londonderry to come over 'with all his tripe about the IRA'. This was her final left hook for Mr. Chichester-Clark and his suspicions that 'IRA and Communist elements' were now infiltrating the movement.

She proceeded to question whether Mr. O'Neill had the courage of his convictions, and even whether he had any convictions. By this time Miss Devlin could do or say no wrong in the eyes of the delighted Labour benches, and they even cheered adoringly when she started clobbering them.

'No, no!' they shouted when she feared, without obvious bashfulness, that she was going to make herself unpopular with everybody. No? Then surely any decent Labour Government would have got rid of all those old Unionists by now. 'Hear, hear!' they roared.

Her final fierce joke about the irrelevance of any possible agreement between 'the two arch-Tories of Ireland' was rewarded with a grin from Sir Alec Douglas-Home; but both Mr. Callaghan and Mr. Heath looked as severe as Sir Knox Cunningham. Even smiles, in these explosive times, can have a backlash. Mr. Callaghan found Miss Devlin's speech over-negative. Apart from that he was as fervent in his praise as everybody else, and even looked to the day 'when she may be standing here'.

The prospect, however distant, of the Rt. Hon. Bernadette Devlin as British Home Secretary made Sir Knox and some others visibly blanch. As for the heroine herself, she looked safe from the reformer's deadliest enemy of all. The intelligent girl knew, no doubt, that the days when Westminster could disarm its plain speakers with flattery are fast drawing to a close.

NOËL COWARD

—

Hunter Davies
Sunday Times Magazine
16 November 1969

Noël Coward's 'talent to amuse' lasted for the best part of sixty years. Though much of what he wrote was, by his own admission, second or even third rate, his reputation hardly faltered. At his best, with Hay Fever *or* Blythe Spirit *or* Private Lives, *he had few equals.*

Montreux. I went up to Les Avants last night to see Noël Coward as arranged. It's fantastically high up this steep, winding road right over the lake. When I came down afterwards my ears went funny, the way they do when you land too fast in a jet. I'm now sitting in this mausoleum of a hotel, the Montreux Palace, wondering if I actually interviewed Noël Coward or was it someone acting Noël Coward. This hotel is like something out of *Marienbad*, great enormous reception rooms dripping with chandeliers, corridors leading into the distance and I'm about the only one here, though somewhere up on the sixth floor the hotel's mystery permanent guest, Vladimir Nabokov, is said to be working away. Unless it's another actor.

The hotel is very sad with no people, like a great stately home that's had its day. I expected Noël to be a bit sad. He's just not Switzerland, is he? He should be permanently prancing between the Ritz and Drury Lane, the Savoy and Ivy, not washed up here in this toytown country. Perhaps he is sad? I couldn't tell. I broke through once or twice, but not often. He's been through it all before, so many times. I think the paper sent me here because they couldn't think of anyone less appropriate. Perhaps he sensed it. Several times he dragged in that one of his pet hates was snide journalists.

You couldn't be snide about him, could you? He's a living legend. Of course I grew up looking upon him as a joke legend, as we all did, when it came to their heroes, like Winston Churchill and the Royal Family. I've always kept this feeling that Noël, Winston and the Queen are as real as William Hickey, or worse, perhaps even plastic blow-up figures which they let down every evening and pack away for the night. I tried to tell him this, not in those words of course, after dinner and a few drinks. He simply picked up the word Churchill and carried it off, telling me yes, they did have a lot in common. You could never be snide about him because he's cool, always has been. He knows what he is and what he's saying. Success hasn't spoiled him. He was spoiled before. He *always* thought he was good. And he was. He still is. But is there anything under the cool, charming mask? I mean apart from being the most professional and successful theatric of the century?

I was met at the Chateau Coward by his bloke, his secretary, Mr. Cole Leslie. I made the mistake of getting him going on how he met the master in the first place. He really does call him The Master. It was in 1936 and was a complicated saga of having his fortune told. It took so long to tell that I almost missed The Master's Entrance. No, he wasn't in a dressing-gown. He had on a bright blazer as if he'd been to Henley with a white silk pullover and yellow cravat. He advanced across the room, his smile enormous, pushing his eyes even tighter together so he could hardly see. His face has the beauty of a boxer who's seen better days. For a minute I thought he was going to speak broad Cockney. He didn't of course. But I was surprised and delighted when later all the four-letter words came tripping out as a normal part of his conversation. I wish I could get them into the paper, though it would rather dent his public image.

I decided to get the boring stuff over with first, you know, all this seventieth birthday thing, which I thought would please him as it must be wearing him down as well. He's got a whole week, leading up to 16 December, in which every Tom, Dick and Larry is giving him a big do, with the TV pumping out appreciations, Binky doing his bit and play and film revivals all over the place.

'It's all terribly flattering,' he said. 'We now call it Holy Week. At the Savoy Banquet I'll have to listen to all the tributes then get up on my hind legs and smile graciously. It's very fortunate that I've never been shy. Some members of the Royal Family are awfully shy.'

On the piano it was standing room only for lines of personal photographs of Noël with Queen Mary, the Queen Mother and loads of other queens and suchlike.

'Why should I be surprised by the scale of the celebrations? I have had a very successful sixty years. I remember in Cape Town in 1940 there were 42,000 people shouting and me doing a lovely wave like this. Back at the hotel nobody came near me. I don't expect 42,000 people at the Savoy. I'm not exactly an absolutely crashing novelty in England today. I think England has grown rather used to me.'

And fond. He's been up and down like a yoyo in his times, but he's been welcomed back with shrieks of delight more times than most playwrights have had hot Foyle's lunches. I was reading Sheridan Morley's book of his career on the plane (*A Talent to Amuse*), and apparently they were doing Coward revivals from as early as 1926. Now his revivals are of National Theatre proportions. By getting to seventy he's seen every conceivable phase of success, even the ones usually reserved for the dead and gone.

'I'm not seventy of course. I can't get it out of my head that I'm still a precocious boy of nineteen, highly talented. But sixty years in the theatre isn't bad. I started as a boy actor at ten. I've no deafness or any other afflictions. Perhaps they'll come later. Age is very curious. You must accept it yet ignore it at the same time. You should never try to be younger than you are. It's a mistake, except for women.

'I wouldn't like to be beginning again now. It would be very hard, but it's never easy to get in. Things have changed so much, with all this permissiveness. In 1924 with *The Vortex* the Lord Chamberlain wanted me to knock out the word damn. I acted it to him, awfully nicely, and he agreed.

'I'd always thought I was talented. I knew it from five. It was obvious. I felt destined for the theatre, which was strange, as none of my family were in it. By seventeen I had a leading part in an important West End play.'

But these juvenile parts – playing the Juve as he calls it – didn't last long. It was being out of work which made him turn to writing plays, giving himself big juicy parts. He wrote ten plays before his first was produced – *I'll Leave It To You*, in 1920 when he was twenty.

'It got wonderful notices, and ran for five weeks. My second play got good notices and ran for eight weeks. *The Vortex* and *Fallen Angels* were both attacked as decadent and ran for months and months. I realized the critics can do damage, but if a thing is good, they can't really hurt it.'

He also realized something else, although it's very hard to disentangle it now. He started to act the part of Noël Coward, playing along with the image the Press had got hold of as the fast young writer of decadent plays.

'I was thought personally to be decadent. The papers thrust this image upon me. I made one dreadful mistake when I was photographed sitting up in bed wearing a Chinese jacket. I looked fiendish. You would have arrested me if you'd seen me in the street. I wasn't decadent. Never have been. It's not me. I'm about as decadent as a suet pudding.

'I was also supposed to be on drugs, just because of Nicky in *The Vortex*. This was really ridiculous. I couldn't have played eight exhausting performances a week if I'd been on drugs. But what do you do? If you decide in the cradle, as I did, to be a big, whacking star then you have to take the rough with the smooth. You get stuck with the labels. People have prejudices about you, picked up because they want to pick them up. I once suffered an unprovoked attack from a silly New Zealand woman who accused me of lowering the whole tone of the aristocracy by writing *The Stately Homes of England*. I told her it was very eccentric behaviour, to give a party in my honour and then be so rude as to attack me. I said I was going to be also rude and leave, which I did.'

His 1920s image also included being a dilettante, which was true in a way, with his smart clothes and smart remarks. He told reporters that *I'll Leave It To You* had taken just three days to write, 'whereas some of my plays take up to a week'.

His fluency was always there and he maintains now he was always sophisticated. He didn't affect anything, not even his accent, so he says, which is strange coming from an impecunious family in Teddington with a father who was a piano salesman.

'I always talked as I talk now and always liked to wear nice clothes. I like being . . . (he paused, tilting his chin to enunciate the word) . . . chic. The young enchanters of today may have talent but why must they look so grubby? I think you should always look your best. I know it's not important, but it's silly to deliberately be grubby. I have always had a feeling for being an attractive public figure. I would do nothing to spoil it.

'Being witty was also part of the image, but I haven't minded having to be that. I am. I've always been quick with a comeback. I remember one splendid thing I said when I was twelve. I was with Gertrude Lawrence in Liverpool in a play produced by Basil Dean. I'm fond of him now, but I wasn't then. He came snarling down the aisle and ticked me off pretty cruelly for something I'd done. 'Mr. Dean,' I said, 'if you ever speak to me in that tone again I'll go straight home to my mother.' The effect was wonderful. It was the perfect answer. The company applauded.

'But I must have been absolutely dreadful a lot of the time. The only work I could get once, despite being so talented, was two pounds and ten shillings touring in *Charley's Aunt*. I had no reverence for the old actors or directors. One old director was telling me, 'Now, here is where you'll move over to the window.' I said, 'No, certainly not. I wouldn't. I'm staying here because the part needs . . .' and I'd tell him how to direct his play. I wasn't popular.

'But Charles Hawtrey always encouraged me, though I drove him mad, talking to him all the time. He knew I had talent. He was the biggest theatrical influence in my life. His timing was perfect. I watched him like a lynx.'

The Master called for one final Rub A Dub Dub from Mr. Leslie. I waited with interest. It turned out to be a glass of Dubonnet. Then we went down for dinner. Halfway down, he started sniffing loudly, complaining there was a smell of paint. He sat at the table and said he felt sick. Mr. Leslie said really, in front of a guest. I suggested a window could be opened but Mr. Coward said certainly not, we'd freeze. Mr. Leslie appeared with a deodorant spray and went round with it, spraying the air and muttering several times that it was a very good one, came from Paris, very expensive. Mr. Coward gave exaggerated sniffs and said it was worse than the paint. He ate hardly anything.

He asked about my hotel and I mentioned Nabokov. Mr. Coward snorted and said he'd dragged all through *Dr Zhivago* and found it a bore. I wasn't going to say anything. (Had it anyway been a cool ironic mistake?) But Mr. Leslie corrected him.

'My greatest advantage in my life has been my lack of education. I had no real schooling after ten. Instead I devoted my life from ten to the age of twenty to learning my job as an actor. I haven't missed not being able to quote Cicero. I didn't know at the time I was going to write. What a writer needs is an interest in human beings.

'I write for pleasure. When it's going well I feel pleased. I have nothing on the go at the moment, except my autobiography which I will get back to after Holy Week. I haven't an idea for a play at the moment, but one will come. I probably will do some more acting, in films though perhaps not on the stage. I don't want people to say, "Isn't he wonderful, prancing up there every night, you wouldn't think he was seventy." That's not the praise I crave. The moment people think of your age, don't do it.

'I've always worked in the mornings, from seven to one o'clock, as Maugham did. He told me never go back in the afternoon, even if you want to. All my plays have been written quickly. I wrote *Private Lives* in four days in the Cathay Hotel, Shanghai. Perhaps the quickest was *Hay Fever*. I began it on the Friday and finished it on the Monday – then it was turned down.

'*Design for Living* took quite a time, ten days. Prose is much harder. It's more words. I work for days then think, Christ, I'm only on the third chapter. I could have a done a full-length play by now.'

Mr. Leslie asked if The Master remembered when they passed Shakespeare. He made him sound like a bubble car. He meant in number of titles. The total today, counting plays, films and books of all sorts, is fifty-three.

'I've had my disasters. I have been spat at in the street. All over my tailcoat as well. It had to go to the cleaners. *Sirocco* was the most astounding flop. They went on booing for a solid seven minutes. My mother, poor dear, had become a bit deaf and thought it was cheering. I let them boo on then I went on stage and congratulated the cast, turning my back deliberately on the audience. Poor Frances Doble, the star, started a speech saying it was the happiest moment of her life. It was the only speech she'd prepared. Yes, I've had some basheroo flops, often when I was beginning to think I was really splendid.

'It's a most difficult thing to have a big success early. You're the belle of the ball, then chop chop. You find your real strength is personal conviction and self-discipline. I've said to myself afterwards, that was a real bugger, I must do better next time. Success can make you self-indulgent, if you're not careful, which is fatal. I've never been that. I wanted to create plays with a beginning, an end and a middle which would entertain and give pleasure. I hate my untidy plays.

'But I know I've written some shockers. There's those lines about Japan which are just banal:

Love like a sigh
Is passing by
Each maid and man
That's the tale of love
In old Japan

'If that had even been true there would have been a remarkable fall in the Japanese birthrate. Yes, I've done some buggers in my time. But now I've become a classic.'

I complimented him on his Liverpool accent. He said it was meant to be Manchester, a city he adores.

It was over dinner I made the remark about Churchill which became a cue for several Churchill stories. 'He had a wonderful sense of humour, which is why I liked him and he liked me. I was never frightened of him, though we did have one terrible drama. The dear *Daily Express*, which shall be nameless, said I'd been sauntering down the Rue Royale in naval uniform. I heard Churchill was very annoyed by the report, so I got a seat on the Cabinet plane to London and went to see him. I was furious that he'd believe it without checking. I told him that next time you read that I'm your Admiral and you're the cabin boy, don't believe it. He was perfectly livid. I later played six-pack Bezique with him and knocked the living shit out of him. It ended up with him owing me something enormous, like seventeen and six. "England can take it," he said.'

He was offered a knighthood about twenty years ago, at least he says it was indicated that it was in the offing. He made it clear he'd really prefer something else. Today he wouldn't say no to an OM or at a pinch a CH, but no one's offered one yet. One of the reasons is thought to be a minor currency offence he was involved in a few years ago, but he doesn't know whether it's true or not. He was a bit touchy about any suggestion that he'd left England for tax reasons.

'I've hardly ever lived in England in my life, not since 1920. I've always been travelling. As I've never lived there, why should I pay English tax? And to a Government I didn't vote for. An Englishman is the highest example of a human being who is a free man. As an Englishman I have a right to live where I like.

'But I must say the tax people have been most awfully nice. I've no complaints. I'm only allowed three months in Britain a year, but the other year, because of acting in my plays, I needed to be there seven months. So I went to the tax people and told them the problem. They said go ahead, as long as I made it up in the following years by staying away. Money fascinates me as a commodity, if it's used with common sense.'

He has a talent to amuse. Had he thought of anything amusing to do with his money in the end? 'No. It's more fun to spend it now. I have a very well-ordered will and all my friends are looked after.'

He tries to go to most plays when he is in London. He still thinks Larry is the best actor, head and shoulders above everyone else. Of the younger ones he likes Daniel Massey. 'But I'm prejudiced as he's my godson.' He couldn't think of the names of any other younger actors he liked. He admires Elizabeth Taylor among film stars. 'She was two minutes late on the set and kissed me and apologized. I've sat on sets for five bloody hours waiting for stars to have their hair done.'

The younger playwrights he likes are Osborne, Pinter and Schaffer. He was very funny at Arnold Wesker's expense, though he seemed genuinely fond of him.

'He came out here to see me a few years ago, about *Centre 32* or *42* or something. A sweet little man. I told him not to waste his talent trying to bring culture to the masses. Fuck the masses. They'd rather play bingo any time. So would I. I said he should concentrate on writing plays. He looked at me a bit pityingly. But he hasn't done much since, has he? Oh, but a gentle creature, Arnold. Just completely wrong, that's all. The moment a playwright becomes cause-conscious, that's the end. When propaganda rears its ugly rear the play goes down the drain. Once an audience feels it's being got at, close on Saturday.'

What about Shaw? 'Yes, but he was unique. He's very difficult to play. I was in *The Apple Cart* once and had that thirteen-minutes speech right at the beginning. I was rehearsing it at my home in Jamaica. Every Jamaican seagull now knows it. They call it out as they go past. A playwright is meant to entertain.'

He's very proud, and justifiably, of his success as an entertainer, though he likes referring to it ironically. 'The most I've had is just a talent to amuse,' as he wrote in *Bitter Sweet*. But wouldn't he have liked to have done more than just amuse? Not necessarily change the world. Perhaps just move people?

'Dear boy, I have had a few causes. In *The Vortex* I did. There was a great deal of morality in that drama. I disapproved of elderly ladies having young lovers.'

But that isn't a cause, not in a social or political sense.

'All right. I have had no social causes. Do I have to? I wanted to write good plays, to grip as well as to amuse. I have a built-in sense of humour, I can laugh at myself, which is more than Arnold Wesker does.'

I felt I'd pushed it a bit far, especially as we were still on the partridge, so I laid off a bit. On the way upstairs he returned to the topic.

'No, I've had no great social causes. I can't think of any offhand. If I did, they'd be very offhand. But I have done some very valuable things, you know. Changed the face of things completely. Do you realize I stopped the fashion for taking curtain calls after every act? A great revolution. It used to fuck up every play.'

Over brandy he said how much he'd loved that picture postcard I'd sent confirming my arrival. It was an Edwardian theatrical pin-up I'd bought in Camden Passage. It had been the perfect one for his collection. Mr. Leslie scurried to get it and for an hour there were giggles all round as we turned over the sepia beauties of yesterday. Lots of funny memories came out with each star. When we came to a postcard of some dewy-eyed boy actor he sighed and said, 'Oh dear, I fear there's no hope for him.'

I was getting on fine now and thought I was well away. Then I happened to mention the John Lennon remark at the Royal Command Performance. When he told those in the stalls to clap their hands while the ones upstairs could rattle their jewellery. The giggles suddenly stopped.

'I consider that the height of bad taste. It must have put the Royal Family at a terrible disadvantage. Perhaps they did laugh. That doesn't matter. They're well trained. It just isn't funny. I'm not at all amused.

'Taste can be vulgar, but it must never be embarrassing. There is no need to embarrass anyone. I deplore the bad manners of today. I did see the Beatles once in Rome. I'd enjoyed their concert and went backstage. I met John McCartney who was very charming. I said I wanted to come to the dressing-room. He came back and told me the others didn't want to see me. I marched straight in and told them what I thought of them. Would I have come to their dressing-room if I hadn't liked their work?

'If you're a star you should behave like one. I always have. Naturally you get asked for your autograph at awkward times. I was once saying goodbye to a dear friend and a woman interrupted to ask me for my autograph. I could have throttled her, the silly bitch, but I signed. The public are very demanding. They have a right to be. I believe in good manners. It is frightfully bad to make people like reporters wish to Christ they'd never come which I know some stars do.

'If you leave a theatre after a big success you must be prepared for people to stick their bloody books at you. They've taken the trouble to wait and see you, so you must never brush them aside.

'In Australia one lady stopped me as I was getting into my car. She had a baby with her and stuck it through the window for me to kiss. The car started to drive off so I did the only thing. I hit the woman to keep her off. I was left holding the baby. Needless to say, the baby peed all over me. I had to wipe myself and stop the car.'

It was all jokes again so I got on to something harmless, his health. He was looking very fit, though there was a bit of breathiness coming upstairs. He has a habit of breathing a tuneless whistle after a particularly good remark, which might be getting his breath back, or perhaps nervousness, perhaps boredom.

It emerged while discussing his health that he loved watching other people's operations. If he is in hospital for some reason he always asks to see anything good that's going on.

'Lord Moynihan used to let me watch a lot of his operations. He once took an enormous stone out of my kidneys. I've always been fascinated by surgery. In New York I used to go to the hospitals to see them at work. Perhaps some people couldn't bear that sort of thing. I love it. The violence on the operating table is terrifying. I've seen most operations, hysterectomy, ovariectomy, childbirth, death. I've witnessed death many times. I once had a man die in my arms. He was still talking. It was rather upsetting.

'The ovarian cyst I saw removed was from an actress I knew. I had tea with her later at five o'clock. No, I don't think it's strange or morbid. Why should it be?'

I felt for the first time he'd given something away, thought I didn't know what. It was something from inside his head, something apart from the charm and wit. I kept on about *exactly* what sort of pleasure did he get from watching operations, did he know why he did it?

'I'm interested in seeing a perfectionist at work. I'm interested in human beings, the physical side as well as any other. I'm fascinated by people, that's all there is in it. It's quite normal.'

But aren't they more like animals, when they're unconscious on the operating table?

'Have another brandy.'

I asked if he felt that the public should know the truth about famous people. He said no. 'One's real inside self is a private place and should always stay like that. It is no one else's business.

'The public is very fond of me. They're proud of me. I've done well by them, given them a lot. I'm proud that I'm popular and I've tried my best not to spoil it. I don't crave praise, but there is more pleasure in being loved than hated. I have taken a lot of trouble with my public face.'

Why want to be liked?

'Most people do. They must be very funny people if they don't want to be liked. The fact remains, I am liked. I'm very grateful for it. I'm grateful for Holy Week.'

I left by saying that I hoped he wouldn't have too many of the same old interviews to go through in the next few weeks, having to answer the same old questions about himself. It must be very boring.

'Not at all. I'm fascinated by the subject.'

THE OFFICE CHRISTMAS PARTY

—

Jilly Cooper
Sunday Times
21 December 1969

By the end of the Sixties, almost a decade after Lady Chatterley had been found not guilty, the public was ready for a columnist who saw the funny side of sex.

It's Christmas Eve in the workhouse: the typing pool has been transformed into a fairy grotto. The typists are red-faced from the hairdresser's and blowing up balloons – they have been making furtive trips to the Ladies all afternoon to see if their dresses have hung out properly. Excitement seethes. This is the night when supertax husbands are hooked. In other parts of the building the higher echelons anticipate the evening with trepidation and veiled lust. The building already reverberates with revelry. The Art Department, having declared UDI, held their party before midday and are still going strong.

At 4.55, when it's too late to rush out and get her something, the Office Crone makes everyone feel a louse by handing out gaily wrapped presents. At 5.00 everyone stops typing in mid-word and thunders down to the Ladies which soon resembles the changing room at Biba's. The office junior has used hair lacquer under her arms instead of deodorant and is walking round like a penguin.

The party begins with everyone standing under the fluorescent lighting wondering what to say next – strange, considering they find no difficulty during working hours. Miss Nitwit-Thompson, who has been putting her Christmas cards through the franking machine all afternoon and telephoning her friends to say what a bore the party is going to be, has not bothered to change out of her grey jersey dress. She will be leaving after five minutes to catch a train home to Daddy.

In an attempt to please everyone, the £40 collected for drink has been spent on one bottle of everything from Brown Ale to Babycham. The caretaker who is manning the bar has assembled a strange collection of glasses: flower vases, toothmugs, bakelite cups. The Office Wolf is busy lacing the typists' orange juice with vodka.

Neatly displayed in out-trays is food cooked by members of the staff – curling sandwiches, flaccid cheese straws with baker's droop, and an aggressive-looking Christmas cake covered in festive robins baked by the Office Crone. The Piggies have already got their heads down in the trough.

Conversation is still laboured, but the arrival of the Production department, who've been boozing all day on free liquor, helps to jolly things along. Soon, members of the Board drift down from Olympus, genial from a succession of long Christmas lunches.

The Receptionist, who is not famed for the strength of her knicker elastic, is making a very alive set at the handsome director of Public Relations. Miss Nitwit-Thompson discovers she's met the Managing Director's son at a number of dinner parties. Soon they are nose to nose.

People are relaxing. Someone puts on a record and two typists dance together. One of the young men on the make is overheard boasting about his expenses by the Financial Director and loses his chance of promotion. The office cat has wriggled out of his green Xmas bow and is thoughtfully licking fish paste out of the sandwiches.

Faces are reddening, backs are being slapped, people are passing round packets of fifty cigarettes. The Managing Director needs little encouragement to get up and say what a big happy family they all are.

The Office Junior swells with pride at the thought that she and about 400 other people are entirely responsible for the firm's turnover. The Caretaker takes the opportunity to rinse some glasses in the fire bucket.

A packer arrives from the warehouse with shiny blue suit and horny hands, and claims a dance with one of the senior sekketries, who bends over backwards to avoid his four-ale breath. The Receptionist and the Director of Public Relations are having private relations behind the filing cabinet.

The Managing Director's wife, who has come to collect her husband, has taken a piece of Christmas cake in deference to the typing pool. She didn't realize the robins were made of plaster, and is now desperately trying to spit out a beak.

Lust is rising in the vast jacked-up bosom of Miss Hitler from Personnel, and she is jostling the newest trainee towards the mistletoe. The Office Boy has hiccups and is trying to roll cheese and chutney sandwiches into an electric typewriter.

'God bless you all, Merry Christmas,' cries the departing Managing Director.

Now he's gone the fun is unconfined. There is a general unfastening of chastity belts. The Sales Director is playing bears round the furniture, the Office Wolf keeps turning off the lights. Squeaks and scuffles break out in nearby offices. The oldest member of the staff is telling anyone who will listen how the firm grew from a tiny two-room business to the 'great concern we are today'. The Director of Public Relations is in the Gents desperately scrubbing lipstick from his shirt front.

The drink has run out. Miss Nitwit-Thompson, who is now quite giggly, is being taken to Annabel's by the Managing Director's son. She'll be lucky if she gets home to Daddy before Boxing Day.

Reluctant to end the evening, people are making plans to meet in pubs or the backs of cars. Others are saying 'Merry Christmas', exchanging beery kisses and taking uncertain steps towards the nearest bus stop.

The caretaker, who has appropriated several bottles of drink, shakes his head over the pair of rose-pink pants in the Gents. Under a pile of forgotten coats and umbrellas lies a doll's tea set and a mournful-looking turkey. As he locks up, a telephone rings unaccountably in one of the lifts.

Jilly Cooper still sees the funny side of sex. She is now an extremely successful novelist.

ACKNOWLEDGEMENTS

—

The editor wishes to thank the following for their kind assistance in the preparation of this book: Peter Preston, Jocelyn Stevens, Max Hastings, Maureen Cleave, Peter Crookston, Jilly Cooper, Philip Norman, Hunter Davies, Christopher Booker, Auberon Waugh, Francis Wyndham, Michael Frayn, Hugh McIlvanney, Keith Waterhouse, Richard West, Claire Tomalin, Arthur Hopcraft, Irma Kurtz, Alan Coren, John Mortimer, Germaine Greer, Philip Evans, Geoffrey Irvine, Diane Courtney, Jennifer Sharp, William Rees-Mogg, Don Short, Patricia Burge, Terry Mansfield and Jeremy Deedes. A debt of gratitude is also owed to Charlotte Delaney who retyped the text for publication, and most of all to Dominic Connolly for his many months of research at the British Newspaper Library in Colindale.

The editor and publishers also wish to thank the copyright holders of all the articles in this book for their generosity in allowing them to be reprinted. Should, in view of the complexity of securing copyright information, any copyright holder have been inadvertently overlooked, or should the copyright have been wrongly ascribed, the editor apologizes and undertakes to correct any mistakes brought to his attention in future editions.

Eye-Witness At Sharpeville by Humphrey Tyler, © the *Observer*, 1960; The Friendless Ones by Penelope Gilliatt, © the National Magazine Company, 1960; Lady Chatterley's Trial by Kenneth Tynan, © the *Observer*, 1960; The Man In The Glass Case by James Morris, © the *Guardian*, 1961; Taking Pains With Pinter by John Gale, © the *Observer*, 1961; Tristan da Cunha: Little World Lost by Michael Moynihan, © the *Sunday Times Magazine*, 1962; Review of *Lawrence Of Arabia* by Dilys Powell, © the *Sunday Times*, 1962; Home For Christmas by Marian E. Davies, © the *Guardian*, 1961; Floodlit Frontier by Richard West, © the *Sunday Times Magazine*, 1963; The Last Days Of Macmilian by Christopher Booker and accompanying cartoon by Timothy Birdsall, © Pressdram Ltd, 1963; Mac The Man by Jocelyn Stevens, © the National Magazine Company Ltd, 1963; Antique Antic by Arthur Hopcraft, © the *Guardian*, 1963; The Four Phases of the Profumo Affair, © the *Sunday Times*, 1963; Nightmare Republic by Graham Greene, © the estate of Graham Greene, 1963, administered by David Higham Associates; An American Tragedy by James Cameron, © the *Daily Herald*, 1963; What Songs The Beatles Sang by William Mann, © the *Times*, 1963; Review of *Dr. Strangelove* by Dilys Powell, © the *Sunday Times*, 1964; Would You Let Your Daughter Marry A Rolling Stone by Maureen Cleave, © the *Evening Standard*, 1964; The Electric Man by Margaret Laing, © the *Sunday Times Magazine*, 1964; The Funeral Of Winston Churchill by Patrick O'Donovan, © the *Observer*, 1965; The Most Exciting City In The World by John Crosby, © John Crosby, 1965; the Case Of The Satirical Personals by Auberon Waugh, © Auberon Waugh, 1965; Come With Flowers by Norman Shrapnel, © the *Guardian*, 1965; P.J. Proby by Francis Wyndham, © the *Sunday Times Magazine*, 1965; Joan Hunter Dunn by Peter

Crookston, © the *Sunday Times Magazine*, 1965; Aberfan by Tony Geraghty, © the *Guardian*, 1966; John Lennon by Maureen Cleave, © the *Evening Standard*, 1966; The Men Who Never Were by Michael Frayn, © the *Observer*, 1966; The Moors Murders by Maurice Richardson, © the *Observer*, 1966; Light And Hard And Ready To Rumble by Hugh McIlvanney, © the *Observer*, 1966; Memoirs Of A Televiewer by Keith Waterhouse, © *Punch*, 1966; the World Cup Final by Hugh McIlvanney, © Hugh McIlvanney, 1966; Fragment from a review of the Edinburgh Festival by Ronald Bryden, © the *Observer*, 1966; Now there Is Only One by Cassandra, © Daily Mirror Newspapers Ltd, 1966; Mao's Bold Stroke by Victor Zorza, © the *Guardian*, 1966; The General Goes Zapping Charlie Cong by Nicholas Tomalin, © the *Sunday Times*, 1966; Paul McCartney by Hunter Davies, © the *Sunday Times*, 1966; Nell Dunn by Hunter Davies, © the *Sunday Times*, 1966; Report From The Six Days War by James Cameron, © the *Evening Standard*, 1967; Who Breaks A Butterfly On A Wheel? by William Rees-Mogg, © *The Times*, 1967; The Permissive Society: Mary Quant by Alison Adburgham © the *Guardian*, 1967; The Last Journey Of Che Guevara by Richard Gott, © the *Guardian*, 1967; How Do You Plead, Mrs. John Bull, © Irma Kurtz, 1968; Inside Khe Sanh by David Leitch, © the *Sunday Times*, 1968; My Name Is Ivy Benson by Arthur Hopcraft, © the *Sunday Times Magazine*, 1968; A Mule Cortege For the Apostle of the Poor, © Alistair Cooke, the *Guardian*, 1968; Something About A Soldier by Alan Coren, © *Alan Coren*, 1968; At Midnight In Bratislava by P.G. Cerny, © the *Guardian*, l968; Training for Armageddon by John Mortimer, © Advanpress Ltd, 1968; Jane Fonda's Curious Menage in St Tropez; © IPC Magazines, 1968; A Groupie's Vision by Germaine Greer, © Germaine Greer, l969; The Stonehenge Heavy Acid Test by Ray Connolly, © the *Evening Standard*, 1969; When the Bullets Started Flying by Max Hastings, © the *Evening Standard*, 1969; The World of Charles Atlas by Philip Norman, © the *Sunday Times Magazine*, 1969; Milady by Neville Cardus, © the *Guardian*, 1969; MPs Hear A Voice From The Barricades by Norman Shrapnel, © the *Guardian*, 1969; Noël Coward by Hunter Davies, © the *Sunday Times Magazine*, 1969; The Office Christmas Party by Jilly Cooper, © the *Sunday Times*, 1969.

The lines from John Betjeman's 'A Subaltern's Love Song' are reprinted by kind permission of John Murray Ltd.